Indian Voices in ELT

8

Indian Voices in ELT

Edited by

Francis Peter

Reader
PG and Research Department of English
Loyola College, Chennai

Viva Books

New Delhi | Mumbai | Chennai | Kolkata | Bengaluru | Hyderabad | Kochi | Guwahati

Publisher's note

First Published 2012

Viva Books Private Limited

4737/23, Ansari Road, Daryaganj, New Delhi 110 002
Tel. 42242200, 23258325, 23283121, Email: vivadelhi@vivagroupindia.net

76, Service Industries, Shirvane, Sector 1, Nerul, Navi Mumbai 400 706
Tel. 27721273, 27721274, Email: vivamumbai@vivagroupindia.net

Jamals Fazal Chambers, 26 Greams Road, Chennai 600 006
Tel. 28294241, 28290304, Email: vivachennai@vivagroupindia.net

B-103, Jindal Towers, 21/1A/3 Darga Road, Kolkata 700 017
Tel. 22816713, Email: vivakolkata@vivagroupindia.net

7, GF, Sovereign Park Aptts., 56-58, K. R. Road, Basavanagudi, Bengaluru 560 004
Tel. 26607409, Email: vivabangalore@vivagroupindia.net

101-102, Moghal Marc Apartments, 3-4-637 to 641, Narayanguda, Hyderabad 500 029
Tel. 27564481, Email: vivahyderabad@vivagroupindia.net

First Floor, Beevi Towers, SRM Road, Kaloor, Kochi 682 018
Tel. 0484-2403055, 2403056, Email: vivakochi@vivagroupindia.net

232, GNB Road, Beside UCO Bank, Silpukhuri, Guwahati 781 003
Tel. 0361-2666386, Email: vivaguwahati@vivagroupindia.net

www.vivagroupindia.com

ISBN: 978-81-309-1780-1

Published by Vinod Vasishtha for Viva Books Private Limited
4737/23 Ansari Road, Daryaganj, New Delhi 110 002

Printed & bound by Raj Press, R-3, Inderpuri, New Delhi 110 012

G0000/S0000

Contents

Preface

India missed the industrial revolution and is now paying the price for it; and if this time it misses the communication revolution, nothing can save the country for ages! This critical compulsion is the reason why there is an all round attempt at steering education in K. Sibyl's words, along a new path of 'expansion, inclusion and excellence'. The one answer to the many questions that plague the country today seems to begin with English. In this knowledge era, a large pool of young, competent, English speaking workforce can make all the difference that can pull the country by its bootstraps out of the mire we have let ourselves in to. Of the rest, we may reasonably feel assured but English is an area of concern.

At this juncture one question that concerns the ELT profession is 'how are we to respond to the challenge of the times'. Is there any role for us in the emergence of a resurgent India? Are we lagging behind or are we ahead of the curve in the teaching and learning of English; what is happening in the academia – do we notice alternate theories, new experiments emerging; is there any attempt to question the question, to dare to think differently? Is a process of evolution, an attempt at sloughing off some old skin and going through stages of metamorphosis evident? Is there a collective Indian voice or like everything else here, is it a fractured, fragmented voice that we hear?

This book is a humble attempt at lifting a corner of the veil and letting us take a fleeting look at what is happening to ELT in India and to invite us to introspect, theorize and encourage serious, sustained and synergized action in favour of the issue at question. I must hasten to add that there is no pretense of a comprehensive or a representative collection. Here subsequent volumes could reflect the range and variety of theoria and praxis many in this country are engaged in. This could be a beginning of an effective response to the challenges ahead of us.

In fact, this amazing subcontinent with its mosaic of colours, cultures and crazy contraries, its hoary tradition and perception of teaching and learning as well as its long ambivalent attitude to English is a veritable laboratory for ELT experiments. Much is expected from India, a country of linguistic and cultural diversity with an English using population that is amazingly larger than that of many countries of native speakers.

This vast country for years has been playing 'the credulous ape' largely replicating the efforts carried out in the West; the ELT pendulum has been swinging relentlessly keeping pace with the dictat form elsewhere. There have also been meek attempts at affirming of and searching for indigenous and effective models of teaching. Innovations by pioneers like West, Maley, the S-O-S approach promoted by MEL, the insights of the tangential reasoning culminating in the efflorescence of N.S. Prabhu's CLT are proofs that more is both possible and necessary.

The assortment of articles in this collection throw up some recurrent issues that are both indicative and interesting: (a) there is greater appreciation of the perceived usefulness of English as a language of opportunity and of emancipation allowing millions to escape from poverty (b) the problems associated with the ambivalence of teaching a most useful but least loved language are being indexed (c) attempts are thought of to compensate for the absence of sustaining environment for learning English in implementing the communicative methodology (d) English across the spectrum and the inclusion of non-conventional authentic material is becoming popular (e) the possibility of complementing the restricted of teacher competence with affordable technology and blended learning.

The chaos the profession experiences is also reflected in some lingering doubts, hankering after the 'garlic and onion' of the bygone days, the endless waiting for the winds of change and the feeling of being 'caught between two worlds, one dead and the other powerless to be born'.

What cannot be denied is that what we hear is the first rumbling of a giant waking up and that augers well for the country, the profession and the word at large.

Chennai
15 April 2010

Francis Peter S.J.

1

Teachers' Growth

N.S. Prabhu

In this paper, I want to outline a concept of language teachers' professional growth and speculate about what conditions or activities might be of value in furthering it.

I am thinking here of teachers' growth as something that arises from the ongoing activity of teaching – from the daily engagement in the classroom – rather than from any professional inputs to the teacher from the world of professional specialism. Specialist inputs to the teacher are generally meant to alter or improve the teaching that takes place and/or promote an understanding in the teacher of the nature of/need for such improvement, rather than start a process of growth based on whatever teaching happens to take place. Growth arises from and is sustained by experience, not training or knowledge.

It has been suggested that such growth is brought about by reflective teaching, that is to say, repeated reflection by teachers on their ongoing classroom experience. Reflective teaching is indeed a suggestive description, but it is not easy to see what would count as reflection and what circumstances are likely to bring it about. Reflection is not a process that one can bring about or engage in by intention – it is something that may happen, rather than something that one can do.

I think it is more useful to think of growth as a process of thinking about and making sense of one's classroom experience and bringing to bear the resulting understanding on one's further teaching. I wish to indicate four kinds of activity that are likely to start or prompt such a process.

Viewing Instances of Teaching

The first activity is viewing someone else's teaching, either live or video-recorded. I do not mean classroom observation for the purpose of identifying, categorizing or counting events of particular kinds, much less seeing someone's demonstration of a particular method of teaching. I mean just seeing classroom lessons as they take place, whichever the class and whoever the teacher. We all know that teachers hardly ever do this, probably because seeing other teachers teach is not a part of the prevailing concept of what is good or proper for a teacher to do. Equally, however, those of us who have seen a video lesson being played to teachers have been struck both by the immediate interest it evokes and by the effect it has in raising the level and quality of pedagogic discussion (see, for instance, Ramani, 1987). There seems to be something in the viewing of a lesson that touches a teacher in a way that talking about teaching does not. It links up with something in the teacher's pedagogic make-up, and brings to the fore some pieces of memory, past perception or understanding which are not otherwise open to recall.

I think there is an analogy between this and the reading of literature, especially fiction. What one reads is a depiction of life and one's interest in reading it stems from the fact that one has been living one's own life. The life one reads about makes connections in some way with the life one has been living, evoking elements in one's experience which are not normally open to retrieval. Reading fiction touches one's understanding or perception, though very inexplicit, of one's own life, with an immediacy and success that reading, say, philosophy does not.

Further, reading literature can be considered a way of living life vicariously, as it were, and, as a result, free of the immediate pressures and tensions that inevitably attend the actual living of one's life. There is, that is to say, both a similarity between life and fiction, which is essential, and a difference or distance which is equally helpful. I think this relationship holds between the teaching one does and the teaching one views: the distance and freedom from immediate pressures of decision-making or attendant feelings of anxiety, insecurity etc. are as productive as the linkages that can be made with one's own teaching.

Perhaps as a result of such freedom and distance, there is a likelihood of making more sense of what one reads or views than can be made of raw experience. By 'making sense' I mean the occurrence of such things as seeing some new connection between one part and another, or a new significance to some event, or a pattern to the different parts or events that one had not seen before. One begins to see a shape to the sequence of events and consequently to develop an understanding of those events. Then, at some point, one begins to make sense of one's own experience in similar terms, thus achieving an understanding of what one has been doing and facing in the classroom. The meaning that is seen to what is vicariously experienced is then transferred to what is actually experienced.

I am of course not suggesting that the meaning that is seen in this way to either vicarious or actual experience is the 'real' or 'true' meaning in some sense. It is just the meaning that one is able to see – or simply happens to see – at a given time. Different persons can see quite different meanings, and the same person can see different meanings at different times. The important thing is that a meaning has been seen – an understanding has been achieved – or, even more importantly, a process of seeing, meaning or achieving understanding has begun. Further, the understanding one has of past teaching operates in one's present teaching, lending new meaning to ongoing classroom events and, equally, being influenced and modified by those events. A teacher's understanding of teaching is thus always in a state of development or change; when it is not, it is no longer be active or alive. The important difference, then, is between teaching that is informed by an active and developing pedagogic understanding and that which is not so informed, rather than between true and false, or superior and inferior, understanding by some criterion. As far as I can see, the term 'reflective teaching' can only mean teaching that engages an understanding of past teaching and has the effect of influencing/changing/developing that understanding.

Making Classroom Decisions

A second activity I wish to suggest is the teacher making pedagogic decisions in the classroom in the light of what happens and how he perceives it at the time. A lesson is normally based on a plan, and needs to be. But a plan is based on a prediction or expectation of how things develop in the classroom and how the learners respond at a particular stage or step. There are always instances of the actual events not matching the prediction and the teacher having to decide what to do differently from the plan. Such on-the-spot decisions are perhaps guided sometimes by alternatives envisaged in plan itself, by memories of other things done on other occasions, or simply by opting for a course of minimal risk. But they can also be guided by a form of pedagogic intuition, that is to say, the significance the teacher perceives to the event concerned, the judgment he/she makes of the learners' current state or readiness for a possible activity, and the larger context of the pattern he/she can see to the progress of the lesson. This latter will involve an engagement of the understanding we have talked about in discussing the effect of viewing instances of teaching. Classroom decision-making can thus benefit from the teacher's pedagogic understanding and, more importantly, it can help to further such understanding – strengthening it, making it more and more readily accessible, adding to it and of course modifying it in different ways. The more decisions the teacher makes, the greater the chance that he engages and advances his current pedagogic understanding.

I am not assuming here that the decisions the teacher makes are likely to be pedagogically sound or good, by some accepted criteria – or even that the teacher himself will find them good or successful by his own standards, all or much of the time. Decisions will often prove to have been wrong in the teacher's own eyes, but that is likely to be a positive input to the further growth of the teacher's understanding. It is by making wrong decisions, and by perceiving them to have been wrong, that a capacity for making better decisions can emerge and strengthen itself. Also, making decisions differently from past decisions involves a modification of the pedagogic understanding that prompts such decisions, resulting in further growth of the understanding. Perhaps, as a teacher's understanding changes and develops in this way, it will come closer to other teachers' understanding of teaching, and the resultant decision-making will then approximate to what is good by more widely accepted standards – or, indeed, have an influence on those wider standards. Classroom decision-making by the teacher is thus productive both of learners' learning (in that, such decisions are responsive to the immediate classroom context, the learners' readiness, etc. instead of a prior prediction or preemption) and of the teacher's pedagogic understanding and growth. There is in fact a strong argument to be made for designing curricula in a way that minimizes prediction and maximizes the scope and need for teachers' classroom decisions.

Teachers are an immediate and constant presence at the place where learning takes place, even if it takes place occasionally, sporadically and not in keeping with the teachers' expectations. Such repeated presence, and continuous involvement in the contexts in which learning happens, often enables teachers to develop a sense or feel for the occurrence of learning – an ability to tell when things are going well and when they are not, quite independently of whether the teaching is going according to plan or not. Many teachers have the experience of coming away from a classroom with a sense of satisfaction or fulfillment on some occasions, and a sense of frustration or failure on others, for no clear reasons that they can see. When teachers make decisions in the classroom at variance with earlier plans and in response to their perception of the immediate context, at least some of those decisions are likely to be guided or influenced by their intuitive feel for the occurrence and non-occurrence of learning. Further, the perceived results of decisions so made are likely to be an influence on the feel for the occurrence of learning – firming it up, perhaps, or making it more readily accessible, or increasing a teacher's confidence in acting on it. Such a feel for learning is an input of great value to teachers' developing understanding of pedagogy and to their professional growth.

Articulating Pedagogic Perceptions

A third activity that can help teachers' growth is attempting to communicate one's current pedagogic understanding to a fellow teacher. This can be very difficult to do when one's understanding is still at a developing stage, perhaps dormant, uncertain and less than accessible. But that is in fact what gives value to an attempt to articulate it. The value is of two kinds. First, attempting to articulate a vague or half-formed idea, perception or understanding is a very good way of making it less vague, better-formed, more accessible to oneself and more open to articulation at the next attempt. Further, an attempt to articulate a half-formed idea often has the effect of making that idea grow and change, in the sense of being seen to be differently formed or differently inter-related to other ideas. As the literature on what is called 'process writing' has brought out powerfully, attempting to say what one means is a very good way of realizing more fully what one means and, equally, of realizing that what one means is different from what one thought it was (see also Malderez, 2003). In a real sense, saying what one has in mind is a way of knowing what one has in mind and also of having more in the mind to say. A teacher's attempt to articulate his/her pedagogic understanding at a given time can thus be very useful both in clarifying that understanding and in furthering it. And there is also a second kind of value to it – the possibility of conveying it to a fellow teacher, leading to a gradual sharing of pedagogic perceptions between teachers. Here too the difficulty of articulating emerging perceptions can be a hurdle to success in communicating them, but it can also be a help. When what is being articulated is something genuinely felt or sensed and when it is being articulated with an effort or struggle, causing several tentative and varied rewordings, it tends to have a particular power to convey itself, especially to someone who similarly has half-felt or half-sensed pedagogic perceptions which are difficult to articulate. The communication that results will certainly fall short of academic standards for explicitness or rhetorical convention, but it will have the valuable effect of making different teachers' perceptions link up and exert an influence on each other, as well as strengthening each teacher's perception and helping it develop further.

Interacting with Specialists' Perceptions

The fourth and last activity I want to suggest is for teachers to try to interact with the more explicit pedagogic perceptions of specialists in the field as they appear in the professional literature. This can be regarded as an extension from a sharing of perceptions between teachers which we have just talked about, but there is a major difference and a further difficulty. Teachers' perceptions are not only in a formative, uncertain and inexplicit state but they are also, necessarily, personal and subjective. Although specialists' arguments and claims too are in many cases based ultimately on their own individual pedagogic perceptions, they are moulded to fit the conventions of academic discourse, and stated as part of a search for some more general, objective truth or knowledge. This makes the specialist's underlying, personal perceptions largely inaccessible to teachers, in addition to the fact that the appurtenances of academic discourse tend to have a discouraging, intimidating effect. The result is that specialist literature is looked on as a distant debate unrelated to teachers' personal experience in classrooms or at most as a body of superior knowledge to be received and retained as such. But teachers who have identified and developed their personal understandings over a period of time – those, that is to say, who have achieved some degree of growth – can perhaps approach the professional literature with a measure of confidence, withstanding the intimidation, working their way through the discoursal manners and making contact with the basic pedagogic perceptions. When this happens, teachers can truly interact with specialists, that is to say, identify the specialists' understandings, interpret them in the light of their own personal understandings and in the process sharpen or modify those personal understandings. The result is not that the teachers have absorbed some academic knowledge, nor that they have gained entry to some academic debate, but simply that they have used some academic literature to strengthen and further their individual pedagogic perceptions. I think this can be a valuable source of teachers' growth, well worth the difficulty involved and carrying the potential of bridging the current gap between teachers and specialists, or even perhaps influencing academic discourse so as to bring it closer to teachers' understandings and make it more directly relevant to teachers' growth.

References

Malderez Angi, 'Alternative Discourses – an interview with Julian Edge', *ELT Journal*, 57/4, 2003.

Ramani Esther, 'The Role of Classroom Interaction in the Integration of Theory and Practice', in Bikram K. Das ed.: *Communication and Learning in the Classroom Community*, Singapore: Regional Language Centre, 1987.

2

Condemned without Crime—Grammar-Translation Method

Shreesh Chaudhary

Robert (Bellarmine) classifies backwardness into four kinds – cultural, economic, educational and regional. In many ways, the first three tie together. The fourth is very different. It implies that even an upper class and caste family in rural areas can be educationally disadvantaged. Backward caste and working class families in rural areas are likely to be doubly or three times more backward, in this sense.

In my village, near Indo-Nepal border in Bihar, I see evidence for this theory of Robert. My village has no electricity[1], no all weather roads, limited access to telephone, hardly any newspapers or television and hardly any use of English. Children growing up there even today have little or no exposure to the English language, no access to a library, etc. Hardly any one speaks English there. No English movies arrive there. The little exposure that a student has to the English language there is limited to the classroom. And even the so called English medium schools, of which we have some now, do not use only and always English. In many schools and colleges, even an English class is taught in Hindi, or in Maithili, the regional languages.

There also are attitudes against English. On the one hand, getting good marks in English is appreciated. I was poor in Mathematics and was seen as a low achiever, a straggler. But I rose in popular esteem when I achieved the class highest in English. Yet the community frowns upon those who speak English among their 'own people'. Though English words are getting into local languages in ever-increasing numbers, few people speak this language anyway. Relatively many people can, therefore, be found to be there who that can write with reasonable fluency and accuracy of grammar, vocabulary and spelling in English. The number of people who can speak in idiomatically acceptable English in acceptable pronunciation is far fewer.

But my village is not the only one of its kind. There are many places of this kind in India even today. Much of the Himalayan region from Kashmir to Mizoram including Nepal, Sikkim and Bhutan, that includes nearly all of Eastern UP, North Central Bihar, Jharkhand, North Bengal and all of Orissa, North Eastern states, Central Indian tribal region from Chhattisgarh to Chambal Valley, and then isolated pockets like Telengana in AP, and some hilly regions in Tamil Nadu, Kerala and Karnataka also meet more or less this description. That roughly accounts for over three fourths of India's population.

Similar regions are there all over the world. There is Bangladesh, Sri Lanka, China, much of South East Asia, North Central Africa and newly independent Central Asian and Eastern European Nations, all of them wanting English, and wanting it in no time. At Anna University, Chennai, just to cite an example, every year hundreds of students return disappointed from special placement camps. They are found professionally competent, but lacking in 'communication' skills'. In simpler words, they have inadequate English. They come from backward castes, classes and regions.

How We Teach them English is a Big Question

Which method would work here? How can we ensure maximal input for everyone so that they have adequate exposure to English? Where are we going to get so many 'competent' teachers from? Or, are we going to abandon the prospective students in these regions telling them you can do without English, just as you have always done, and to say this to them at a time when denial of English is seen as equal to the denial of education[2], when English is practically the only difference between advancement in life and their absence?

Compared with 50 years ago, today there are numerous students from non-English using backgrounds. We can no longer close our eyes to their dream. And yet today we do not know what will help them best.

A good way to answer these questions, Alan Maley[3] rightly says, is to look into history. Briefly, Maley says, history is not a bag of dead and irrelevant facts. It is also a store-house of community's collective experience of what has worked and what has not. There are, Maley says, at least four reasons to consider about history:

- When we look at our past, it becomes clear that many of the current ideas which we think of as being so innovative have, in fact, been around for a long time.
- A second reason for cultivating a sense of history is that it gives us perspective. There is a sense in which we cannot know where we are going without an appreciation of where we have been.
- Much of our current effort is expended on innovation: more new ideas, more new materials, more new research. It could be that much of this frenzied effort is misdirected and even counter-productive.

- Finally, the past offers us a rich source for generating new ideas. We can use it as a stimulus for our own present thinking.

Maley's approach to history appears to be most significant to our present situation for teaching English to vast numbers of learners in schools and colleges in backward areas described above.

History[4] of non-native language learning shows that grammar-translation method has been the most successful method in situations where language had to be learned with limited exposure and little aid. This is how all the foreigners who came to India learnt Indian languages. Most recently, many Christian missionaries learnt Indian languages through translation. They mostly translated the Holy Bible into these languages and then they translated works in these languages into their own. Thus, it is significant that they learnt these languages within months of coming to India that they were able to use them. It is also notable that they learnt these languages so well that soon many of them wrote the first grammars and dictionaries of these languages.

This is how a large number of Indians learnt and still learn English. This is an interesting aspect of the history of the English language in India. Though the English came to India in the early part of the 17th century, hardly[5] any Indian other than those who worked in their factories or elsewhere with them knew even a word of English. Actually, it was the British who learnt the Indian languages then. The situation remained more or less unchanged until about the last quarter of the 18th century. But after the British won some battles[6] in India and acquired political power, Indians had no doubt which way the tide had turned. They knew that the Muslim power was almost gone from India now and the British were the new rulers of this country. The British also created a Supreme Court in Calcutta in 1774 for the administration of justice to the population in the territories under their control, and made English the language of this court.

Suddenly, there was a huge demand for people who could read and write English. Petitions could be read and written only by those that knew this language. Copies of petitions could be made only by those that knew this language. Within the next 50 years, in 1830s, East India Company replaced Persian with English as the language of administration at the higher echelons. The Company announced in 1839 that preference in appointments would be given to those that knew English.

But, suddenly, such large numbers of English knowing Indians were not available. There was a spurt in the number of people who began learning English. But hardly any books or journals were available. Englishmen or women had little interaction with the masses of Indians, and the little that happened took place in Persian or Hindustani. Neither were there many schools and colleges or teachers to help these Indians. But Indians were curious and eager. They made use of anything that helped. Grammar and translation method (GTM) became popular in such a situation.

The History of the English language in India shows few books for learning English before 1774, but after this date there was a spurt in the production of these books. Some popular titles and dates of their publication are given below[7].

Dyches, Thomas 1716 *A Guide to the English Proper for Beginners, Showing a Natural and Easy Method to Pronounce and Express both Common Words and Proper Names in which particular care is taken to show the Accent for Vicious Pronunciation*, Published by the Danish Mission.

Hadley, Capt. George 1772 *Grammatical Remarks on the Practical and Vulgar Dialects of the Indostan Language, commonly called Moors with a Vocabulary English and Moors*[8].

Hadley, Capt. George 1776 *Introductory grammatical remarks on the Persian Language, with a Vocabulary English and Persian.*

Richardson, John 1777 *Dictionary of Persian, Arabic and English in two volumes.*

Gladwin, Francis 1780? *The Persian Moonshie: The English Persian Vocabulary.*

Gladwin, Francis 1780? *The Epitome of Modern Law: English Translation of Alfaz Adwiyeh* A Dictionary of Medical terms by N.N.A. Hai Shiraji, Physician to the Mughal Emperor Shah Jahan.

Forster, H P 1779 *Vocabulary in Two Parts: English and Bengali and Vice Versa, Calcutta*[9].

A Dictionary of English and Hindosthanee, Calcutta, 1786.

A New Spelling Book, Calcutta, 1787.

An English Bengali Vocabulary together with Grammatical Introduction, Calcutta, 1788.

Ingreji O Bengali Bokebilari (English and Bengali Vocabulary), Calcutta: The Clarendon Press, 1793.

A Vocabulary in Two Parts: English and Bengali, Calcutta, 1799.

A Vocabulary – Persian, Arabic and English, Calcutta, 1799.

Even these books were not easy to come by. So by 1820s, Book Societies appeared in different parts of India to produce affordable and useful books. A record of sale of this kind at Calcutta School Book Society is given below[10].

Table 1: Sale of Books by Calcutta School Book Society in 1834.

Books in	*Copies sold*	*Books in*	*Copies sold*
English	31,640	**Bengali**	5,754
Sanskrit	16	**Hindi**	4,171
Arabic	36	**Anglo-Asians**	4,525
Hindustani	3,384		

The books that sold most were *The Elements of English Grammar* and *The Geography of Hindustan*. The result was that in less than 50 years, there were enough English knowing Indians to man the offices of the Imperial Government of India and of the English and Indian merchants trading in India and overseas. By early 20th century, there were close to 10 million English knowing Indians enough to overwhelm the English in India and to demand independence from them. Much of the credit for producing so many English knowing Indians should go to the GTM.

GTM works through modules. The first module is grammar. It teaches, from the point of the learner, the grammatical 'peculiarities' of the language to be learnt. The next module is translation which gives English equivalents of mother tongue expressions. The third module is writing. It teaches spelling, punctuation and other aspects of short and long pieces of formal writing such as business letters, essays, reports, paragraph, etc.

In Addition, it has Two Optional Modules

Students are encouraged to read. Reading is expected to impart vocabulary and idiomatic expressions. Most popular reading in this section have been, besides *Lamb's Tales* from *Shakespeare*, retold, abridged, or in many places, even original works of great prose writers and novelists of English such as Walter Scott, Thomas Hardy, Charles Dickens, Mark Twain, George Eliot, Arthur Conan Doyle, Jane Austen, O'Henry, etc. Many in India believe that a non-native language is learnt best through enjoyable reading. Many Indians are living proof of this claim.

Yet another optional component for GTM is the speaking module. On a periodical basis, events like elocution, recitation, debate and arguing are organized so as to get the learners into the habit of using a formal spoken language. In this manner, GTM helps with all aspects of language, substantially and in a short period of time.

The backbone of the GTM, of course, is its grammar-translation module that teaches all the sentence patterns and essential vocabulary. GTM recognizes that there are only four kinds of sentences, as described below, from the point of view of meaning.

1. (a) Declarative: (i) Affirmative
   (ii) Negative
   (b) Imperative
   (c) Interrogative
   (d) Exclamatory

GTM also recognizes that languages of the world have only four kinds of sentences from the point of view of structure, as shown in (2) below.

2. (a) Simple
   (b) Compound
   (c) Complex
   (d) Mixed

GTM makes similar assumptions about tense and aspects of the grammars of natural languages. For instance, it is assumed that there are only three kinds of tenses, as follows.

3. (a) Present
   (b) Past
   (c) Future

Each tense has four aspects, as follows.

4. (a) Simple (or, Indefinite)
   (b) Progressive (or, Continuous)
   (c) Perfect
   (d) Perfect Progressive

So the equivalent of English Simple Present Tense is traced in the learner's mother tongue (MT), and the learner is given some general principles for translating particular kinds of sentences from his mother tongue into particular ways in English. In Hindi, for instance, all sentences ending in *–taa hai, te hain,* or *tii hai,* constitute simple present tense. Thus the following are simple present tense sentences in Hindi.

5. *raam aam khaataa hai.*
6. *siitaa gaanaa gaatii hai.*
7. *ladke maidaan mein khelte hain.*
8. *ladkiyaan patra likhtii hain.*

Then a principle, such as the following, is presented.

9. (a) All sentences ending in *taa hai/tii hai* exhibit subject-verb-object/ complement order and they add *–s* or *–es* to the verb.

   (b) Sentences ending in *te hain/tii hain* have the same order as in (9a), but they add no extra particle to the verb.

Following the principles (9a) and (9b), the sentences from (5) to (8) are translated as follows.

10. Ram eats a mango.
11. Sita sings a song.
12. Boys play on the ground.
13. Girls write letters.

Similar principles are cited for other tense and aspect types within different meaning and structural classes, and the basic syntax and vocabulary are successfully taught in a short period of time, usually in less than two years. After these two years, translation still continues, but grammar and writing take primacy. Beginning with parts of speech and parsing, curriculum includes clause analysis, synthesis, conversion of sentences from direct to indirect speech, also known as narration, followed by conversion of sentences from active to passive voice, etc. By this time, writing module graduates from simple letters to friends describing a festival and simple applications requesting leave of absence to longer essays on the importance of books, patriotism, etc[12]. Finally, students move to recitation, elocution, debate, arguing, etc. Reading in various forms continues through all the years of English education.

The problem with GTM arises not from the grammar-translation module, but when other modules are not implemented thoroughly. Otherwise, for the kind of learners described above, GTM works better and faster.

I have no clue as to why India began apologizing for this method and almost abandoned it. Whatever else GTM lacked, it certainly did not lack in positive results. The evidence for this claim may come from the sale of grammar, translation and bi-lingual dictionary books. Books like *LIFCO Tamil-English Dictionary* and *LIFCO English-Tamil Dictionary* sold thousands of copies. In the North, it used to be *Bhaskar Hindi-English Dictionary* and *Bhaskar English-Hindi Dictionary.* In South India, generations of English learners were brought up on Wren and Martin's *Grammar and Composition in English.* In the North, that honour went to J.C. Nesfield's *English Grammar* and *Composition*, which was available in both English and in bi-lingual, i.e. Hindi-English, editions.

But beginning with late 1970s, and this period coincides with the British Council sponsored Summer Institutes for quick training to teachers in using direct method, communicative method, phonetic method, etc. the prestige of GTM began declining. These summer institutes gave free[13] copies of *Advanced Learner's Dictionary of English*[14] that emphasized 'correct' pronunciation of words and gave meaning of English words in English. Steadily the sale of the ALDs rose[15], and those of LIFCO and Bhaskar declined. School students of today, even in places such as the ones I described above, do not even seem to have heard of these books. Neither have they seen the new ones, they are expensive and they use strange ways of non-native language teaching. This trend must be reversed. English must come also to the disadvantaged, as Robert has desired all his life.

References

1. Electric wires have arrived now, and occasionally some electricity is also supplied, but it is hardly worth thc name.
2. UNESCO has a proposal suggesting absence of opportunity to learn English may be considered equal to denial of education. See Phillipson, Tom 1997 *Linguistic Imperialism*, London : Oxford University Press.

3. During early 1980s Alan was the Director of the British Council at Madras, and is a good friend of Robert and many other English teachers in South India. For his views on the relevance of history for finding answers to ELT questions, see Maley, Alan 2001 'A Matter of Time' in *English Teaching Professional*, Issue Eighteen, January 2001, pp. 5-8.
4. See, for instance, Chaudhary, Shreesh 2008 *A Sociolinguistic History of Foreigners' and Foreign Languages in India*, New Delhi: Cambridge University Press.
5. At the lower echelons, Tamil and Telugu in Madras, Marathi and Gujarati in Bombay, and Urdu and Bengali in Calcutta presidency became the language of administration.
6. Notably, the British prestige in India went up from that of a mere trading company to a politically and militarily powerful group of foreigners after the British won the Battle of Plassey against Sirajuddaulah in 1757, and the Battle of Buxar against Mir Kasim in 1764.
7. See Chaudhary 2008, cited above, for more on this issue.
8. The manuscript had been ready since 1765 itself, but it took time for publication.
9. The author of this book held the post of Senior Merchant in the Company.
10. Ayyar, Chandrika, *Educational and Intellectual Pursuits*, Kanpur: Prajna Prakashan, 1987.
11. See, for instance, Thakur, K.P. 1997/2006 *A Practical Guide to English Translation & Composition*, Patna: Bharati Bhawan, p. 11.
12. Sinha, Surendra Prasad, *English in India : A Historical Study with Particular Reference to English Education in India*, Patna : Janaki Prakashan, 1978, pp. 161-2.
13. In the 19th century when English companies introduced tea in India, they used to offer it free at street corners. Interested customers could take free sachets and some money as well with which to buy sugar and milk which are essential parts of a good cup of tea in India. Now India is the largest tea-drinking country in the world.
14. Hornby, A.S. (first published 1948, sixth edition appeared in 2000) *Advanced Learner's Dictionary of English*, Oxford : Oxford University Press.
15. Friends in the Oxford University Press tell me that OUP sells above a 100,000 copies of ALD every quarter in South India alone. Now other dictionary publishers, such as Cambridge University Press, Collins-Cobuild, Longman, Macmillan, etc. also have their ALDs.

3

To Use or Not to Use Technology for Teaching English

M.N.K. Bose

Technology: A Friend or Foe?

I'm choosing a risky question, risky because we, teachers, as any literate persons, have already married technology and life without it is empty. We wake up with it, start our day with it, go to office and work with it, have lunch and dinner with it and go to bed with it. We have fallen for it, yet we fall apart when it 'hits' us. So, the question is justified, I think. Have we gone all out for technology or do we still have to stand away and think? Does technology offer solutions to all our problems of teaching for all of us? Is it a solace or a source of more problems? Is teaching possible without technology? The National Survey of Information Technology in Higher Education in 1994 notes that the colleges in India have been using information technology poorly, the percentage varying as follows:

WWW based resources: 9%, CD ROM materials: 9%, computer lab/classroom: 24%, commercial courseware: 19%, multimedia: 11%, Email: 25% and presentation of handouts: 28%; this confirms what Geoghegan pointed out in 1994 that only a very small proportion of faculty are actively using instructional technology, and these tend to be 'innovators' or 'early adopters' rather than 'mainstream' faculty.[1]

Teaching without Technology

In the 1960s, Sydney Pressy came up with the idea of a teaching machine, in order to replace a teacher, using technology as a substitute for a teacher. The idea as well as the machine was rejected but has come back with a bang in another 'avatar' called computer. Indian educational history tells us that teachers were successfully teaching languages (more difficult than English) and subjects more complicated than those we teach nowadays without recourse even to printed books. The methodology used was rough-tuned and not backed by finer shades of linguistic and psychological principles borne out by researches (at least not known to have been supported by them at that time). The success rate was so high that the teachers' methods never came under any scanner nor was there severe criticism against them. Generations of students passed out without 'annual or semester examinations' but after severe, nerve-racking examinations.

Teaching with Technology

In these days of information explosion and the technological do how, on the other hand, we are pushed into using technology (whether we like it or not) for the benefits it allegedly has; it is claimed that teacher's work is made easier and learners' performance is enhanced. Starting from the use of chalk and blackboard up to the use of palmtops or iPods, technology lends a helping hand to us, not only inside the classroom but also outside, more in the distance learning programmes. We have become so dependent on technology that we can never think of a classroom without a book or notebook or a dictionary or a calculator; electronic dictionaries are no longer rare in classrooms, not to mention the use of cutting edge technology – the hi-tech virtual classrooms.

How You Use Technology Matters

The secret of success is not in using or not using technology but how you use it and how the technology you use supports human learning processes. If two lessons —digital or face-to face—include all the elements of learning, learning will occur in both. Alternatively, if the latter is interactive and the former is not, then learning will successfully take place in the latter and not the former. Clark and Mayer[2] provide support to this, showing that there are hardly any learning differences between digital and face-to-face delivery in the 300 studies comparing learning with various forms of electronic distance technology to learning in face-to-face classrooms.

The following tips are provided by the researchers to use technology usefully:

- **Use relevant visuals to promote learning:** use of relevant graphics with words has been found to enhance learner performance by 89% in 9 experiments by Mayer (ibid).
- **Use audio to describe complex visuals:** use of words and visuals overloads the eyes (visual centres of working memory) and the absence of audio leads to the under use of the ears (the auditory centre of working memory).

- **Make your language personal:** use of 'you' and 'we' resulted in improvement in learning in Mayer's (ibid) experiments.
- **Lean lessons more successful:** Mayer (ibid) also found the lesson of 80 words with illustrations resulted in better achievement than the lesson of 600 words with illustrations.

CALL – A Brief

Computer has taken several 'avtars' since its invention; from a room-occupying main frame to one sitting on the top of your palm increasing its power to the extent of sending the entire Encyclopaedia Britannica in two seconds at the rate of 2 Gigabits per second. However, the father of Computer, John Von Neumann, should feel shocked to see its (mis)uses, if he were alive now. It is no more the prerogative of the computer scientists to make use of computers; in fact, computers are used to a threatening extent in some schools and colleges that teachers seem agitated about them fearing that they might make them redundant[3]. The myths of computer I wrote about[4] in 1986 remain no longer myths. Nevertheless, it is true that when I suggested Computer Assisted English Language Learning (CAELL) as an optional course for the Postgraduate Diploma in the Teaching of English (PGDTE) programme at the then Central Institute of English and Foreign Languages (CIEFL), Hyderabad in 1986-87, about 30 years after its establishment, there was stiff opposition from senior professors and it took a lot of sweet-talking and arm twisting before it was accepted. Teachers and learners of languages now find them more useful in their business of language learning with the materials produced exclusively for this purpose. Since 1960s, the use of computers in the field of education has been flourishing; having begun as CAI (Computer Assisted Instruction), it has branched off to CALL (Computer Assisted Language Learning), exclusively to assist the language learning process. Van Campen at Stanford University produced the first programme in the 1960s to learn Russian, followed by Curtin et al. producing PLATO (Programmed Logic for Automated Teaching Operation) in the 1970s and Dartmouth College provided BASIC for the novice programmers.

Why CALL?

Kumar (2000) along with Higgins (1984) and Ahmed et al. (1985) list the following as the major advantages of Computer Assisted Learning,

- Students learn at their own pace and test themselves, leading to learner autonomy.
- The materials are broken down into manageable units taking the burden off the learner's mind.

- Feedback received is so personal that the affective system of the learner is made use of.
- Several time-tested theories of teaching/learning back up this system of teaching/learning.
- Learners learn at their own time and place and learning becomes more and more individualized.
- Computers are unbiased, consistent and untiring 'teachers'; adding novelty.

Communicative CALL (CACLL)

Dissatisfied with the materials that created monotony because of the 'drill' type and lack of learner initiative, language specialists turned out programmes that get the learners interact with it to a large extent; these programmes immersed them in the activities providing much scope for a lot of interaction[5]. The result was more interactive and challenging materials for the learners to tackle at the computer. In addition to all the above advantages, CACLL materials

- aim at acquisition practice, making the input comprehensible.
- allow the students to generate original utterances, grammar taught implicitly unlike in the earlier materials.
- help them to correct their errors themselves.
- provide a lot of challenge as well as fun; learning is no more a tyrannous experience.
- use as natural English as possible so that the students experience life-like situations.

The CALL programmes are not without disadvantages; they most often leave the learner alone, depriving him/her of the opportunity to interact with his/her peers; they present to the learners predetermined uses of language based on the imagination of the programme writer of what would take place rather than what people really say in real situations, and it wastes a lot of time especially when the learners do not have the basic computer skills. However, it is claimed by many practitioners in India and abroad that CALL and CACLL materials have a lot of potential for developing the learner's reading skills. Why is it so? Is it because the fun and the challenge elements in them? Is it because reading itself, utilizing the peculiar power of the brain, requires such materials for its development? Let's see what's reading and how it is not developed properly in the present classes before we look at how these materials help develop reading. Pardon me for this little digression.

Reading: Gymnastics for the Brain[6]

Most of us are not aware of and do not appreciate what our brains do when we read; while we are reading, for a few seconds, we are putting our brains through gymnastics so complex that no scientist has yet described them fully. Indeed, trying to understand it involves ophthalmology, pedagogy, neurology, linguistics, psychology, computer science, cybernetics and more. Reading occupies our life so much that we take it for granted; even going for a stroll means reading posters, sign boards, street names and etc. But reading became commonplace very recently. The Greeks and Romans had professional readers who read aloud and in the Middle Ages monks did the job. Who would take pains to read, if the text is written like this?

FURTHERDOWNTHE STMARTINCAN-
ALWITHBOTHLOCKSCLOSEDDISPLA-
YEDASTRAIGHTLINEOFINKYCOLOU-
REDWATERINTHEMIDDLEOFITWAS

This was how the whole book was written and not until around the year 1000, did reading become more visual than oral, because of better manuscripts and around 1400 A.D. printing came into being to make the reading matter more legible. However, reading was the privilege of a tiny minority even in the West till about the 19th century.

Unfortunately, reading continues to be the casualty mainly because many learned adults read not only slowly but also have the habit of pronouncing the words as they read. Emile Javal, an ophthalmologist discovered that, while we read, our eyes divide each line into six or seven portions of some ten letters each, bouncing from one segment to the next in a mind-boggling one-250,000th of a second. So, we need less than a quarter of a second to identify each group of letter (we never identify letters at all!). For example, when we read this text, we don't add B + O + O + K or M + A + K + E to recognize 'book' and 'make'; only unfamiliar words are read letter by letter. In fact, it has been found that if words were cut in half horizontally, the upper half was still sufficient enough for us to recognize the meaning. You can think of words written on the wall, parts of which are rubbed out, yet you can read those words, as long as they are in a language you know.

How do we Understand what we Read?

It is our brain's extraordinary capacity that comes to our help. As the 17th century philosopher Rene Descartes once wrote, 'when we see a hat moving from our window we deduce from it that a man is going by', similarly, the signposts in the text we read such as 'and', 'so', 'thus', 'in fact', 'however', 'fortunately' warn us of what's coming and help our understanding of the text. What comes to our minds when we read the following sentence?

When he saw the rope, he got a shock.

It would mean different things to different readers, but if we are told where the action took place, say, in a forest, suddenly all differences disappear. Understanding means coordinating the text with our cognitive map, built by our memory. Our short-term memory is weak and is unable to remember more than 15 words for more than 20 seconds after reading them, whereas our long-term memory is perplexingly powerful doing the jobs of sorting, blending, deducing, assimilating and filing, all done at unimaginable speed. Psychologist Michel Denis concludes after his experiments that 'the sentence is always *less descriptive* than what we see'. For example, when we read a sentence

The Prime Minister hoisted the national flag,

we see (in our mind) the Prime Minister standing near the flag post, the tricolour flag going up slowly, unfurling, flowers falling down, etc. None of that is in the sentence, though.

Understanding what we read need not have anything to do with intelligence. It is an aptitude, like being able to run fast and readers who visualize the most have the best memories. Balzac, who was said to 'devour' books, Bergier, who needed less than 30 minutes to read a 200-page book, Kennedy, who used to read at dizzying speed had amazing memory. 'Reading', says Elisabeth Badinter, philosopher and historian, 'is a way of living more richly, with greater satisfaction.'

Reading in CALL and CACLL

Reading is definitely the biggest beneficiary in CALL and CACLL, probably next to writing; software market is flooded with materials for developing reading skills. Moreover, studies reveal that learners show greater inclination to use these materials for reading rather than other skills or for learning grammar or vocabulary, though materials are available for all of them, probably because these materials have a lot of challenge as well as flexibility in them[7]. CALL/CACLL materials such as STORYBOARD, TEXTBAG, CHATTERBOX, have been found very useful for developing reading skills.

Multimedia in Teaching/Learning/Reading

The 21st century option for teaching/learning is not just using the computers with readymade or tailor-made software, which are most often text-based (single medium) but using multimedia packages (MPs) on the computer. Multimedia is a notion of using multiple channels of communication such as text, graphics, animation, pictures, video and sound to present information under the control of the computer. Though this idea is not quite new as it has been the practice followed in printing calendars and signboards and textbooks (with texts and pictures), it has come back with a bang in the field of education. Multimedia packages, no doubt, help the learners understand the information, as learning is aided by various mental processes but reading is often the casualty as learners have recourse to other means of understanding and may fail to exploit their reading skills. It is like someone listening to the news bulletin over the radio has a better opportunity to develop his/her listening skills than the one who watches it on the TV, as the latter provides visuals and helps the understanding even if his/her listening is not fully exploited.

Many researchers have found that the use of MPs results in better learner performance compared to traditional classrooms, topics ranging from language, chemistry and biology to the procedures for the operation of complicated instruments in the fields of engineering and technology[8]. They have also proved that it is not so much the media types used that affect the learner performance but the information they are used for presenting; for example, combining animation with verbal narration has been shown to be effective in problem solving tasks. Because of the vast possibilities provided by MPs these days, they are used in children's education, especially children with neural disabilities such as autism, dyslexia and rett syndrome, to a large extent under the new category of 'edutainment', educating them with entertainment.

Why do CALL and MPs succeed more than the traditional classroom teaching in enhancing learner performance? The following have been pointed out as possible reasons:

- The information is necessarily structured and this facilitates learning since structure and organization facilitate information processing in human beings.
- Both of them provide instruction in an interactive way and this in turn improves retention and speed of learning.
- Novelty associated with them has been found significantly decreasing the differences in learning performance between students.
- The 'Hawthorne Effect' i.e. the tendency to improve their performance due to subject being studied or being paid extra attention.

These are in addition to the advantages of CALL and CACLL mentioned above.

In Close

I began this paper with a question that has been nagging many minds, not only of teachers but also of parents. I have attempted to present my ideas of how technology can be put to use in English classes, but I am still not convinced that teachers are at home with technology. Even today, with a lot of computers around us, a lot of noise made about the use of EDUSAT and the like, teachers are not clear about their use in teaching nor are they comfortable with them; distance education institutions, where technology has a big contribution to make, use computers for delivering materials and calculating the results only! Technology will succeed on the day when teachers, irrespective of where they teach and what they teach, replace the textbooks with CDs or their materials on their websites for the learners to download at their own will and pace, when the printed books in the libraries are replaced with CD ROMs, when the blackboards in the classrooms are replaced with the touch screens. We look forward to that day.

References

1. Popli A. and Popli S., 'Advanced Technology in Teaching', Paper presented in the National Conference on English Language Teaching, Vellammal Engineering College, Chennai, 2006.
2. Clark R.C. and R.E. Mayer, *e-Learning and the Science of Instruction*, 2nd Edition, San Francisco: Pfeiffer, 2007.
3. Dhaif H.A., 'Can Computers Teach languages?' *English Teaching Forum,* July, 1989.
4. Bose M.N.K., 'A few computer myths', *The Hindu*, 1986.
5. Dutt P.K., 'Teaching with and without CALL materials: a comparison', Unpublished M. Lit. thesis at CIEFL, Hyderabad, 1988.
6. Most of the information in this section on reading comes from Javron J., 'What happened when we read', *Reader's Digest*, June, 1986.
7. Dutt P.K., ibid.
8. Lawrence T., *Challenges of teaching with technology across the curriculum. Issues and Solutions*, Information Science Publishing, 2003.

Bibliography

Ahmed K.G., Corbett M. and Sussex R., *Computers, language learning and language teaching*, Cambridge: CUP, 1985.

Higgins J. and Johns T., *Computers in language learning*, London: Collins, 1984.

Kumar K.L., *Educational Technology*, New Age International (P) Ltd. Publication, 2000.

4

Can We Dispense with R.P. in ESL Classroom 'Here and Now'?: An Indian Perspective

Stanley Mohan

> *The position and prospects of R.P. today, then, it seems to me are not very bright. If I may venture a prophecy, R.P. is slowly but surely on its way out.*
>
> (*David Abercrombie:1991*)

David Abercrombie's gloomy prediction is based on the sound argument that R.P. has ceased to be phonetically stable as it has never been homogenous. The trend at the beginning of the 21st century is to replace R.P. or NRP. The suggested alternatives are General American or the Scottish Accent. But in the absence of an acceptable alternative model, is it easy to dispense with R.P. right now, totally? Abercrombie's prophecy comes at a time when globalization has started renewing the strength of English as a global language. There is stiff competition among Asian nations to gain working knowledge of English so that they can become the 'ultimate destination' of Multinational Companies. The MNCs seem to prefer Received Pronunciation or General American. But, it is the predicament of teachers of English all over the globe as to which model they can use for teaching English, in case R.P. is displaced as a model.

Received Pronunciation is the ideal which is approximated by an average Indian. India is a large multilingual country with no Indian language to become its link language. Though Hindi has a greater number of users in India, the North-South divide displaces its preference as a link language. In this scenario, English continues to integrate India as a nation. Though the system of education in India is still largely Macaulayian, the goals of teaching English have changed dramatically over the years. English is no longer viewed as a colonial hangover. To put it succinctly, English has gone so deep into the Indian sensibility that even an illiterate Indian prefers to use English words in place of pure Indian equivalents in their day-to-day conversation. For instance, 'Carry out your own bag, Avoid to use polythene bag' (John: 2007) – the admonition in 'english' at the entrance of Mother Dairy Booth in Delhi has preference over the Hindi version. But the question is, whether varieties of English – called 'englishes' in postcolonial parlance- can lock horns with R.P. as a desirable model. Caught in the midst of multitudinous languages coupled with dialectal variations, in India, it is difficult to arrive at a single acceptable model of pronunciation like RIP (Received Indian Pronunciation). Moreover, most of the seminal texts used in language classes are authored by westerners and even books written by Indian authors invariably use R.P. as a model.

The question remains, do we have an acceptable model of pronunciation to be taught in Indian schools and colleges at the present time? The question continues to haunt educationists and curriculum designers all over India. It may sound politically incorrect, to urge learners to take up GA as a model. Though it is controversial to sustain R.P. which smacks of colonialism, there seems to be no way out. Often English Language experts talk about decolonizing English education in India. It can be done content-wise but not accent-wise at the present moment. Can a single variety of Indian English emerge as an acceptable model on the lines of Received Pronunciation? Can we communicate with world users of English with perfect intelligibility? Developing General Indian English (GIE) or Indian Variety of English (IVE) or Standard Indian English (SIE) has tormented Institutes of English in India. But, replacing R.P. with any other single indigenous English model at this point is a risky proposition. It will engender another Babel.

The following issues may be considered seriously to perceive the deep-rooted problems inherent in the use of English in India.

1. Complexities of multilingualism
2. Prevalence of bilingualism
3. Cultural diversities
4. Inconsistency in the use of English in India
5. Immensity of ESL material to be prepared

It has to be appreciated that an average Indian is a polyglot, but the influence of Indian languages on the use of English has to be handled discreetly. Cultural diversities also add complexity to the issue on hand. As culture plays a strong role in the acquisition of language, cultural diversities certainly account for the multi-pronged diversities in the use of English in India. Indians are so used to code-switching and code-mixing that they are left with an inconsistent, non-standard form of English which is the result of too many languages, dialectal variations, diverse cultures and subcultures. The biggest problem that is foreseen is the immensity of ESL material that has to be prepared using standard Indian English.

Some of the nuances and oddities of Indian English should be considered before embarking on a unified model. Though English is spoken as a second language in India, it has around hundred million users which is relatively higher than the number of native speakers in a single geographical location. These are the features which may affect 'intelligibility' of Indian English at an international level:

- Indian English has only one phoneme /ə/ corresponding to RP's /ʌ/ /ɜː/ and /ə/[1]
- Similarly it has one phoneme /ɒ/ corresponding to RP/ɒ/ and /ɔː/[2]
- Monopthongs /e:/ and /o:/ replace the diphthong /ei/[3]
- Often no distinction is maintained between /i:/ and /I/. There is a tendency to replace /i:/ with /I/[4].
- Some Indian speakers tend to replace /ei/ with /e/[5].
- Most of the vowels of English are approximated to vowels of local Indian languages. So often 'lorry' becomes /la:ri/ rather than /lɒri/.
- Most of the consonants in the Indian languages are retroflex; naturally English consonants are also retroflexed.
- The dental fricatives /θ/ /ð/ are often replaced with /t/ and /d/
- The consonants /v/ and /w/ are very rarely distinguished.
- /z/ is replaced with /dʒ/[6]
- /z/ is replaced with /s/[7]
- Initial and medial /r/ sound is a strong tap. Indians are so fond of /r/ that they tend to pronounce /r/ wherever and whenever they come across the sound. In other words, in words like 'shirt' where /r/ becomes /ɜː/ is rarely followed by the common man. The comfortable pronunciation of shirt is /ʃərt/.
- Very often /p/ and /b/ are not properly distinguished, because some Indian languages like Tamil have only one letter of the alphabet to represent both the voiceless and voiced forms of the phoneme
- /v/ and /w/ are replaced by one phoneme /v/ realized as frictionless labio-dental or weakly rounded /w/
- /f/ is often used to replace /p/ – for example 'pants' is pronounced 'fants' and 'pleat' becomes 'fleet'
- In Indian English /p/ is invariably unaspirated in all positions.
- Influenced by the mother tongue, Indian users indulge in epenthesis, so that they pronounce 'film' as /filim/ or /filem/ and 'school' becomes /iskool/.

- Indians also tend to remove syllabic consonants and add an extra syllable. Instead of saying /bʌtn/, they say /bətən/ and /mʌtn/ becomes /mətən/.
- Indian English is syllable-timed as many Indian languages are, resulting in strange stress patterns and rhythm in the use of English.
- Transliteration of English sounds into Indian languages also plays havoc. Certain sounds that do not exist in the Indian languages are approximated. For instance, the English vowel /æ/ does not exist in Tamil. Transliterators use either /ma:n/ or /mane/ to represent /mæn/. This works in reverse to affect the local Indian languages too.
- English accent is often sacrificed for the Indian accent. Even word stress is changed. It is no longer tech'nology but techno'logy.
- English words have been assimilated into a form of Tamil which is commonly used by illiterate natives. For instance, **office** is pronounced /a:bi:s/ and **coffee** is pronounced /ka:bi/ and **tiff** as /dib/. Interestingly, some such forms are given primacy over equivalents in Indian languages.
- In English, accentual pattern depends on whether the word is used as a noun or an adjective or a verb. In Indian English, the feature of change in accent according to the function of the word is not always found in Indian English.
- In connected speech, words that are normally accented in native English are sometimes left unaccented in Indian English.[9]
- In intonation, Indian speakers sometimes do not divide their sentences into groups correctly. sometimes, they place the nucleus on the wrong word.[10]

This is just the tip of the iceberg. How can all these differences be discounted. Some are very enthusiastic about the authenticity of Indian variety of English. But if there are too many differences, English will not be English but Tanglish or Hinglish or sometimes half-baked English. If these features of Indian English are pushed further, perfect intelligibility will be called into question.

If such is the condition of Indian varieties of English, how can we arrive at a standardized Indian model of English which can be taught in schools and colleges? Hence, it is not feasible to replace RP in the Indian context here and now. Binoo John's *Entry From Backside: Hazaar Fundaas of Indian English* tickles the readers with funny examples of Indian English hoping against hope that Indian English will gain respectability and acceptability as a 'subgenre' of English. Even then, till such time, we cannot pronounce **'R I P'** for RP in India.

Notes:

1. /bʌs/ becomes /bəs/ and /bɜːd/ becomes /bərd/ /h ɔː s/ becomes /hɒrs/.
2. /geit/ becomes /ge:t/.

3. field becomes 'filled'; 'sleep' becomes 'slip' & 'feet' becomes 'fit'.
4. later becomes letter.
5. /z əʊ ɒ l ə dʒ i becomes /dʒ əʊ ɒ l ə dʒ i/.
6. *falls* becomes *false*, *fears* becomes *fierce* and *peas* becomes *peace.*
7. In the case of 2 *absent* (adj and verb) the accent is on the first syllable; 2 *object* (noun and verb) both accented on the first syllable.
8. *Several other things & 'Indian students' Hostel'.*
9. *'Good Evening', I know what you mean.*

References

Abercrombie David, *Fifty Years in Phonetics*, Edinburgh: Edinburgh University Press, 1991.

Bansal R.K. & J.B. Harrison, *Spoken English for India*, Bombay: Orient Longman Ltd., 1980.

Collins Beverley and M. Mees Inger, Practical Phonetics and Phonology, London: Routledge, 2003.

John Binoo K., *Entry from Backside Only*: Hazaar Fundaaș of Indian-English, New Delhi: Penguin, 2007.

5

Linguistic Aspects of ESL Listening—Some Observations

R. Usha

Introduction

What's Listening?

Listening is a complex process wherein the auditory system, the brain and language interact. This interaction converges for the realization of one goal, i.e. comprehension. It appears that some listening can occur in spite of difficulties with physiological, neurological and cognitive functions, but not without linguistic functions.

Listening comprises an intricate chain of events. Sound waves, which are nothing but minute changes in air-pressure, are meaningless and convey no information until they reach the ears. Here, they are converted into nerve impulses to be interpreted by the brain. The understanding of speech mostly occurs instantaneously.

Language, being a means of human communication, plays a pivotal role in the process of listening. Effective listening is an important prerequisite to acquisition of knowledge and language learning. In ancient times, knowledge was imparted only orally and handed down from generation to generation. There were no written documents. The Vedas in Sanskrit, the scriptures in Greek and Latin and epics such as Homer's *Illiad* and *Odyssey* were recited and not read. The Vedas have been rightly called 'Shruta' meaning, 'the heard'. During the recitation of the Vedas, one had not only to reproduce the sounds accurately but also adhere strictly to the intonation patterns, because even the slightest change in intonation brought about a difference in meaning.

Language necessarily requires its learners to be sensitive to the sound patterns and to relate them to context and meaning. Listening correctly or accurately is necessary if one expects to speak a language properly. This is largely proven by the fact that hearing

–impaired children are invariably born mute. A child with a hearing loss attempts to match his speech with the 'distorted' utterances he hears from others. If he is to make his speech intelligible, then he has to undergo special training.

Some Theoretical Issues

Hearing: The first faculty

It is an ubiquitous fact that man's contact with the environment is established through his senses. Dr Alfred Tomatis (1987), a French scientist, says that language learning begins even when the baby develops inside the mother's womb. He finds it amazing and remarkable that the only fully developed faculty of the newborn baby is its hearing. He says that the foetus begins to hear the mother's voice transmitted down the spinal column and through the amniotic fluid. The unborn child even acquires intonation patterns and language-specific hearing habits. The shock of birth, Tomatis claims, is largely caused by our being propelled from the environment where sound is transmitted through liquid to the one where it is carried by air.

Dichotomy between Hearing and Listening

Though very often used synonymously, hearing and listening are not identical activities. Hearing is just one of the five sensory mechanisms and involves a passive reception of sounds while listening may be defined as an active meaning-construction process. While listening, one receives spoken words and formulates them into ideas or concepts. The following analogy clarifies the distinction between hearing and listening: Assuming that A and B are two friends talking to each other in a crowded and noisy market street, we say that A or B 'listens' to the other friend who is talking, and simultaneously 'hears' the cacophony of noises in the street. Listening thus involves not only reception but also 'paying attention to', comprehending, re-creating, interpreting, evaluating and responding to what is being said. It is as much a mental phenomenon as it is a physiological function. The goal of a listener is to hear what the speaker says, understand what he says and retain information or respond to it.

The Listening Process – An Overview of Contributions from Diverse Disciplines

Listening and Reading

Listening is often considered to be parallel to reading. The reader and the listener are both viewed as active participants in the creation of meaning. However the processes of understanding are different. Spoken texts have features such as variations in pronunciation, pauses, hesitation, repetition, half-formed sentences and back-tracking etc. which are practically non-existent in a written text. Yet the grammatical and lexical parsing skills essential for reading are also necessary for listening, since written English and spoken English texts are based on nearly the same linguistic norms. The underlying linguistic 'competence' is the same for the written and spoken modes of languages. As a result of this and the vast number of researches in reading skills, the understanding of listening in language learning has been directly influenced by the understanding of reading skills. Some of these influences include factors like the presence or absence of schemata or background knowledge (Long 1989), interactionism in language processing (McClelland 1987) and the organization and complexity of materials.

First and Second Language Acquisition Research

Listening development promotes the accessibility dimension of language acquisition according to Klein (1987). First language acquisition researches show that developing sensitivity to the sounds and patterns of sounds in any language quickens language acquisition. Studies of Krashen (1977), Hatch (1983), McLaughlin, Rossman and McLeod (1983), and Chaudron (1985) emphasize the key role that listening plays in the development of a learner's second/foreign language particularly in the initial stages of development.

Psycholinguistics

Psycholinguists offer many valuable insights into the process of listening comprehension. According to them the process of comprehension begins with a sound wave arriving at the hearer's ears. Sound waves are continuous, not in chunks that correspond to discrete sounds in printed words. In order to find the meaning of an utterance in his mental lexicon, the hearer breaks the continuous wave into word-like chunks. He identifies discrete sound units – phonemes. The meaning of an utterance thus depends on the meaning of the words it contains and on the morphological, syntactic and semantic decoding.

Neurolinguistics

Neurolinguists are now trying to discover how the brain performs the function of receiving and understanding spoken language. Studies in neurolinguistics are yet to explain how exactly people understand spoken language or what brain cells are associated with language processing. Information about parts of the brain which would probably be associated with language ability and in particular, the ability to listen, has been obtained from patients suffering from brain damage.

As a result of certain kinds of brain injuries, such as those caused by a stroke or head injury, the patient seldom loses all language abilities. Only a part of language abilities is impaired while others remain intact. Detailed examinations of aphasic patients reveal that they can perceive vowel sounds well but are poor in identifying consonant sounds. Their perception of speech improves when the rate of speech is very low.

The Present Study

Since the 1950s many important and useful insights have been gained about the numerous factors that influence comprehension of spoken language. But most of them have been derived only from logico-deductive reasoning and classroom-teaching experience. There has been a need of empirical research to investigate the ways in which a number of various factors affect comprehension, i.e. how each factor functions in promoting or hindering listening comprehension especially of ESL listeners belonging to different levels of language proficiency.

A study was therefore conducted to meet this requirement. In India, researches in listening seem to be in the embryonic stage. The importance of listening as a skill imperative for language development and as a skill that requires systematic training and practice cannot be over emphasized. Its importance has been realized only in the past decade or so and schools and colleges have incorporated a listening comprehension component in their English Language Teaching Curriculum. But there do not seem to be any research to identify the problems these ESL listeners encounter while listening to varieties of spoken English.

The objectives of the study were:

- To understand the process of listening comprehension of some ESL users of different proficiency levels in India.
- To identify the linguistic factors and analyse how each of these linguistic factors functions in promoting or impeding listening comprehension of ESL learners in India.

The experiment conducted to achieve these objectives had two parts. The first part aimed at assessing the influence of phonetic factors of speech such as tempo of speech, length and frequency of pauses, fundamental frequency and amplitude variations on ESL listening comprehension. The second part investigated the influence of other linguistic factors i.e. phonological, lexical, syntactic and semantic on listening.

During the course of this study, visits were made to one of the Area Flight Control Centres at Madras to observe the communication between pilots and air-traffic controllers.

This paper confines itself to only a part of the study conducted and presents the following:

1. A brief account of the real life communication between pilots and air-traffic control officers.
2. The experimental method, analysis and observations pertaining to the phonetic aspects of listening comprehension of some ESL users in India.

A quantification of the prosodic features of the listening texts used in this study is also presented.

Communication between Pilots and Air-Traffic Control Officers: A Real Life Experience

During the course of the present study, visits were made to one of the Area Flight Control Centres at Chennai to observe the kind of interaction that takes place between pilots on the ground and in the air, and the air-traffic control (ATC) officers operating from ground control. The long-range communication between the pilots and ATC officers was observed from the control towers and some ATC officers were asked to share their experience as listeners. This led to some significant insights about factors influencing listening comprehension. They are briefly reported below.

The pilot in the cockpit, flying the aeroplane, is virtually blind. He is ignorant of where he is in the vast expanse of the skies, of the atmospheric pressure in the region where he is flying; he does not know whether there are other aircraft flying in the same region. He is totally dependent on the commands he receives from the ATC. The slightest mishearing, or breakdown in communication, can lead to disastrous consequences, and, hence, both pilots and the ATCs function under a high level of concentration and stress and with a highly standardized, inflexible and internationally accepted code.

English is the internationally accepted language of civil aviation. However the ATC uses no particular language (in the sense of using sentences and phrases used in other situations). It uses Roman script and the phonetics of English. The commands or requests are usually a group of sounds generally known as radio telephony (RT) and these are transmitted and received by the pilots and the ATC, through mechanical and electronic devices. The ATC uses a specialized set of phraseology. Most often commands or ideas are compressed and indicated by a single word. For instance, the word 'ROGER' means 'I have received all your transmission' and the word 'WILCO' means 'I have received, understood and will comply with your transmission'. The phraseology also includes figures and numbers. An excerpt from a conversation between a pilot and the ground control officer at the Radar Control section from the Chennai-base is presented in Appendix 1.

The interaction between aircraft IAC 540 and the ATC (see Appendix 1) at the Radar Control Tower at Chennai shows that though both the pilot and the ATC were operating with a high level of concentration, the ATC failed to understand the pilot's request and the pilot failed to hear the ATC's command, on two occasions within two minutes. These breakdowns could be due to some meteorological disturbances or mechanical failure. At the same time, the possibility of the interference of other factors such as expectation or linguistic confusions cannot be ruled out. It is also evident that in case of doubt or mishearing, the commands or requests were repeated till they were received correctly.

The RT phraseology has been coined in such a way that the same syllables or words are not used in different commands. One instance of similar syllables used in different commands and which gave rise to complications was the usage of 'affirmative' and 'negative'. On one occasion, when the initial sounds were blurred owing to some defect in transmission, the pilot misheard the ATC's signal 'negative' as 'affirmative'. Both words have 'tive' as their final syllable and in the absence of initial sounds gave rise to misunderstandings and some serious consequences. Henceforth, the 'tive' was dropped and the current RT communication phraseology contains only 'affirm' and 'negative'.

One notable fact is the rapidity with which the verbal signals are received and transmitted by the pilots and the ATCs. This implies that a very high level of concentration, quickness of reception, comprehension and response are imperative if breakdown in communication is to be avoided. Other factors that seem to influence the listening process are force of habit, familiarity with content and expectation. But expectation can also lead to misunderstandings because very often we come across situations in which the hearer hears only what he wants to hear irrespective of what the speaker says. For instance, a pilot, once, waiting for clearance for take off received a 'negative' command but thought that the ATC had given him the clearance to take off. This misunderstanding ended up in a serious mishap, as reported by one of the ATCs. Since the enquiry reports about these mishaps are strictly confidential, we cannot refer to them.

Stress and irritation also influence their performance. Deviation from the use of prescribed phraseology, constant repetition, coping with less than the ideal equipment, with many sources of sound at the same time and incessant background noise lead to increased stress and irritation and appear to lower their listening comprehension levels significantly.

Though physiological, psychological and mechanical factors play an important role, the communication between pilots and ATCs is primarily linguistic. Gestures and other non-linguistic clues have no place in this interaction. The phonetic structure of the RT code is such that it eliminates the possibility of linguistic confusions. The phraseology uses no single sounds, i.e. no monosyllables. Most of the commands are disyllabic and one of the main reasons for the effectiveness in such communication is strict adherence to the agreed code. This reiterates the fact that communication depends largely on language. Interestingly, it was also observed that the longer the phrases, the lesser the possibilities of misunderstanding them.

The Experimental Method

Materials

Two short first person narrative passages from O'Connor (1973) (ref. Appendix 2) were chosen for the study. Both passages have eight sentences each. The first passage has 99 words and the second passage has 121 words. These passages were read aloud by two ESL speakers and were audio-taped. Each passage was spoken in two different ways and each was different from the other with regard to tempo of speech, and length and occurrence of pauses. They also perceptibly differed in their stress and intonation patterns.

Due to constraints of space, the analysis and observations made with respect to the first passage alone are considered here. Also, it would be relevant to point out here that the experiment yielded similar results in the case of both Passages 1 and 2 with no major deviations.

The following table describes the phonetic differences between the two versions A and B of Passage 1.

Version	*Phonetic Characteristics*		
	Tempo	*Pause*	*Stress & Intonation*
A	Normal rate of speech Time taken: I minute 5 seconds	Occurrence appropriate; 19 pauses	Appropriate word and sentence stresses. Appropriate use of the four basic tunes.
B	Rapid rate of speech Time taken: 36.098 seconds	Erratic occurrence; 24 pauses	Inappropriate word and sentence stresses. Faulty intonation.

Speakers and Listeners

Two ESL speakers participated in this study. They were undergraduate students from the Indian Institute of Technology, Madras. They used English as their second language and had at least ten years of exposure to English. They spoke the same variety of English viz. standard Indian English as is spoken by many educated people in India. Their pronunciation styles did not differ greatly and did not have any significant mother tongue influence.

Version A of Passage 1 was spoken by the first speaker and audio-taped after he underwent a training course in Spoken English at the Institute. Version B was spoken by the same speaker and audio-taped before he underwent the above-mentioned course.

The subject listeners were students from schools and colleges in Chennai. They belonged to 3 levels of language proficiency. They spoke the same variety of English spoken by the two speakers selected in the study. The following table gives the proficiency levels and number of listeners who participated in the study.

Levels	*Proficiency Level & Number of Listeners*
L1	ESL learners with minimum 5 years exposure to English and aged between 10 and 12 years. N = 33

L2	ESL learners with minimum 10 years exposure to English and aged between 15 and 17 years. N = 114
L3	ESL learners with minimum 15 years of exposure to English and aged between 21 and 24 years. N = 95

Testing Protocol

Listeners belonging to each level listened to the two different versions of each of the two passages. There were 12 sessions in all and in each session, the number of listeners was between 11 and 35. No listener heard the same passage twice. As they listened to each version of the texts, listeners performed a blank-filling exercise. The blanks in the questionnaire were distributed in such a way as to assess the listeners' comprehension of certain key words necessary for understanding the passages. The tape was stopped at frequent intervals to enable the listeners to fill in their responses.

Analysis

The analysis was done in three stages.

Stage 1: Sonographic analysis of the spoken texts
Stage 2: Analysis of listeners' responses
Stage 3: Analysis of the influence of segmental and prosodic features of the spoken texts on comprehension.

Sonographic Analysis of Spoken Texts

The four versions of the two passages were examined using a DSP sonograph (Model 5500). The Fo contours, pitch levels, pitch movements, relative amplitudes and tempo of speech and the length of pauses were scrutinized and their values obtained. The utterances were then digitized and stored in a computer disk. The information was then graphically presented. Due to constraints of space only some graphic displays of the various prosodic features are included in this paper. The graphs present a quantification of the Fo contours and levels in hertz and the amplitudinal variations in decibels. Bar graphs show the duration of each sentence in seconds. The time taken to utter each sentence differed between the two versions of each passage.

Analysis of Listeners' Responses

The listeners' responses were evaluated. The erroneous responses were noted and the percentage of errors was calculated. The following tables present the data obtained.

Passage 1 Version A Task : Blank-filling No. of blanks : 13

No. of Errors	*Percentage of Error Occurrence*		
	L1 N = 33	*L2 N = 114*	*L3 N = 95*
Zero	36.36	46.49	83.15
One	39.39	32.45	14.73
Two	15.15	21.05	2.1
Three	9.09	Nil	Nil
Four to Thirteen	Nil	Nil	Nil

Version A

Correct Response	*Erroneous Responses*	*Percentage of Listeners who Misunderstood*		
		L1	*L2*	*L3*
Novice	Enormous; modest; novelist; nervous; obvious	100	38.63	6.12
Ladies size	Ladies' eyes; latest size; ready size; ladies' side	85	Nil	Nil
Wood work	Good work; book work	36.1	Nil	Nil

Passage 1 Version B Task : Blank-filling No. of blanks : 13

No. of Errors	*Percentage of Error Occurrence*		
	L1 N = 33	*L2 N = 114*	*L3 N = 95*
Zero	Nil	Nil	4.2
One	Nil	2.63	5.26
Two	5.12	Nil	14.73
Three	17.94	20.17	18.94
Four	28.2	14.03	17.89
Five	12.82	25.43	14.73
Six	12.8	11.4	17.89
Seven	5.12	Nil	6.31
Eight	2.56	15.78	Nil
Nine	10.25	10.52	Nil
Ten	5.12	Nil	Nil
Eleven to Thirteen	Nil	Nil	Nil

Version B

Correct Response	*Erroneous Responses*	*Percentage of Listeners who Misunderstood*		
		L1	*L2*	*L3*
Did his best	Is best; made his best; its best; it best	35.1	24.9	12.9
Fifteen	Three; team; fifty	51.6	41.8	26.08
Kinds	Things; no response	10.6	Nil	Nil
Jobs	Jaws; jokes; cause	41.4	31.2	Nil
Want it for	Want sir; wanting for; wanted for; want to firm	13.7	15.3	Nil
Bookshelves	Bookshells; bushels; bookshops	67.2	39.5	31.1
Ignorant fool	Impudent fool; arrogant fool; indolent fool; no response	63.3	54.5	Nil
Experts	Expose; exports	42	38.6	24.1
Novice	Enormous; nervous; novelist; obvious; modest	100	63.6	34.7
Should need	Should mean; should meet; should be; should lead; should read	77	36.2	15.3
Ladies size	Ladies eyes; latest size; ready size; ladies side	83	54.8	41.7
Wood work	Good work; good word; book work	79.5	36.1	18.1

The above tables show that Version A of Passage 1 was better understood by listeners compared to Version B. They also reveal the words that were frequently misunderstood and the erroneous responses. It appears from the data obtained that only few words were misunderstood and only by a few listeners in Version A whereas a large number of words were misunderstood in Version B by a large number of people.

Analysis of the Influence of Segmental and Prosodic Features of the Spoken Texts on Listening Comprehension

The major point of difference between the two versions A and B of Passage 1 is phonetic, i.e. the versions differ with respect to the tempo of speech, length and frequency of pauses and the fundamental frequency and amplitude variations. That these differences are significant enough is evident from the sonographic analysis of the spoken texts and the analysis of the listeners' responses. Given below is a detailed analysis of some phonetic equivalents of well-understood and least-understood speeches.

Tempo

Tempo of speech seems to be a critical factor in listening comprehension even when the speakers and listeners have the same pronunciation styles, or, in other words, use the same variety of English and belong to the same or similar linguistic communities. Tempo of speech, as is observed from the present study, can effectively promote or impede comprehension. A visual representation of the differing rates of speech in the well-understood and least-understood speeches was made during the study. Due to constraints of space, only one such sample is given below.

Tempo – Passage 1 – Sentence 3
But we have fifteen different kinds for different jobs (14 syllables)

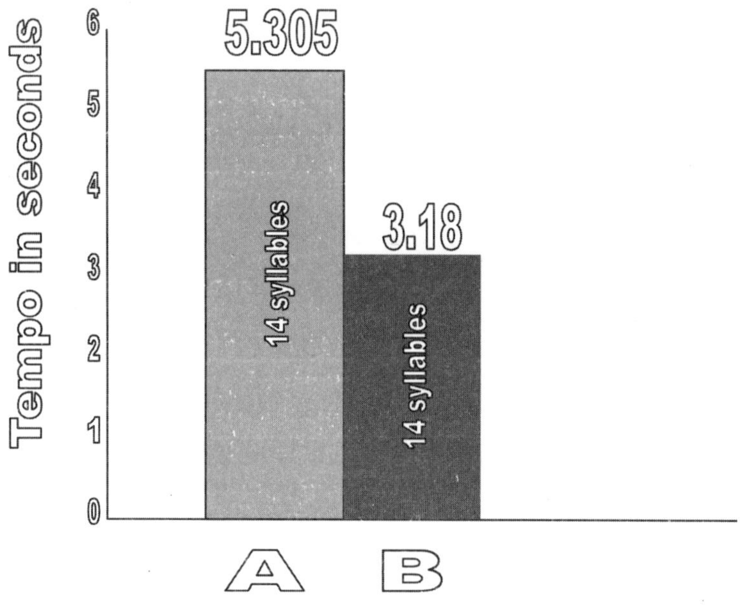

The graph shows that sentence 3 of Passage 1 was spoken in 5.305 seconds in Version A and 3.18 seconds in Version B. A large percentage of listeners misunderstood many parts of this sentence in Version B whereas all parts of the sentence in Version A were understood correctly by most of the listeners. For instance, in Version B, the words 'fifteen', 'kinds', and 'jobs' occurring in the sentence were uniformly misunderstood by almost all listeners of the three levels. Similar is the case with other content words in the rest of the sentences in Passage 1.

The study also reveals that utterances at a slow tempo of speech, i.e. less than three syllables per second are better understood than utterances at a rapid tempo of speech, i.e. five or more syllables per second. Tempo of speech affects the duration of vowels and consonants, of pauses and co-articulatory effects upon contiguous sounds. Rapid tempo of speech alters the phonological and morphological structure of words and phrases in such a way that the listeners get an entirely different idea from what was intended by the speaker.

The present study gives evidence of some phonological departures or deviations that occur in rapid speech. Some of these are discussed below:

Reduction of Vowels

Generally in connected speech, the length of vowels is much reduced as against the length of those that are pronounced in isolation. But in connected speeches spoken rapidly, this reduction of vowel sounds in words is greater in degree, resulting in the misperception of words by listeners, as in the following examples.

Word	*Misunderstood as*
ladies	ready
fool	full

Long vowel /i:/ changes to short vowel /i/ and long vowel /u:/ changes to short vowel /u/ in the listeners' perception.

Disappearance of Distinction between Front, Back and Central Vowels

Word	*Misunderstood as*
but	bet
experts	exports

The centralized vowel /^/ changes to the front vowel /e/ and the central vowel /:/ changes to the back vowel /o/ resulting in misunderstanding of the words.

Deletion of Consonants

Word	*Misunderstood as*
should need	should be
bookshelves	bookshells; bookshops; bushels
jobs	jaws

Listeners fail to perceive one or two sounds in consonant clusters. For instance, in 'bookshelves' and 'jobs', the fricative /v/ and the plosive /b/ are dropped from the cluster in which they occur and the listeners misunderstands the words as 'bushels' or 'bookshops' and 'jaws' respectively.

Substitution of Consonants

Sometimes, consonants which are minimal pairs or when they occur in unstressed positions, tend to be replaced by other consonants, thus resulting in a misunderstanding of what is said.

Word	*Misunderstood as*
ladies	ready
woodwork	goodwork
wood	good; book

/l/ and /r/ are both liquids and tend to substitute each other in the listeners' perception. The consonant /w/ in the unstressed syllables in the above examples is replaced by /b/ or /g/.

Nasalization of End Phonemes

Word	*Misunderstood as*
want it	wanting
need	mean

The dental or alveolar plosives are replaced by homorganic nasals.

Confusion of Voicing and Juncture

Word	*Misunderstood as*
a novice	an office
ladies' size	ladies eyes

Disappearance of Word Boundaries

Word	*Misunderstood as*
want a saw	want Sir
a novice	enormous
want it for	wanted for

Elision of Syllables/Words

Word	Misunderstood as
fifteen	fifty; team
did his best	is best

Misplacement of Stress

Rapid speech does not necessarily trigger the wrong stresses. However misplacement of main stress added to a rapid tempo of speech often causes misperceptions as in the case of the following words.

Word	Misunderstood as
fifteen	fifty
woodwork	goodwork; bookwork
experts	exports; expose

The above words were stressed wrongly on the initial syllable in Version B and hence gave rise to misperceptions. Even then, misunderstanding of 'experts' is difficult to explain.

Misperceptions seem to occur more often with syllables that are unstressed whereas the stressed syllables are generally well understood. These phonological deviations do not occur in Version A. This perhaps explains why many listeners have not committed errors in comprehending the content words in Version A.

Pause

Much of the intelligibility of spoken words depends upon the short silent intervals called pauses which occur between phrases, clauses and sentences. Pauses can either promote, or turn out to be barriers to, effective communication as found in the present study. In Version A (well-understood text) of Passage 1, there are 19 pauses. They occur in appropriate places. The length of the pause varies from .8 to 1.1 seconds between phrases and clauses within a sentence. The pause between sentences varies from 1 second to 1.3 seconds. In Version B (least-understood text) of Passage 1, there are 24 pauses in all. They occur erratically. The length of the pauses between phrases and clauses ranges from .08 to .1 seconds and between sentences from .88 to .93 seconds.

In this version some sentences have too many pauses and some do not have the required number. Between phrases and clauses, pauses were effective in increasing the intelligibility of the spoken texts while too many pauses occurring erratically inhibited the comprehensibility of the sentences. Speech became too jerky and, so, difficult to comprehend. For instance, the sentence 'He told me what I should need and advised me to have a ladies' size' was well-understood and least-understood depending upon the number and duration of pauses that occurred in the two versions.

Version A (Well-Understood)

He told me what I should need/and advised me/to have a ladies' size.

(1 sec) (.9 sec)

Version B (Least-Understood)

He told me what / I should / need and / advised me / to have / a ladies' size.

(.08 sec) (.1 sec) (.08 sec) (.09 sec) (.08 sec)

Similar instances were observed in other sentences in the two versions.

Voice Dynamic Features

Every utterance has some variations in fundamental frequency and amplitude. But some utterances are better understood than others. This study also examined the patterns of utterances in both well-understood and least-understood versions of the passages, with regard to fundamental frequency and amplitude.

Fundamental Frequency

Pitch and amplitude are the underlying physical properties of the observable features of stress and intonation. Generally stressed syllables are signalled to a listener by means of pitch prominence and higher amplitude levels. Accents are indicated by a change of pitch direction and pitch level. The stressed syllables, when accompanied by higher pitch levels, tend to acquire greater prominence than the syllables with lower pitch levels. The accentual patterns of the content words in the passages selected for the study are examined with reference to pitch and amplitude.

Pitch fluctuation is one of the most significant features of voice dynamics. Pitch fluctuations are not random movements. They follow some patterns which are common to the specific linguistic community. Again the fundamental frequency (Fo) contour or pitch contour for any one utterance appears to differ with different speakers. But there seem to be certain features of pitch which can be considered characteristic of well-understood and least-understood spoken texts. Some of these features observed in the present study are briefly listed below:

Fo Variations – Well-Understood Version A

1. Pitch levels of content words are higher than the preceding or following words.
2. Pitch levels are lower for function words.

3. Pitch fluctuations show significant rise and fall.
4. Pitch range, i.e. the difference in the pitch levels between the syllable with the lowest pitch and the syllable with the highest pitch in any sentence varies from 100 hz to 230 hz.

Fo Variations – Least-Understood Version B

1. Content words more often have lower pitch levels than their neighbouring words. Even if they have higher pitch levels, they are not sufficiently marked or distinguished from those of the neighbouring words.
2. Function words, sometimes, tend to have higher pitch levels.
3. Pitch fluctuations do not show significant rise and fall and the utterances sound like monotones.
4. Pitch range is limited and varies from 40 hz to 75 hz between the syllables with the lowest and the highest pitch in the sentences.

The fundamental frequency variations of the well-understood and least-understood spoken texts are illustrated in the sample graph given below:

Fo – Passage 1
Sentence 3 – But we have fifteen different kinds for different jobs.

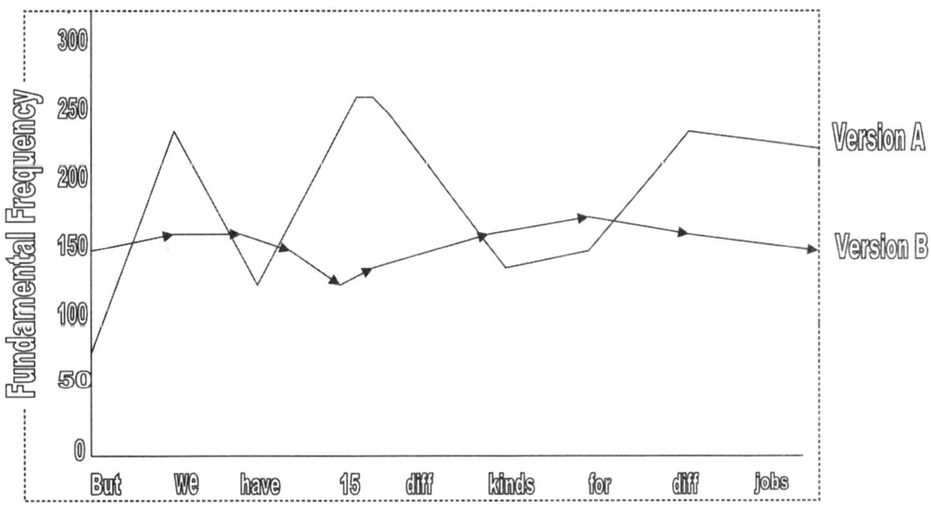

Amplitude

Amplitude by itself does not seem to affect the comprehensibility of the spoken texts. However the content words in well-understood texts have higher amplitude values than their neighbouring words. The amplitude variations also correspond directly to the variations in pitch i.e. the relative amplitude values for content words with higher pitch values were higher and lower for those with lower pitch values. The tables and graphs showing these characteristics are not presented here.

Conclusion

The study has helped us to understand the nature of some phonetic and phonological changes that occur in rapid speeches, which significantly affect the listeners' perception. It has also shown how the place of occurrence, number and length of pauses influence understanding of spoken language. It further illustrates that acoustic patterns of well-understood spoken texts widely differ from those in least-understood ones.

Pitch levels and variations appear to be important in that they provide efficient cues of prominence of content words to the listeners. The study further reveals that variations of amplitude correspond directly to variations of fundamental frequency.

In short, this study shows that phonetic factors are crucial and affect listening comprehension in a definite and predictable manner.

Applications of this Study

The process of listening is of interest to experts and researchers in various fields, such as psychology and cognitive science, sociolinguistics, neurolinguistics, language pedagogy, artificial intelligence and speech technology. A quantification of the phonetic features of speech, as performed in the present study, seems to be of special significance in artificial intelligence and speech technology.

Curriculum designers can frame suitable syllabi for teaching both listening and speaking skills to ESL learners in India on the basis of the kind of problems the latter encounter while trying to comprehend different varieties of spoken English.

Computer scientists and speech technologists are presently trying to develop speech understanding systems i.e. to enable the computer to recognize and comprehend natural language spoken by human beings. The problems in enabling the computer to understand speech, lie both in the 'lower level' areas of phonetic identification and grammatical parsing and in the higher level inferencing of speaker intentions and assumptions. The basic problem, however, lies in the paradox that speech is a continuous stream of sounds with no obvious discontinuities at the boundaries between different sounds and yet speech is perceived as a set of discrete symbols. Identification of these problems can help to discover knowledge application routines that can be used by computer and other intelligent machines, such as robots, in comprehending spoken language.

Neurolinguists can study the brain cells associated with the function of spoken language recognition based on the kind of linguistic processes involved in comprehension.

Psycholinguists and cognitive scientists are engaged in trying to discover how the mind processes spoken language. The linguistic features during the various stages of spoken language processing would help them create models to represent these processes.

None of these issues has been addressed in any great detail in the present study though its results have a bearing upon all these subjects.

Appendix 1

Communication Between Pilot (IAC 540) and Air-Traffic Controllers at the Madras Region

Time	From	To	Text
16:29	IAC 540	MM RDR	MADRAS IAC540 GOOD EVENING
	MM RDR	IAC 540	IAC 540 MADRAS RADAR GOOD EVENING REPORT VOR RADIAL DISTANCE FROM MMV DME AND HEADING
	IAC 540	MMRDR	SIR WE ARE 48 DME RADILA 342 AND OUT OF 125 FOR 110
	MM RDR	IAC 540	ROGER IDENTIFIED REPORT HEADING SIR
	IAC 540	MM RDR	HEADING IS 164
	MM RDR	IAC 540	ROGER IDENTIFIED TURN RIGHT HEADING 180 VECTORING ILS APPROACH RWY 07 DESCEND TO F 65
	IAC 540	MM RDR	SAY AGAIN THE HEADING SIR
	MM RDR	IAC 540	180 TURN RIGHT HEADING 180 VECTORING ILS APPROACH RWY 07 DESCEND TO F 65
	IAC 540	MM RDR	ROGER SIR DESCEND TO F 65 AND TURN RIGHT HEADING 180
	MM RDR	IAC 540	AFFIRM
16:30	IAC 540	MM RDR	WHAT IS THE SURFACE WIND
	MM RDR	IAC 540	WE HAVE GOT TWO DEPARTURES ON RWY 07
	IAC 540	MM RDR	REQUEST SURFACE WIND
	MM RDR	IAC 540	WE HAVE GOT TWO DEPARTURES
	IAC 540	MM RDR	I AM ASKING YOU THE SURFACE WIND
	MM RDR	IAC 540	I COULD NOT MAKE OUT PLEASE SAY AGAIN 540 IS ASKING SURFACE WIND SIR
	MM RDR	IAC 540	---CONFIRM
	IAC 540	MM RDR	SURFACE WIND
	MM RDR	IAC 540	SURFACE WIND IS 180 DEG 08 KTS
	IAC 540	MM RDR	THEN WE WOULD LIKE TO USE 25
	MM RDR	IAC 540	ROGER CONTINUE WILL ADVISE YOU WE HAVE GOT TWO DEPARTURES
	IAC 540	MM RDR	ROGER
16:31	IAC 540	MM RDR	MADRAS IAC 540

	MM RDR	IAC 540	IAC 540 WIND 150 DEG 10 KTS RWY IN USE 07 AND CONTINUE HEADING 180 VECTORING ILS APPROACH RWY 07 RWY 25 NOT APPROVED DUE TRAFFIC
	IAC 540	MM RDR	ROGER SIR AND CONFIRM MAINTAINING 19 ... 180
	MM RDR	IAC 540	AFFIRM MAINTAIN HEADING 180, VECTORING ILS APPROACH RWY 07 RWY 25 NOT APPROVED DUE TRAFFIC
	IAC 540	MM RDR	ROGER WE ARE MAKING OUR OWN APPROACH WE ARE VISUAL
	MM RDR	IAC 540	ROGER
16:32	IAC 540	MM RDR	WE ARE 65 MAINTAIRING 180
	MM RDR	IAC 540	ROGER
16:33	VWJ	MM RDR	MADRAS APPROACH GOOD EVENING VWJ
	MM RDR	VWJ	VWJ MM RDR IDENTIFIED TO DEPARTURE. AT 2000 FT TURN LEFT H340 CONTINUE CLIMB TO F 100 STANDBY FOR FURTHER CLIMB

Appendix 2

Tape Transcripts of the Spoken Texts Used in the Experiment

(Slant lines indicate the occurrence of pauses)

Passage 1

Version A

I said to the man / behind the counter / 'I want a saw'. / He was a nice man / and did his best for me. / 'Yes Sir. / But we have fifteen different kinds / for different jobs. / What do you want it for?' / I explained about my bookshelves / and felt like an ignorant fool / in a world of experts. / He saw that I was a novice / and was very kind. / He told me what I should need / and advised me / to have a ladies' size. / 'Easier to manage for the beginners, Sir.'/ He also sold me a book on woodwork / for schoolboys. (19 pauses)

Version B

I said / to the man behind the counter 'I want a saw'. / He was a / nice man and did / his best for me. / 'Yes Sir. But we have fifteen different / kinds for different / jobs. What do you want it for?' / I explained / about my bookshelves and felt / like an ignorant / fool in a world of experts. / He saw / that I was a novice and was very kind. / He told me what / I should / need and / advised me / to have / a ladies' size. / 'Easier to / manage for the beginners, Sir.' / He also / sold me a book on woodwork for / schoolboys. (24 pauses)

References

Chaudron C., 'A method for examining the input/intake distinction', In Gass, S. and Madden, C., ed., *Input in Second Language Acquisition*, Rowley, MA.: Newbury House, 1985.

Hatch E., *Psycholinguistics: A Second Language Perspective*, Rowley, MA.: Newbury House, 1983.

Klein W., *Second Language Acquisition*, Cambridge: CUP, 1987.

Krashen S., 'The Monitor Model for Adult Second Language Performance', in Burt, M. Dulay C. and Finocchiari M., ed., *Viewpoints on English as a Second Language*, New York: Regents, 1977, pp. 152-161.

Long D., 'Second Language Listening Comprehension. A Schema – Theoretic Perspective', *Modern Language Journal*, 1989, p. 73, pp. 32-40.

McClelland J., 'A Case for Interactionism in Language Processing', In Coltheart M., ed., *Psychology of Reading*, Hillsdale, NJ: Erlbaum, 1987.

Mclaughlin B., Rossman T. and McLeod B., 'Second Language Learning: An Information Processing Perspective', *Language Learning*, 1983, p. 33, pp. 135-158.

O'Connor J.D., *Better English Pronunciation*, Cambridge : CUP, 1973.

Tomatis A., 'L'Oreille et la vie : Itineraire d'une recherché sur l'audition la langue et la. communications', Paris : Robert Laffont, 1987.

6

Technical Speaking

S.P. Dhanavel

Introduction

Technical communication must include all the four language skills – listening, speaking, reading, and writing. However, the teaching of technical communication in our colleges seems lopsided as it tends to focus on writing to the sad omission of other the three skills, especially speaking. Even when textbooks include a unit on speaking or specify some speaking tasks, it is not given much importance. This paper, analyses the equally important dyad, i.e. speaking and writing in technical communication and suggests that valorizing writing over speaking has led to a skewed development of technical communication. Hence, it argues that a corrective course is the need of the hour for professionals and teachers of technical communication. It also outlines some efforts made by some colleagues in the US to impart speaking skills to technical students. Further, it suggests some ways to incorporate speaking skills meaningfully in the curriculum, textbooks, and classrooms and in the Indian examination system.

Communication

Communication is the process of sending and receiving information and ideas through both oral and written medium via any channel with proper feedback from the receiver to the sender. Naturally then, teaching technical communication should focus on both oral and written communication. Syllabus designers, teachers, and textbook writers of technical communication understand this fact. That is why, they touch upon some elements of all language skills – listening, speaking, reading, and writing – in the syllabus, in the teaching, and in the textbook on technical communication. However, in practice, both listening and speaking, for many practical reasons seem to be given step-motherly treatment in teaching technical communication. Two major reasons are practical exigencies and problems in implementing these in the large classrooms with fixed furniture and unwillingness or inability to accommodate teaching of these skills. Other chief reasons relate more to conducting examination in listening and speaking than with academic and real life requirements for the students. Hence, convenience and practicality drives us to confine ourselves to teaching and testing just technical writing. So much so, technical communication has come to mean technical writing as is evident from the many books with this title.

Technical Communication

Technical communication refers to workplace communication. It is also called professional or business communication and is taught in business and engineering institutions. It is usually contrasted with academic communication that is taught in the general English classrooms. Importantly, the goals of technical communication are different from those of academic or general communication. While the former emphasizes immediate and prompt action for decision-making and problem-solving, the latter focuses on the content with less attention to practical problems. In short, technical communication has to achieve a target set for itself in the form of positive and prompt action.

Technical English

English for specific purposes pertaining to the field of science, engineering, and technology is called Technical English. The focus here is more on preparing the students for the intricacies of workplace communication, rather than just to increase the general competence of the students as it happens in General English classes. The goal is clear but the execution is constrained and compromised in the sense that the ghost of examination conditions on how the course is implemented in the classes. Unfortunately, it is the question paper pattern that determines the nature of technical English taught in the class, and not the goals of the course that decide the question paper pattern. This is a serious issue that has to be sorted out sooner for the benefit of the students, the industry, and the country as a whole.

The Path Traversed

Anna University Chennai has two courses on Technical English for the first year B.E./ B.Tech. students. These are language skill-based courses designed and implemented with the expert guidance of the British Council. Three Anna University teachers had been to Thames Valley University for training (incidentally Robert was the Special Officer, English studies at that time in the Council) and professors from UK also visited Anna University under the Key English Language Teaching (KELT) Project of the British Council, South India. The syllabus design and the production of course materials were done by the staff of the Department of Humanities and Social Sciences. Two volumes of textbooks, one for the first semester and another for the second, were published by Orient Longman, Chennai, in association with Anna University and finally the courses were put into operation from 1990. Over the years, the syllabus was 'revised' occasionally to fulfil the mandate of the university. But the textbook remained the same. The books were revised in 2002 but the content and the structure did not change much. Some outdated reading passages were replaced. In 2006 the two volumes were combined with some replacements of reading passages. The new edition of the same book was prescribed again for the first year students in 2007.

With the passage of time, Anna University, succumbing to the pressure from the industries which recruit students from engineering colleges, introduced a course on Communication Skills Laboratory. The course aimed at improving their spoken fluency-enabling students to face interviews and get better job opportunities. This meant that the students had to develop their oral communication skills to help them face interviews and participate in discussions. Topics like Group Discussion, Presentation Skills, Interview Skills, etc. found a place in the syllabus. These were perhaps 'taught' in the classroom also. The driving force of the educational system, however, was not developing oral communication skills in students but fulfilling Anna University requirements for passing the examination in the lab course. Interestingly the lab course was mandatory for affiliated colleges and not for the constituent colleges of Anna University. Again to fulfil Anna University's exam requirements testing of the students is still based on written components, however not on paper as in the conventional examination system but on the computer. Whether paper or computer is used for examination, the ultimate goal of developing oral communication skills in students is likely to suffer the same fate in the current system.

Course on Technical Speaking in the US

Many US universities have made serious efforts to introduce a course on Technical Speaking to their students of undergraduate programmes in Science, Engineering, and Technology. For instance, Colorado State University offers a 3-credit course entitled 'Business and Technical Speaking' during 1991-1998. Similarly, Idaho State University came up with a 2-credit course on Applied Technical Speaking to its students of Graphic Arts and Printing Technology. Purdue University also has a course on 'Technical Speaking'. However, the most interesting attempt in this direction has come from the University of Pittsburgh at Johnstown (UPJ).

UPJ Professors John Thompson, Stephen Curran, Susan Wieczorek, and Michael Ferencak have jointly undertaken a project called 'Development and Implementation of a Technical Speaking Course in Mathematics'. This project is aimed at developing technical, discipline-specific, verbal communication skills in the students of Mathematics. The basic premise of this project is that most students do not think about theorems and proofs in their jobs but make presentations almost on a daily basis. Hence, the professors adapted the public speaking course to suit the professional needs of the mathematics students.

The Technical Speaking Course at UPJ covers five kinds of speeches in a gradually increased difficulty level from least technical to most technical topics. These are: (i) autobiographical speech, (ii) commemorative speech, (iii) applied problem solving speech, (iv) persuasive speech and (v) technical speech. Obviously, if the students progress gradually from the personal level to most technical level, they will be able to acquire all the skills required for verbal communication in both general and technical or business contexts.

An Experiment at Anna University

Breaking away from the traditional path of using a textbook in the class, as part of an M. Phil. Research project, an attempt was made at Anna University in 2007 to develop the speaking skills of Part-Time First Year B.E Civil Engineering Students. Initially the students were asked to introduce themselves, and then they watched some selected clippings from two films of Rajinikanth and a film of actor Livingston. After watching the clippings, the students performed role plays based on the situations they watched: asking for guidance on the street, conducting a meeting, attending an interview, lodging a complaint with the police, meeting a friend in a restaurant, buying some clothes in a shop, managing workers in a worksite, etc. Amazingly, the students performed all these roles very creatively. Finally, the students were asked to introduce their friends to the class. Naturally, there were time and other constraints. What cannot be denied is that the extra effort put into this experiment brought about great satisfaction to the students, the teacher and the research scholar. If only the specific and practical syllabus and testing pattern can be designed for Technical Speaking, many problems relating to time, administration, and logistics can surely be overcome.

An Outline Syllabus

The foundation for a course on technical speaking has necessarily to be presentation skills – a reinvention of its older form public speaking. Therefore, all elements of a presentation and public speaking have to be brought into the syllabus: planning, audience awareness, purpose of the presentation, logical development of ideas with a variety of inputs like anecdotes, humour, evidence, technical details, non-verbal communication, and so on. The course components may tentatively be arranged as follows:

I. Presentation: Definition, Purpose, Kinds, Structure, Feedback, Adaptability
II. Listening: Active Listening, Empathetic Listening, Interpretation, Evaluation
III. Introduction: Self, Other, Product, Place
IV. Business presentations: Sales, Report, Proposal
V. Everyday Interactions: Inquiry, Clarification, Explanation, Social participation

A section on listening is included here because both the speaker and the listener must understand each other for effective communication. Some more relevant topics and points can surely be included to make the course comprehensive enough.

Evaluation of Technical Speaking

In some of the discussions with academics, it was clearly agreed that speaking must be given adequate importance in the curriculum. But the major problem encountered was how to evaluate the students' performance objectively. It was suggested that a listening task could be done with the help of a tape recorder. It was also suggested that a presentation seminar could be organized. Tasks like group discussion, role play, debate, etc. could be given to students in the classroom. However, the acute problem in the Indian context and in many other countries is the large number of students and the lack of time to evaluate the students. Even if time is available, how to be fair and objective is the crucial question that is difficult to find a satisfactory answer from the academics and administrators.

A possible solution to overcome this problem is to introduce continuous internal assessment of the speaking tasks carried out in the class for the whole semester. Again a variety of tasks performed by the students can be evaluated fairly with the help of a checklist commonly agreed upon by the teachers of English. If some more class time is required for English classes due to spoken English assessment, it is the duty of the English fraternity to convince the administrators to allot one or two more hours in a week for English. They cannot ignore this move because the industries want to have students who can speak and write reasonably well.

Of course, technology can be of great help to evaluate the spoken performance of students. The 'tests' can be recorded by a handycam and fed into a computer for automatic evaluation against a set of commonly agreed parameters. It is not a wild dream. It is possible in the present age of high technology for everything on earth. If such a mechanism is not available, it is necessary to develop such software in collaboration with the software industry.

Conclusion

If the objective of the courses on Technical Communication and Technical English is to include oral communication skills as the industries expect, then the educational administrators must think differently and must be willing to introduce a course on Technical Speaking along the line of what the four professors at the University of Pittsburgh at Johnstown have done. Experiments of the kind done at Anna University with part-time B.E students should be carried out. Just as the American professors get institutional support, the Indian teachers must also receive support from the Management of Educational Institutions. The students are eager and willing to speak in English in both their personal and professional life. Then, what prevents the teachers from giving them what they want? The only impediment that is possible is the ghost of the Indian examination system. There is no other way to handle this monster than to adopt innovative and fairly acceptable methods of evaluation. Who is the best judge to evaluate the speaking skill of the students, the teacher in the class or the man on the street?

Works Cited

'A Technical Speaking Course in Mathematics', University of Pittsburgh, 11 Feb. 2011, <http://www.pitt.edu/~ciddeweb teachingtimes/SEP2004/math.htm>.

Anderson Paul V., *Technical Communication: A Reader-Centered Approach*, 6th edn, India edition, Delhi: Thomson Wadsworth, 2007.

Anna University, *English for Engineers and Technologists*, Revised edn, Vol. 2, Chennai: Orient Longman, 2002.

Anna University, *English for Engineers and Technologists*, Combined edn, Chennai: Orient Longman, 2006.

Day R.A., *Scientific English: A Guide for Scientists and Other Professionals*, 2nd edn, Hyderabad: Universities Press, 2000.

Gerson S.J. and Gerson S.M., *Technical Writing: Process and Product*, 3rd edn, Delhi: Pearson Education, 2001.

Frarahathullah T.M., *Communication Skills for Technical Students*, Chennai: Orient Longman, 2002.

Herbert A.J., *The Structure of Scientific English*, London: Longman, 1995, [1965].

Houp K.W. Pearsall T.E. Tebeaux E. and Dragga S., *Reporting Technical Information*, New York: Oxford University Press, 2006.

Livingston G., 'Using Tamil Films for Developing the Communication Skills of Engineering Students', M.Phil. Thesis submitted to Anna University Chennai, 2007.

Mishra Sunita and Muralikrishna C., *Communication Skills for Engineers*, New Delhi: Pearson, 2006.

Mitra B.K., *Effective Technical Communication. A Guide for Scientists and Engineers*, New Delhi: Oxford University Press, 2006.

Pickett N.A., Laster A.A. and Staples K.E., *Technical English: Writing, Reading, and Speaking*, 8th edn, New York: Longman, 2001.

Riordan Daniel G., and Steven E. Pauley, *Technical Report Writing Today*, 8th edn Indian adaptation, New Delhi: Bizantra, 2006 [2004].

'Teaching Excellence Fair: Speaking of Numbers', University of Pittsburgh, 11 Feb. 2011, <http://www.mac10.umc.pitt.edu/u/FMPro?- db=ustory&-lay=a&-format=d.html&storyid=4176&-Find>.

7

(In)Significance of Teaching Writing in General English Curriculum

K. Elango

An analysis, even if casual, of the General English Curriculum, be it at a high school or tertiary-level, is enough to reveal that of the four skills (LSRW), writing is given the least importance. To make it worse, writing tasks assigned to learners usually revolve around just three types: writing paragraphs, essays and letters. In case other kinds get mentioned in the curriculum, they merely remain at the periphery. The writing skill at all levels is thus highly restricted, stereotypical and repetitive.

The positioning of 'W' at the end of the acronym of LSRW clearly signposts two aspects the natural acquisition order of the skills and the progression of the difficulty level, writing being the most difficult of the four. Hence, instead focusing more on this skill, the syllabuses, quite sadly, tend to marginalize it. In an attempt to offset the imbalance, the study here attempts to highlight the wide range of writing that is carried out by professionals and to make out a case for a possible inclusion of a variety of genres of writing in the curriculum to enable learners to try their hands at all kinds of writing and to identify the one type they are most comfortable with.

Contrary to the current classroom practice of confining writing to just three kinds, in real life, writers constantly indulge in a wide range and varieties of writing. Significant among them can be classified into the following seven categories, viz. academic writing, creative writing, journalistic writing, scientific writing, business writing, legal writing and spiritual writing. Learners could familiarize themselves with all these varieties and to find out genre of writing they have a flair for. Rather than imposing certain genres on learners, they have to be enabled to zero in on the ones they are passionate about and develop those specific genres. Such focused learning is to be encouraged as even the professional writers themselves earn their reputation mostly in one genre of writing. Salman Rushdie or J.K. Rowling can only be novelists; just because they are creative, one cannot expect them to be reputed dramatists or poets or journalists, although there are exceptions such as T.S. Eliot, Graham Greene, and Rabindranath Tagore, to name a few.

The General English curriculum, it must be emphasized, has to include all the seven genres; either all of them taught at the same level with certain specific areas or in a phased out manner across the years of formation, that is, certain genres at certain levels but including all of them at some level or the other. Let us deal in some detail, not necessarily in any order of importance, with each of these categories.

Academic Writing

Academic writing includes assignments, projects, reports, examination answers, classroom notes and at a higher level, synopsis, theses, abstracts, research papers, etc. It often involves aspects such as researching a topic, arguing, evaluating, making inferences, paraphrasing, summarizing, quoting and organizing information and ideas. Academic writings often have a very specific structural design, although a conventional one. They contain an introduction, a body of several paragraphs, and a conclusion. Each of these parts has a specific function: introduction presenting a thesis statement, conclusion summarizing the main ideas and restating the thesis and the meat of the writing being the body broken down into paragraphs. Learners are required to handle paragraphing skilfully with each containing a topic sentence, ideas and sequenced logically with appropriate cohesive devises. It is indeed a feat to accomplish through repeated practice and mastery of this art is a sure sign of effective communication because as it is stated, 'Sloppy writing instantly reveals the sloppy mind'.

Creative Writing

Creative writing, obviously, incorporates all the four literary genres, viz. prose, poetry, drama and fiction. And each of these embraces a wide variety of writing. Prose for instance, takes on different forms such as discursive essays, biographical and autobiographical writings, diary writing, travelogues, anecdotes, jokes, puzzles, copy writing including slogans, script writing, dialogue writing, criticism, etc.

Learners often engage in creative writing on their own, and with some formal training and encouragement that hones their latent talent, they are bound to reach great heights. Creative writing, as the phrase suggests, transcends all boundaries and barriers; not just poets, but every creative writer has a 'license' to think out of box and break conventions. Conformity and status quo are anathema to most creative writers.

As creativity is mostly intuition ignited and is spurred by a spark of imagination rather than the result of laboured scholarship, youngsters can be motivated to capitalize on their innate creative impulses. Many literary writers confess that their creative spark is rarely deliberate but mostly spontaneous which often, 'in vacant and pensive mood', flash upon their inward eye. So learners need to cultivate a culture of creative visualization, a kaleidoscopic perspective capturing often the transitory feelings or thoughts and transform them into felicitous phrases and expressions. Once learners begin to identify and value their own creative instincts stemming from reflected experience, observation, and simmering imagination, they would well be on the royal road to creativity.

Journalistic Writing

Journalistic writing is any kind of writing meant for all the five mass media. The print media, for instance, includes writings such as titbits, letters, cartoons, editorials, features, reviews of films, plays, concerts and books, profiles of celebrities, interviews, articles on current trends and happenings, advertisements (display and classified) and the electronic media embracing scripts, lyrics, dialogues, serials, talk shows, news casting, etc.

Learners today are inundated with limitless media material and have no reason not to be able to identify the types that inspire them and model after them by constantly reading/watching them. Journalistic writing predominately adopts a style called, inverted pyramid style wherein ideas, facts or details are organized according to their significance. It also compels them to dig for details with the formula of 5Ws and the 1H. The spirit of Rudyard Kipling's lines are followed to the hilt,

> I keep six honest serving-men
> (They taught me all I knew);
> Their names are What and Why and When
> And How and Where and Who.

Journalistic writing does not call for extraordinary efforts, for instance, an interview with a celebrity can be kicked off with stock questions provided one has access to them. Or review of films or books can be easily attempted. With wide access to publishing or broadcasting one could with minimal effort become a freelancer. Hooked on to the right type they would soon take to it like duck to water.

Scientific Writing

Scientific writings include reports, procedures, manuals, research articles, etc. Unlike other genres of writing, scientific writing makes heavy demands on the writers, as it involves a combination of three kinds of competencies i.e. subject competency, linguistic competency, and organizational competency. Further, this genre of writing is characterized by features such as technical content, specialized vocabulary, formal style, total objectivity, use of graphs, charts and diagrams, and a specific audience. All these aspects make any form of scientific writing very challenging.

Learners in schools are mostly assigned to do only lab reports but not the other forms of scientific writing. But today the whole world has turned out to be a global market and the transfer of technology is playing a vital role in economic growth; in this emerging context different forms of scientific writing have become all the more significant. Practice in scientific writing would enable learners to possess in-depth subject knowledge, appropriate and adequate language skills and the ability to present scientific facts or information with clarity and precision, and the ability to organize technical information in a logical and structured way. It is a highly disciplined style of writing wherein unlike literary writing, liberty with content, language and organization can hardly be tolerated.

Business Writing

Business writings encompass office memos, minutes of meetings, proposals, letters, notifications, resumes, project descriptions, product or service brochure, etc. Business writings aim at different functions, the important ones being informing, managing and persuading which necessitate multiple styles of writing. Learners in classrooms today are unfortunately directed *ad nauseum* to write only business letters to the sad neglect of the other more exciting forms of business writings suggested above.

The seven C's that theoreticians recommend for effective communication – courtesy, clarity, conciseness, concreteness, correctness, consideration and completeness – apply more to business writings than to any other form because it often not merely aims at passing on information but also attempts to create harmonious relationships between business houses and clients, and to retain goodwill. Further, business writings attach equal importance to all the three components of writing: context, language, and format. While content and language are common to any kind of writing, the format has a special significance in business writing as it has to enable ready retrieval of information. So it is common to find devices such as subtitles, italicization, underlining, indentation, bulleting and numbering, columns, use of expressions such as ref., sub., encl., cc, etc. to glean the required information with minimal effort. This sort of writing makes different kinds of demand on learners compared to other genres of writing.

Legal Writing

It includes many varieties; some of them are documents, statutes, rules, notices, manuals, complaints, judgments, contracts, FIR and the like. Although it is a specialized genre of writing and does not fall under the ambit of learners' everyday experiential knowledge, an exposure to them would enable them to become familiar with a kind of writing significant in the adult world. Some of its characteristic features are use of specific registers, jargons, convoluted grammatical constructions i.e. too many complex structures, over formality, citation, etc. The term 'legalese' encapsulates the stylistic features of legal writings. As the legal writings chiefly target those in the profession and not the laymen, their abstruseness can be justified.

Learners, however, can be introduced to easier forms of legal writings such as FIR (First Information Report), notices and manuals. When a complaint is to be lodged in a police station the first requirement is to submit a written version of it. This in a way creates an authentic context for learners to simulate when they are assigned to draft an FIR on one of the recurring problems in their area that requires police intervention. However, legal writing is perhaps the most difficult form of writing as it attempts to cover all possible contingencies related to a particular issue and at the same time be concise and precise, thereby providing less room for ambiguity. Besides, certain kinds of legal writing value precedent and citations to authority, which are unique to this genre, make it difficult for learners to handle.

Spiritual Writing

This comprises prayers, sermons, discourse, songs, hymns, orations and reflections. Almost all religions produce a high volume of spiritual writings but for some strange reasons due recognition is not accorded to it. When we look at the origin of American literature its strong religious roots cannot be ignored. The early settlers of the seventeenth century, the Puritans, defined good writing as something that brought home a full awareness of the importance of worshipping God and of the spiritual dangers that the soul faced on earth. Although the modern life has been described as highly secular, materialistic and individualistic, in the private domain of every individual spirituality continues to be an obsessive concern; religious discourses continue to be crowd pullers and religious TV channels surprisingly have maximum viewership.

One significant merit of religious writings, even if they may border on superstition, is the values they inculcate among people, such as hard work, dedication, obedience, honesty, and striving for success. Spiritual writings, not smacking of any particular religious tenets, should also be encouraged among learners as the genre lends itself to express their fears, concerns, and intensely felt experiences.

Thus, each genre of writing has its own distinctive features and makes different kinds of demand on writers. With such a variety of themes and topics, teaching and writing in a classroom can be challenging as well as enterprising. With an enlarged scope if our educational constitutions can include the features listed below, students can enjoy writing and would prove themselves to be fit for the emerging job market.

Strategies for Writing

- Make writing totally learner-driven rather than teacher-driven. Permit learners to identify an area of their interest and zero in on a particular topic and try their hand at it.
- Allow learners the choice of the genre to write rather than force everyone to write in a particular genre. They are to decide whether to write an essay or a one-act play or a feature or a lyric or a report, etc.
- Encourage them to shift from product-based approach to process-based approach. As against the current practice of first draft as the final draft, learners are to attempt multiple drafts and actively seek feedback from family members to whoever is willing to offer, thereby moving away from the culture of teacher's feedback alone, which is often sketchy and riveted upon errors.
- Encourage them to write for the 'public eye' rather than the 'private eye' of a teacher. The desire to prove their capability as also the fear of possible ridicule would act as a catalyst to give their best.
- Motivate them to write for different levels and kinds of publications or broadcasts, starting from class to international levels through newsletters, magazines, journals, newspapers, blogs, other innumerable websites, news castings, etc. Added to this mobile novels and other forms of cyber literature are also gaining popularity now.

A complete revamping of the curriculum along the lines suggested above would transform learners' writing experiences to be an enjoyable one as against the current practice of making writing a torture.

8

Teaching Transactional Email Writing: A Contextualized Paradigm

K.S. Antony Samy

Transactional Email: Its Importance

In the context of an emerging globalized world email communication in India is viewed as an important component of corporate communication. It has become so common and significant in corporate communication that professionals use this medium to send and receive messages ranging from highly informal to formal nature. They chat, greet, enquire, advertise, report, make decisions, brain write, and transact many other things. Both the recruiter and the candidate deem it an indispensible mode of communication to be mastered to be job ready. Moreover, the reasons for its popularity are that it eliminates 'telephone tag', saves time, facilitates fast decisions, costs less and provides a written record. The utility of email is so immense that it is even replacing the traditional age-old postal service jovially known in the high-tech community as 'snail mail'. It's just another example of the relentless calculus of the digital revolution. Therefore, training in email writing for learners who aspire to be employed in the corporate world has become an important aspect of English classroom today.

What Makes Transactional Email Unique?

Email writing has acquired the status of a genre and so needs to be specifically taught and learnt. Ever since the commercial potential of emails came to be realized, users have developed certain specific features of this form and soon it got to be singled out as a special genre. The emergence of new linguistic and stylistic conventions is researched and recorded only in a few research papers and textbooks for email users. Academic research has so far not been able to crystallize the issue of stylistic protocol specific to emails. However, a few researchers have established email as a special mode of communication primarily based on the practice and usage of email users. Crystal (2002: 112) who undertook an extensive study of internet language expressed that electronic revolution has brought about a linguistic revolution resulting in 'Netspeak', 'a genuine new medium', referred as the 'dialogic character of e-messaging' in emails. 'Because of its spontaneity, speed, privacy, and leisure value', said Crystal, 'email offers the option of greater levels of informality than are found elsewhere in traditional writing' (pp.127-128).

The use of abbreviations (Swales 1990), the language used in email 'electronic mail has created another novelty: the written conversation' (The Economist (1996:37) contracted forms, abbreviated spelling, and quoted texts (Mallon and Oppenheim 2002) embedded messages – the opening message being initiator and the concluding message being terminator (Gimenez 2006) are a few of the reasons cited as evidence for the existence of specialized discourse. Based on his examination of the features of emails both personal and commercial, Gimenez (2000) suggests emails have simple syntax, co-ordinated ideas and abbreviated spelling. The observation is that email is closer to the nature of spoken language.

It is thus evident that emails combine features of spoken discourse with those of the written. The following table indicates the special features that distinguish email from other modes:

A Table distinguishing e-mode from other modes

S. No	*Features*	*Spoken*	*Written*	*E-mode*
1	Discourse	Oral	Written	Written conversation
2	Grammar	Grammar of the spoken language	Comprehensively correct	Idiosyncratic and novel
3	Spelling	Nil	Correct	Loose and innovative
4	Words	Colloquial	Right	Peculiar
5	Sentences	Simple straightforward syntactic structures	Elaborate formal syntactic structures	Conversational syntactic structures embedding emoticons
6	Information units	Loose sally of the mind	Complete information units	Elliptical forms
7	Organization of messages	Loosely organized	Well organized	Spontaneous

8	Style	Informal	Formal	Conversational
9	Contracted forms	To a great extent	Little	Very much
10	Punctuation	Nil	Correct	Playful
11	Abbreviation	Nil	Standard abbreviation	Informal abbreviation and initialism
12	Norms	To an extent	Well established	Very few guidelines
13	Non-verbal	Exorbitant	Nil	Emoticons and coloured words

Balancing Informality and Formality

Emails written both in personal and commercial contexts are, therefore, creative, different from traditional writing with its own features like elliptical forms and are true to the observation of Hale and Scanlon (1999: 3): 'A well-written electronic missive gets to the point quickly, with evocative words, short grafs, and plenty of white space. Spelling and punctuation are loose and playful (no one reads emails with red pen in hand!)'. Yet a lot of people do keep such a pen in mind, in educational, business, and other workplace settings, where emails are viewed as professional document. Moreover, this mode is, for most of the email users in workplaces, meant for various purposes: sending formal letters, official invitations, greeting cards, reviews and any other formal communications. Hence, it becomes mandatory to modify the structure and elements of email according to the expectations of their correspondents rather than email guidebooks.

Emails in business context should incorporate certain aspects of formal writing, yet retain some of the peculiarities of this specialized discourse like short sentences and conversational style. There are other factors in support of this assertion. They provide a unified permanent record of internal communication within the organization and reports of a variety of work-related purposes—to inform, to request, to respond, to promote, to direct, to praise or scold, and even to chat. Gains (1999: 98) has understood this view and therefore found '... the linguistic conventions for writing email messages appear to be reasonably stable and are largely consistent with the type of business English used between cooperating colleagues. Grammar and punctuation too are generally allied to what may be called standard written English'. At the same time, the contemporary bias towards informality needs to be kept in perspective. There should then, be balance between informality namely conversational, elliptical, and personal style and formality that is, formal openings and closings, organization of the message, and above all error-free language.

A Possible Teaching Procedure

Such a crucial means of communication as Transactional Email is best perceived and discovered through 'learning by doing'. At present, email writing is taught much the same way any other aspect of language is taught i.e. a lengthy instruction and explication by the teacher possibly assisted by some examples. Even evaluation, the reinforcement of learning is, to a great extent, memory-based testing of their theoretical knowledge of the learning item. There needs to be an urgent and swift shift from the instruction to the construction model of learning. The new teaching-learning procedure has to be relevant, interactive and participative.

After a review of the principles behind some teaching methods, a working combination of some of the salient features has been attempted in what is termed a 'learning by doing' approach. This would include insightful notions such as 'noticing the gap' (Schmidt 1990) 'constructivism' (Vygotsky 1986), Community Language Learning (Curran 1976), and 'transfer and reconstruct' (Sweeney 2005). In fine, Notice, Construct, Transfer (NCT) form the basis of the proposed teaching procedure defining the role of teachers who would not so much 'teach' as create a rich environment in which learners can familiarize themselves with the features of transactional email and acquire competence in using it.

The 5 'P' Approach

These principles and insights were integrated to form a practicable approach that would yield more effective and better results. In what can be termed the 5 'P' Approach the learners, after an initial introduction to the basic concepts and objectives of email, are encouraged to respond individually to a genuine business situation through mock transactional email. Step one aims at 'raising the learners' consciousness' (Rutherford 1987) regarding the procedures and the necessary strategies to write email. In the words of Willis and Willis (1996) the approach gets learners to notice particular features of the email, to draw conclusions from what they notice and to organize their views in the light of the conclusions they have drawn. This leads the learners to:

- **perceive** features of an effective transactional email and identify the features that make the text successful,
- **plan** a task individually and in small groups, notice the gap between the model text and their versions,
- after a group discussion, **prepare** a checklist to help future reference,
- **present** an improved version incorporating the insights gained, and
- in the context of 'academia-industry interaction' **perform**
- **progress** by consolidating the gains and employ skills acquired in real time with a real customer addressed and feedback from the expert practitioners.

A Worked out Example

A worked out model tried out in three different places reveals how the much relished procedure has benefitted the learners of transactional email. The learners are prepared with a general introduction about the language and the format of email after which they attempt a task. Many organizations send welcome message to persons joining their workplace. This is an exercise to build goodwill and familiarize them with the organization. The following is the task given to a group of students learning Business English Communication (BEC):

Task: You are the Human Resource Manager of West and Compton in the city. Write a 'Welcome email message' to make a new employee feel wanted and accepted.

The learners attempt the task individually with the experience gained from the orientation. Given below is one of the sample messages composed by a learner. The sample is utilized for contrastive discourse analysis at the stage of perceiving learning. The following version is hereafter referred to as 'Learner's Attempt 1' (LA 1):

To : vidyajothi@india.in From : edwin@sahara.com Date : Nov. 21, 2008 10.00 AM Cc : Bcc :	Prefatory elements
Subject : A warm welcome to you.	Partially complete
Good morning! It's nice talking to you. You are going to start your occupation with our company. We are happy to have you working with us. West & Compton is a well-known company in the city. It has sprouted like a banyan tree and its achievements are inumerable (sic). It is possible because employees are hard working and they are encouraged to venture into new methods and consummate. We are mutually satisfied with each other. As a result, there are no layoff and turnover rates in the company.	Two separate ideas clubbed
We were given an impression that you were very enthusiastic during your employment interview. I want you to show the same interest in the years to come. On our part we assure you of welfare measures and other perks. If you contact our personal sectary (sic), she will explain to you about community atmosphere of the company. We are once again happy to learn that you have decided to associated (sic) with us. We wish you good luck. See you and goodbye.	Not cohesive
Thanking you, A. Edwin Raj	Not a complementary close

An Improved Version

At the second stage LA 1 could be juxtaposed with a better model. Using a contrastive discourse analysis, they work individually to see the extent of effectiveness of their draft and identify areas for improvement. Given below is an effective version of the **welcome email message** furnished by the teacher:

To : Wilson@sahara.com From : mariana@india.in Date : August 21, 2008, 10.00 AM Cc : vijay@india.com Bcc :	*Prefatory elements*
Subject : A warm welcome from a well-established workhouse.	*Short but informative subject line*
Dear Mr Wilson	*Greeting*
Welcome! You have chosen an excellent company with which to begin your professional career.	*Welcome employee*
West & Compton is a well-established company with a good reputation. The company trusts its employees, and they are given freedom and encouragement to use innovative ideas in meeting their daily challenges. The management is so satisfied with our performance that we have almost nil employee turnover rates in the industry.	*Provide information*
As we briefed you during your employment interview, West & Compton takes care of its employees' welfare and provides them with excellent fringe benefits. Please feel free to contact Ms Sophia Seth in Customer Care Department to grab an appointment to learn how the welfare measures can be of value to you.	*Give supporting comments*
Wilson, we are delighted that you have decided to associate yourself with us. We hope that you have many successful and fruitful years with us. If I can be of any help, please let me know.	*Show appreciation*
Regards Sincerely,	*Complimentary close*
Mariana Susan Human Resource Manager	*Name & Position*

Preparing a Checklist

At this stage the learners focus on targeted features in the model text made available to them, and on the gap that exists between their present level of performance and the target form. A comparison of their version with the input model provides them helpful evidence of the yet-to-be-acquired features, and this process of 'noticing is essential for input to become intake' (Irun-Chavarria 2005: 20).

At this stage learners sit in the classic form of 'community' (Curran 1976) with the teacher standing outside the circle as a 'counsellor' or 'knower' facilitating discussion. The community now engages in a critical reflection and highlights what is helpful, what is working, and what needs improvement. It is important that the response is elicited from the learners themselves rather than simply stated by the teacher. Learners are motivated to perceive the meaningful and natural use of language and get a feel of typical business register, style and approach. They also prepare some examples incorporating the basic phrases, formal versus informal language, polite/impolite language and discourse and communication strategy. Once they learn to tease out linguistic and non-linguistic aspects, communication, strategies, specialist vocabulary, etc. they start internalizing them. This exercise is carried out orally too, because this is the way it is done in real life and serves to enhance learners' oral skills. This technique helps them to prepare a complete checklist containing all aspects – features, format, organization of the message, and strategies involved. This checklist would serve as a benchmark for future reference.

Collective Revision Process

If participation of learners is the key at the stage of preparing a checklist, partnership is the guiding force at presenting. Learners at this stage are fairly equipped to revise their drafts. Even things that they are not sure of at the preparation stage would get clarified in small group discussion in which they collaborate and help one another in improving their earlier version on 'Welcome email message', followed by whole class activity of questioning, clarifying and counselling. Feedback from the expert practitioners in the workplace rounds off the process. A copy of 'Learner's Attempt 2' (LA 2) is furnished below for analysis. A noticeable change could be seen in the target learning items. As practice makes things perfect, learners internalize the input better in practice. They also sharpen and tone up their linguistic and extra linguistic competence required for email writing. Therefore, this phase in 5 'P' approach is very vital.

LA 2:

To : vidyajothi@india.in From : edwin@sahara.com Date : November 23, 2008 10.00 AM Cc : vijay@india.co Bcc :	*Prefatory elements*
Subject : A warm welcome from West & Compton.	*Informative and complete subject line*
Dear Ms Vidya Jothi	*Formal salutation*
We heartily welcome you to West & Compton. You have chosen to begin your professional career with a well-reputed company.	*Welcoming*
It is an organization with a good track record. It has over the years, served the consumers to their utmost satisfaction. Therefore, the clients repose faith in our service and the quality of the product. Moreover, the company encourages the employees to be innovative and consider their views in rendering quality service to the clients. The job satisfaction of the personnel is so high that I am proud to say we have almost nil employee turnover rates.	*Providing information*
You may be curious to know about the welfare measures. Our company plans employees' welfare measures well and takes care of their safety and security. There are many opportunities for us not only to improve our career but also to socialize and maintain the working relationship with one another. To know more about our company, you may contact the personal secretary in customer care department and she will tell you about the community atmosphere in West & Compton.	*Showing appreciation*
Vidya, we are happy to have you in our midst and hope to have many successful and fruitful years with us. Please feel free to call me should you need anything.	*Complimentary close*
Regards Sincerely,	*Farewell*
Edwin Raj Human Resource Manager	*Name & Position*

An Analysis of the Improved Version

A simple contrastive discourse analysis of the two versions of 'Welcome email message' (LA 1 & LA 2) shows a marked difference between them:

A learner's First and Second Draft – An Analysis

S.No.	*Specific areas*	*LA 1*	*LA 2*
1	Subject line	Partially complete	Informative and complete
2	Vocabulary	Stiff e.g. 'consummate'	Familiar e.g. 'socialize'
3	Sentences	Indirect e.g. 'we were given an impression...'	Direct e.g. 'the company encourages us to express our innovative ideas'
4	Paragraphs	Two separate ideas clubbed	Built around a single idea
5	Thoughts	Not cohesive	Cohesive in a few places
6	Language features	Spoken and informal e.g. 'See you and goodbye'	Conversational and formal e.g. 'Please feel free to call me for any information'
7	Format	Formal salutation and closing	Formal salutation, closing and farewell
8	Strategy	Welcoming, encouraging the employee and closing with a positive note.	Welcoming, providing information, showing appreciation and complimentary close
9	Elliptical forms	A few instances e.g. 'see you'	Nil
10	Accuracy	Error of grammar e.g. 'you have decided to associated with us'. Error of spelling e.g. 'sectary', 'inumerable'	Free of errors of grammar and spelling
11	Effectiveness	Ideas not very coherently presented	Well argued message
12	Tone	Preaching e.g. 'I want you to show the same interest in the years to come'.	Positive and encouraging e.g. 'opportunities for us ... to improve our career ...to socialize...'
13	Courtesy	Writer-point of view e.g. 'we are once again happy to learn that you have decided to associate with us'.	Reader-point of view e.g. 'you have chosen to begin your professional career with a well-reputed company'.

This contrastive discourse analysis may not be exhaustive, foolproof or scientific however it works. Even a casual comparison of the first draft with the final version suggests that learners have by and large profited by this process. The following table shows the sequence of this workable learning process:

Perceiving • Identifying the features • Attempting a task • Noticing the gap
Preparing • A checklist
Presenting • An improved version
Performing • Working in real life situation
Progressing • Validating the experience with the feedback from practitioners

The Underpinnings of '5 P' Approach: Learning to Learn

This formative process evolves out of experience, observation, interaction, experimentation, analysis, interpretation and inferences. The revelation of the approach is that the teacher facilitates learners pick, practice, perform, discover and own their learning. Hence, there is a swing away from the teacher fronted method to learning by modelling, learning by doing and learning by socializing. Definitely the underpinning of this teaching procedure is 'learning to learn'. 'In a fast-changing world, the most valuable skill is,' said Hugh Cory (2004:2) 'the ability to adapt, re-train and pick up new skills and knowledge. It isn't enough to teach our students today's facts and procedures, because many of these will be obsolete tomorrow.' Therefore facilitators need to help them internalize the learning process and so discover their ability to tackle the learning items themselves.

Works Cited

Cory H., *Learners' Autonomy, Language Matters*, 9 September, 2004, pp. 2-4.

Crystal D., *Language and the Internet*, Cambridge: Cambridge University Press, 2002.

Economist The, 'Language and Electronics', *The Coming Global Tongue*, 21 December, 1996, pp. 37-39.

Gains J., 'Electronic Mail – a new style of communication or just a new medium? An investigation into the text features of Email', *English for Specific Purposes* 18/1, 1999, pp. 81-101.

Gimenez J.C., 'Business email communication: some emerging tendencies in regista', *English for Specific Purposes,* 2000, pp. 19:237-251.

________, 'Embedded business emails: Meeting new demands in international business communication', *English for Specific Purposes* 25/2, 2006, pp. 154-172.

________, 'Embedded business emails: Meeting new demands in international business communication', *English for Specific Purposes* 25/2, 2006, pp. 154-172.

Hale C. and J. Scanlon, *Wired style: principles of English usage in the digital age*, New York: Broadway Books, 1999.

Irun-Chavarria M., 'Doing, reflecting, learning' *English Teaching Professional* 40 September, 2005, p. 20.

Mallon R. and C. Oppenheim, *Style used in electronic Mail*, Aslib Proceedings 54/1, 2002, pp. 8-22.

Rutherford W., *Second language grammar: Teaching and learning*, Harlow: Pearson Educational Trust, 1987.

Schmidt R., 'The role of consciousness in second language learning,' *Applied Linguistics* 11, 1990, pp. 129-158.

Swales J.M., *Genre Analysis*. Cambridge: Cambridge University Press, 1990.

Sweeney S., 'Work-life balance', *English Teaching Professional* 41, 2005, pp. 35-37.

Vygotsky L.S., *Thought and Language*, Cambridge, MA: MIT Press, 1986.

Willis D. and Willis J., 'Consciousness Raising Activities' in D. Willis and J. Willis ed., *Challenge and Change in Language Teaching*, Macmillan Heinemann, 1996.

9

The Semiotics of Communication

Thilagavathi G. Joseph

Communication, the term widely used in many fields of study, is not a simple phenomenon, and there is more to it than the definition, 'any method by which human beings pass information to one another' (Universal Dictionary), which is why a number of theories and models of communication are developed and explored in each stage of human life. Language, being the primary mode of communication, encompasses the highest number of complexities in the field of communication. The least an effective teacher of language needs to do is to become aware of cumulative complexities that can baffle a second language learner.

Communication basically requires a sender and a receiver and a code in which a message is encrypted. The sender encodes a message using a code (in this case a language) which can be understood by the receiver and transmits it through either the oral or the written mode. Communication is said to be successful, only when the receiver receives and understands the message. Though it sounds simple, the process of communication is not as simple as this. If it were so, teaching would be very simple and all input would without any attrition turn into intake. Where lies the problem? What makes communication so complex? Who is the culprit? Is it the code, the channel, the sender or the receiver?

When the sender and the receiver understand the language used, we presume that communication is perfect. For example, if both understand Tamil, and the code used is Tamil, it is presumed there is no possibility for erroneous decoding or misunderstanding. But, everyone knows that even when two people speak the same language there are ever so many problems and glitches in comprehension. This problem arises because of the linguistic phenomenon which Ferdinand de Saussure, the great Swiss Linguist, calls the arbitrary nature of language.

Saussure in *Course in General Linguistics* scientifically analyses the communicative function of language. He considers language as a system of signs, and each word of the language, a sign, is a combination of the signifier and the signified. The signifier is the 'sound' produced when the word is uttered and the signified is the 'concept' that looms in our mind when we hear the sound. For example, when the word 'tree' is uttered, we hear the sound /tri:/ and for one who knows English, the image or the concept 'tree' comes to mind. With the combination of the sound /tri:/ and the concept 'tree', meaning is created. If this combination doesn't take place, the sound remains as sound or the signifier, and there is no creation of the concept or the word or the meaning, and hence communication fails to occur. This is the basic principle behind the function of language as a communicative tool.

However, this function may encounter problems, as there is no one-to-one relationship between the signifier and the signified or the sound and the concept —which Saussure calls the 'arbitrary nature' of the sign. The bond between the two is not natural but is conventionally fixed. The word 'tree' is associated with the object tree not because it is a tree naturally. The tree has never suggested that it would like to be called a tree. It is called a tree because our forefathers have always called it a tree for some reason or the other and the name has come to stay. However, a study of Etymology reveals that not all words have been randomly or arbitrarily encoded. Umberto Eco, in *The Search for a Perfect Language* gives a few examples to prove that many words are 'etymologically right' and not necessarily arbitrary. He refers to Adam's naming procedure and analyses the etymology of the word 'woman':

> In the Vulgate the name is virago (a translation from the Hebrew *ishha*, the feminine of *ish*, 'man'... In Genesis 3:20, he calls his wife Eve, meaning 'life', because 'she was the mother of all living'; it is evident that we are faced with names that are not arbitrary, but rather – at least etymologically – right' (1995:8).

Though we, like Eco, may be able to trace the etymology of a few words, the meaning as such still remains arbitrary going by Saussure's definition of the term, and we can't disprove Saussure's claim that meanings are conventionally fixed.

As the meaning of a word is conventionally fixed, there is the possibility though rarely for the word to shift meaning: When the word 'mouse' is uttered, what is the concept that comes to our mind? Is it the cute little creature that peeps out of the hole to check whether there is a cat around? Or is it the gadget that seems to have become indispensable, the one that attaches itself to the computer with its long tail? This indeterminacy always poses an impediment to communication. There is yet another problem. When a word such as 'mouse' causes confusion, humanity may one fine day decide to change the name of one of the 'mouses', (not mice!!), and which mouse will go and which mouse will stay, only posterity will decide. The history of language has seen many words either changing their colour or getting dropped. In the Shakespearean Age, 'vulgar men' meant common men, who we now refer to as the masses. Though the dictionary meaning of vulgar still remains 'ill mannered, in bad taste' (OED), the word is now used in a different sense.

If a single word, which is only one sign of an entire signifying system, can lead to such 'confusion of codes', then, sentences and discourses embedded in multifarious socio-cultural contexts, may turn out to be more indeterminate and more puzzling, leading to innocent or deliberate misunderstanding. When someone tells a colleague, 'you are coming only now!' he or she may take it either as a casual comment or as an accusation for coming late. The interpretation depends both on the sender and the receiver and the relationship between the two. The tone of the utterance may be sarcastic or accusing or the receiver may have guilt in her/his consciousness, which has induced her/him to access the second interpretation. It is also possible that the sender has intended it as an accusation but the receiver has decoded it as a casual comment. If the two persons involved have a close relationship and perfect understanding, the intended meaning most often successfully reaches the receiver. Even then, there is something called mood, which keeps fluctuating, and this mood also may interfere with the interpretative act. Roland Barthes refers to images, as signifiers with a 'floating chain of signifieds', (1977: 39) and we may attribute this quality to sound images as signifiers as well; they are always in a state of flux, and it is left to the human user to fix them up.

This arbitrary nature of the sign, which leads to multiplicity of meaning, is only one of the many problems, probably the simplest of them all. If the word is a sign, and the language is a system of signification, the signifying system is boundless and the meaning making is unlimited. Moreover, there is not just one language. According to a statistical summary given by Ethnologue, there are 6912 living languages in the world. 'A living language is defined as one that has at least one speaker for whom it is their first language; extinct languages and languages that are used only as a second language are excluded from these counts' (2005:www.ethnologue.com). If each language is a signifying system, governed by different cultural ethos and if each language operates with its own arbitrariness, then we can surmise the depth and the width of the problem.

The cultural background of a person matters a lot in communicative function. Certain words accepted in one culture may sound disrespectful to people from another culture. Any expression, even when it is uttered in a single language, may mean differently to people from different cultures. Eco humorously comments in *Faith in Fakes*, 'If I write the phrase 'no more', you who interpret it according to the English language code will read it in the sense that seems most obvious to you; but I assure you that, read by an Italian, the same words would mean 'not blackberries' (1986:140).

Men and women, linguists say, use the linguistic function in different ways. Women, they claim, encode subtle indirect messages and men decode them in the literal sense;

whereas men put across their messages in a more direct way, which may sound rude to the woman receiver. For example, when a woman asks a man, 'Would it be possible for you to do it?' she expects the man to do it. But the man may conveniently access the interrogative sense and respond, 'No.' In a similar context, the man may just say, 'Do it!' and the woman may consider him rude and impolite. We can neither blame the woman nor the man. The difference in their linguistic behaviour is due to the inherent characteristic difference between the two genders, built up by social and cultural expectations. Woman is expected to be polite and man is expected to be assertive and these culturally fixed gender attributes, called gender roles, have become natural to the two genders. This naturalization process has been a slow and steady one and hence goes unnoticed and so cultural attributes are very often mistaken for nature. This linguistic difference exists not only between men and women but also between employer and employee, teacher and student, parent and child and wherever there is a hierarchical difference.

It is not just the language that we use, but other accoutrements like our gestures, facial expressions, clothes etc. form a part of the communication system. Semiotics, which is a theory of signification as well as a theory of communication, encompasses all fields and its scope is broader than that of language. Even trivial, insignificant objects become signs as they communicate a message. As Roland Barthes explains in *Writing Degree Zero and Elements of Semiology*, 'Often they are objects of everyday use, used by society in a derivative way, to signify something; clothes are used for protection and food for nourishment even if they are also used as signs' (1967:107). Another semiotician Julia Kristeva says, 'Nobody just talks. Every speech act includes the transmission of messages through the languages of gesture, posture, clothing, hair style, perfume, accent, social context etc. over and above, under and beneath, even at cross purposes with what words actually say' (1977:qtd. in Hawkes 125).

Language together with all other signs forms the semiotic system, which in turn can be considered to some extent, the communication system. When a girl or a boy is wearing fashionable clothes, she or he is making a statement and very often they openly acknowledge this. A girl may be fashionable for the sake of being fashionable or she may be telling her parents that she wouldn't go by their traditional dictats and she is not in the least bothered about what any one else thinks. However, it is not proper to judge one by one's clothes. She may be just wearing the clothes that she likes and feels comfortable in. To avoid erroneous decoding of a sign, one has to view the sign not in isolation, but together with other signs, placing it in a system. To understand the 'statement' that a girl is making, whether it is fashion statement or otherwise, we need to view her clothes, together with her verbal communication, her cultural background, etc.

If the act of communication is so complicated, could we ever get our message across to another person the way we intend it to be? We may be successful, if we are careful. The message needs to be encoded using a shared code that is, not just the language but also the style of language and the tone of voice should be carefully chosen. The gestures, facial expression, dress, etc. should create the right impression. Transcending all these complexities if someone successfully communicates, that person is considered a good communicator.

Works Cited

Barthes Roland, *Writing Degree Zero and Elements of Semiology*, Hill and Wang, 1968.

_______, *Image Music Text*, London: Fontana Press, 1977.

Eco Umberto, 'Towards a Semiological Guerilla Warfare', *Faith in Fakes: Essays*, tr. William Weaver, San Diego, Secker and Warburg, 1986.

_______, *The Search for the Perfect Language*, tr. James Feantress, Fontana Press, 1995.

Hawkes Terence, 1977, *Structuralism and Semiotics*, London: Methuen and Co., 1987.

Saussure Ferdinand de., 1915, *Course in General Linguistics*, ed. Balley and Sachehaye, tr. Wade Baskin, London: Peter Owen Ltd., 1960.

(www.ethnologue.com, SIL Publication Web Version, 2005).

10

Identifying the Socio-Linguistic Gap: A Corpus-based Comparative Analysis of Two Young Learner English Textbooks from Tamil Nadu, India

Kirsten A. Anderson

List of Abbreviations

ABL	Action-based learning
EM	English-medium schools
EYL	English for Young Learners
LHR	Linguistic Human Rights
MBT	Matriculation Board Textbook
MDG	Millennium Development Goals
NCERT	National Council of Educational Research and Training
NGO	Non-governmental Organization
PROBE	Public Report on Basic Education in India
SSA	Sarva Shiksha Abhiyan
Std.	Standard (class in school/grade)
TCT	Tamil Nadu Textbook Corporation
TNGBE	Tamil Nadu Government Board of Education
TNMB	Tamil Nadu Matriculation Board

TLF	Three Language Formula Policy
TM	Tamil-medium schools
TN	Tamil Nadu, India
TPR	Total Physical Response
UEE	Universal Elementary Education
UN	United Nations
VM	Vernacular-medium schools

Introduction

The Global Perspective

Shortly after the formation of the United Nations (UN) in 1945 came the Universal Declaration of Human Rights, adopted in 1948. For the first time 'once and for all the right of "everyone" to education' was formally proclaimed (Volio, 1979: 22). About ten years later, the UN signed 'The Declaration of the Rights of the Child'. Principle 7 of this declaration (see Box 1), although sexist in language, describes the child's right to education as (ibid.: 25-26):

- free public elementary education
- compulsory education but with the freedom to choose private institutions

While this declaration of universal elementary education (UEE) provides a minimum baseline for countries to strive for, it does not answer questions about implementation, curriculum, teacher training or teaching materials.

Box 1. Principle 7 of The Declaration of the Rights of the Child (Milarapct, 1979: 257; UN Human Rights Commission, n.d.).

Principle 7

The child is entitled to receive education, which shall be free and compulsory, at least in the elementary stages. He shall be given an education which will promote his general culture, and enable him on a basis of equal opportunity to develop his abilities, his individual judgment, and his sense of moral and social responsibility, and to become a useful member of society.

The best interests of the child shall be the guiding principle of those responsible for his education and guidance; that responsibility lies in the first place with his parents.

The child shall have full opportunity for play and recreation, which should be directed to the same purposes as education; society and the public authorities shall endeavour to promote the enjoyment of this right.

–Proclaimed by General Assembly resolution 1386(XIV) of 20 November 1959

Reassessing the situation at the millennium, the UN set forth the Millennium Development Goals (MDGs) with the hope of ending poverty by 2015. Of the eight goals, number two echoes the need for UEE:

> Ensure that, by 2015, children everywhere, boys and girls alike, will be able to complete a full course of primary schooling (UN Millennium Goals, n.d.).

However, it is the implementation process that is often fraught with complications such as socio-economic disparities (Naik, 1979b) and the hotly debated topic of the language of instruction (Hoffer, 1979; Mazaba & Nthépé, 1979), which each country is left to deal with independently. For countries with a colonial history, the language of education, especially for the elite, has often become the language of the colony. This alienates those in society limited to mother tongue schooling and perpetuates inequality along linguistic lines. To be schooled in your mother tongue is a linguistic human right (LHR) according to Skutnabb-Kangas and Phillipson (1995). In addition, however, LHRs also include 'the right to learn an official language in the country of residence, in its standard form' (ibid.: 71). While the rhetoric of transnational organizations such as the UN supports mother tongue education and policies to preserve all language, the language of the policies allows countries 'to adopt a minimalist approach' while meeting the requirements set forth (Tsui & Tollefson, 2004: 6). Internationally mandated principles and goals are somewhat ambiguous guidelines that each country must implement independently.

The Indian Perspective

In addition to international mandates, the national constitution has also pledged to provide free and compulsory education within 10 years (see Box 2).

Box 2. Article 45 of the Indian Constitution (Constitution of India, n.d.).

Article 45. Provision for free and compulsory education for children.
The state shall endeavour to provide, within a period of 10 years from the commencement of this constitution, for free and compulsory education for all children until they complete the age of fourteen years.

However, issues of access and quality have made achieving UEE unattainable to date. The 86th amendment to the constitution mandated 'making free and compulsory education to the children of 6-14 years age group, a fundamental right' and this universalization of primary education is now being implemented under the programme Sarva Shiksha Abhiyan (SSA) (n.d.) to address the needs of an estimated 192 million children. Working with local state governments the SSA is focused on access, enrolment and retention while improving the quality of education, however, issues regarding the medium of instruction is again left ambigious.

From Macaulay's highly controversial 'Minutes on Education' in 1835 to the anti-Hindi movement in the South during independence, it is predicted that India ranks third after the United States and Britain as the largest English-using country in the world (Bhan Prasad, 2006: 99-115; Crystal, 2003: 47-48; Sheorey, 2006: 14-15). While English is a *lingua franca* in India and 'may be seen as an ethnically neutral move ... it is by no means a politically neutral move' because the unequal power relationship 'perpetuates social, economic, and political inequality' (Tsui and Tollefson, 2004: 5). While English is an established co-official language in India, emphasis needs to be placed on ensuring multilingual education by expanding and enforcing the Three Language Formula that informs India's language education policy (Mathew 1997: 165-66). This policy, in line with LHRs, assures a place for regional languages by emphasizing bilingualism as a minimum and multilingualism as the ultimate goal towards 'equipping Indians with a language of globalization' while also attempting to unify a multilingual country (Vaish, 2008: 14). Recognizing that 'English is here to stay', Ramanathan adds that English is kept within the reach of the middle class and is inaccessible to economically and socially disadvantaged students (1999: 226). Therefore, while English is a permanent linguistic fixture in India, the current quality is abysmal and inadequate to help those students who remain on the outside of the power circles in India (ibid.: 212).

The current system in India offers privately funded English-medium (EM) education and public government funded schools teaching in the mother tongue language, or vernacular medium (VM) (Ramanathan, 2005). This division is often, but not always, along the lines of urban and rural; wealthy and poor; and high-caste and low-caste, exemplifying the idea that language, culture and ideology are inextricably linked with power, domination and social inequality (Baik and Shim, 1995: 122-123). Furthermore, at the university level across India, English is the standard medium of education for the sciences and professional subjects (Ramanathan, 2005: 34). This presents a huge linguistic gap for students who have attended VM schools. Therefore, learning English often becomes the students' burden, forced to learn English on their own (Sheorey, 2006: 70). In theory, the English language could be the language that unifies India, but it has become a medium used to maintain inequalities in society (Baik and Shim, 1995: 123-124) and it 'remain[s] inaccessible to those who are disadvantaged because of their economic situation, their caste, or both' (Ramanathan, 1999: 212). Even if English education is a path towards social upliftment and does not threaten local languages, without adequate access to English, specifically trained teachers and quality materials, the education system is likely contributing to the social divide in TN and in India.

To narrow the gap, state governments in India have recently decided to place more emphasis on English in the government schools. For example, the state of TN decided to implement English as a subject from the first standard (std.) as of the 2004-2005 school year because English is a global language and knowing English will 'open employment opportunities throughout the world especially in IT Industry' (Government of Tamil Nadu, Policy Note 2004-2005). Globalization is transforming education in India, as Vaish explains:

> ...the urban disadvantaged are demanding earlier access to the linguistic capital of English, government schools find that offering English only in secondary school is too late and does meet the demands of the community' (Vaish, 2008: 36).

An increased focus on English is supposed to alleviate societal pressures from parents and students who cannot compete with the private English-medium schools as well as supply the business sector with more proficient English speakers (Government of Tamil Nadu, 'Framing of Curriculum/Syllabus', n.d.). In addition, it is aimed at narrowing the bilingual/multilingual gap between the haves and have-nots, but it is not yet clear if this new language policy will have the intended effect. Therefore, more needs to be understood about English education in general and specifically how the two textbooks for the two systems of education frame the language learning. This paper will now move away from the theoretical debate that does 'little to address the concrete problems of teaching English in difficult circumstances' (Maley, 2001: 2) and look at the socio-educational environment specific to TN.

The Education Crisis in Tamil Nadu

The value placed on English in TN, is both a matter of regional linguistic pride and a reaction to limit Hindi as the national link language of India. While, the vast majority of Tamil speakers remain monolingual, the elite bi/trilingual speakers have maintained a competitive edge nationally and internationally, by choosing English as their language of communication to enhance their education and job opportunities at home and abroad, further advancing the state (Brass, 2006: 356-7).

TN is recognized as being an educationally 'advanced' state (Mehrotra, 2006: 262; Mehrotra & Panchamukhi, 2006: 423; Mishra, 1999: 336). For example, only 1.8% of the teachers in both public and private schools are untrained and TN has one of the lowest teacher absenteeism rates in the country (Mehrotra & Panchamukhi, 2006: 434 & 436). Unfortunately, being an advanced state does not exclude it from the problems facing education in India. Infrastructure and human resources problems are largely confined to the government and rural schools. For example, approximately 35% of the rural schools only have one classroom, 28% are built *pucca* and 38% of the rural schools have no drinking water facilities and often there is no toilet (Mehrotra & Panchamukhi, 2006: 429- 430). Sadly, drop-out rates in government schools also tend to be much higher. See Table 1 for a comparison of government and private school statistics (Mehrotra & Panchamukhi, 2006).

Table 1. A comparison of government and private schools in TN (Mehrotra & Panchamukhi, 2006; NCERT, 2008: 33) * No statistics available.

Types of Schools by Funding and Location	*Government Schools*		*Private Schools (aided/unaided)*	
	Rural	*Urban*	*Rural*	*Urban*
Total State Enrolment (NCERT, 2008: 33)	4,221,560 Rural=2,715,929 Urban=1,505,631			
Enrolment by Funding Type	74.32%	51.40%	25.68%	48.60%
Average Cost Per Child (average of 8 states in the study)	Rs 891	Rs 1100	Rs 1588	Rs 2268
Teacher Ratio	1:42	1:30	1:45	1:37 / 1:24
Teacher Salaries (average yr. salary for ALL India)	Rs 63,000-90,000	Rs 76,000-106,000	1	5
Untrained Teachers	0.9%	0.8%	5.4%	0.4% / 16.7%
Drop-out Rates	17%	*	7%	*
No Drinking Water	38%	*	*	*
One Classroom	35%	*	*	*

Research also indicated that 'a higher proportion of the upper caste children are enrolled in non-government schools', in other words, the socio-economically disadvantaged students are more likely to be enrolled in the non-fee paying schools—the government schools (Mehrotra & Panchamukhi, 2006: 429).

As exemplified with the ambitious goals of UEE, policies and ideals do not always materialize into action or effective changes. Nevertheless, the Department of School Education (Government of Tamil Nadu, n.d.) promises:

- To provide elementary schools in hamlets where there are no schools.
- To provide free and compulsory education for all children of age group 6-14.
- To provide eight years of schooling for all children before 2010.
- To eradicate drop-outs before 2010 fully.
- To improve the quality of education from the pre-school to higher secondary school level.
- To eradicate illiteracy.
- To open village libraries where there is a population of 5000 and above.
- To encourage health education in schools.

1 This number is unknown for the state of TN, but yearly salaries from Bihar and West Bengal are thought to be as low as Rs 6600~10,000 (Mehrotra & Panchamukhi, 2006).

If fully realized, TN would probably be the most educationally advanced state in the country. However, AID India, a non-governmental organization working to organize, educate and empower the poor, believes the state is facing a learning quality crisis. The state has approximately 30,000 primary schools, 10 million school going children and an estimated 98% of children in the state join and attend primary school. Enrolment statistics aside, AID India's website reports that 50% of children in 5th standard cannot read a paragraph in Tamil and 70% of children in 5th standard cannot do simple division problems (AID India-Chennai, n.d.). Enrolment statistics may look impressive but there is obviously a disconnect between enrollment and learning outcomes, resulting in a serious learning quality crisis that includes but also goes beyond English education.

English for Young Learners

This research is focused on first standard textbooks, therefore, the young learner as a unique learning group must be considered. English for young learners (EYL) textbooks are often focused on the interplay between prominent images and their reference to the written, but limited, text on the page. In the first std formal literacy is still in the early stages of development and some grammar constructions may be too complicated linguistically (Cameron, 2001: 12). Furthermore, Pinter notes that:

> ...the general consensus is that children should learn to read in their mother tongue first and when they are reasonably competent they can learn to read in a foreign language. It would be controversial to introduce reading and writing in a second language to children who are not yet literate in their first language (Pinter, 2006: 65).

While reading and writing activities can be positive reinforcement for oral language practice (ibid.: 66), perhaps this is most successful through letter and word focused activities focused on phonics including card games, songs, copying words, and finger writing (ibid.: 71-76). Presenting smaller chunks of language that are recycled throughout the textbook is critical in creating a positive learning environment with adequate exposure and input, while helping students gain self-confidence.

Interdependent categories, vocabulary and grammar, are chunks of language that are considered to be the building blocks towards proficiency (ibid.: 83-84). However, young learners are not cognitively ready for grammar explanations or language manipulation and are most excited by using language in games, songs, or stories (ibid.: 84). Consequently, young learners may 'recognize a vocabulary item without knowing the exact meaning' (ibid.). This may in turn help them to learn other words and realize meanings without explicit explanations. Subsequently, however, vocabulary is crucial in defining culture:

> As small children learn vocabulary, in fact, they are simultaneously learning the world, as it is categorized and described by the culture into which they have been born (Swan, 1997: 164).

Therefore, vocabulary and lexis used in textbooks give insight into the cultural norms presented and taught within the text. The associated images are also keys to understanding the cultural undertones of the text.

Unfortunately, grammar does not always have clear or consistent rules and is not a linear learning process (Pinter, 2006: 85). For young learners, grammar is best learnt through 'meaning-focused input', or where it naturally emerges from meaningful communication (ibid.: 84-85). Deliberate practice of vocabulary and grammar, even encouraging memorization, is necessary to help young learners 'retrieve it quickly and efficiently when needed' (ibid.: 85). Central to this is the need to recycle vocabulary and grammatical structures in different and fun ways in the classroom, language activities and in the textbook (ibid.: 85 & 159). Recycling, or increasing the frequency, is important because it ensures 'learners get the best return for their vocabulary learning effort by ensuring that words studied will be met often' (Schmitt & McCarthy, 1997: 17). In addition, Pinter advises that in environments with young and inexperienced teachers, two key elements are essential (2006: 118):

1. Total Physical Response (TPR): activities, songs, rhymes, and action stories
2. Teacher supported textbooks: detailed notes, simple language, teaching tips, activity answers, game ideas, etc.

With the limited scope of this paper, a critical analysis of the appropriateness of the textbooks for young learners is not possible. However, the vocabulary and grammatical structures presented in the textbooks, explicitly and not, are keys to identifying the sociolinguistic gap between the dual systems of education.

The Research Perspective: A Comparative Textbook Analysis

Implementing English from the first std. requires developing new curriculums, training teachers, creating resources and writing textbooks – a demanding challenge. This research is focused on the textbook; the key classroom resource and aid for both teachers and students[2]. This paper will compare, analyse and assess the differences of two first std. (1st grade, age 6-7) English textbooks from TN. One textbook was published by the TN Textbook Corporation (TNCT) and represents their new curriculum and language policy set forth by the TN Government Board of Education (TNGBE). This textbook

2 The new government activity-based learning (ABL) programme materials were unavailable while doing research overseas. However, the material in the textbooks were converted into the ABL flashcards. Therefore, comparing textbooks is still relevant and is a better comparative tool considering the ABL programme is limited to the government schools.

is used in Tamil-medium (TM) schools. The other textbook was published by the TN Matriculation Board (TNMB) and is used in English-medium (EM) private schools.

This research has been extracted from an MA TEFL/TESL thesis that in addition to the corpus-based analysis incorporated objective analysis as suggested by Littlejohn (1998) and imagery analysis. Given the constraints of this paper, only the corpus-based analysis will be presented. The specific research questions pertaining to this paper are:

1. How do two first standard English textbooks from the educationally advanced state of Tamil Nadu compare linguistically?
    - Word Frequencies
    - Progression of Grammar
    - Explicit Vocabulary
2. Based on the differences found between the textbooks, the following questions will be discussed:
    - Is there a linguistic and/or cultural gap between the textbooks?
    - Are the textbooks encouraging a social or linguistic divide in India?
    - Do the textbooks contribute to the discrepancy in education from the first standard?

Based on eight years of volunteering with 'socially, economically, educationally and locationally' disadvantaged (Bellarmine, 1993-1994: 16) students in TN, I assume social inequality is being perpetuated by the dual education systems and I use it as a point of departure for this corpus-based textbook analysis. However, this paper does not try to assume (yet) that one textbook is necessarily superior. It seeks to engage in a dialogue between the texts in order to better understand the dual systems and the possible implications on students and society because as Dyer notes, there is a 'slim body of research into practices in elementary school classrooms' for policy-makers to draw on (2000: 12). Indeed, there seems to be very little research at the primary level into the linguistic and social chasm being perpetuated.

Methodology

Identifying the Textbooks

The EYL textbooks selected for comparison are both written for first std. students and are specific to Tamil Nadu but they represent two different state-level boards: the TN Government Board of Education (TNGBE) and the TN Matriculation Board (TNMB) (see Table 2).

Table 2. The two textbooks used for analysis.

Title	*Publisher*	*Curriculum Endorsement*	*Abbreviation*
English Course Book 1 (see Picture 1)	Tamil Nadu Textbook Corporation, Government of Tamil Nadu	Tamil Nadu Government Board of Education	TCT
Sunflower Series English Main Course Book 1 (see Picture 2)	Tata McGraw-Hill Publishing Company Limited	Tamil Nadu Matriculation Board	MBT

The underlying assumptions with this selection are: (1) both textbooks are for beginners and (2) they are regionally, and therefore, culturally similar. The government schools are required to use the government published textbooks, but the private schools can choose any number of approved textbooks. Unlike many English language textbooks around the world, these were written and published in India by Indian speakers and teachers of English.

Picture 1. English Course Book 1, Tamil Nadu Textbook Corporation Textbook (TCT)

Picture 2. Sunflower Series English Main Course Book 1, Tamil Nadu Matriculation Board Textbook (MBT)

Creating Corpora

With no scanner available, the two textbook corpora were created by manually typing the text into a txt-file, which was then imported into the AntConc 3.2.1w 2007 software (Laurence, 2008). This is a simple concordance program with the ability to generate concordance lines, word frequencies, and collocates available for free on the Internet.

For this research, the concordance software was used to find the most frequent content words (as opposed to grammatical words), identify grammatical structures present in the textbooks and discover how explicit vocabulary is interweaved throughout the text. Specific corpus lines of interest were then exported to be included as data in following sections.

Results

Word Frequency

The frequency word list from each textbook corpus was extracted using the AntConc 3.2.1w software (Laurence, 2008). Using the AntConc software, the top 50 most frequent words were identified. The content words, those with stand alone lexical meaning (Richards and Schimdt, 2002: 116), from both textbooks were extracted and compared (see Table 3). The function words, those of grammatical importance, are almost identical (ibid). Interestingly, the textbooks do not share a single content word in the top 50 most frequent words. However, both textbooks do cover similar topics such as fruits, vegetables, transportation, animals, actions and classroom objects. In most of these cases the MBT presented more words to the students within each category. Overall, the MBT has almost double the amount of word types and about 2.5x as many total words in the text.

Table 3. Content words from the top 50 most frequent words in the textbooks (see Appendix 6 & 6a).

Frequency	*TCT Content Words*	*Frequency*	*MBT Content Words*
22	say	30	children
17	good	23	exercise
14	come	22	tree
14	go	19	see
14	name	18	days
13	mother	18	words
12	little	17	dog
11	thank	17	Mini
9	baby	16	big
9	farm	16	crow

8 8 8 8 7	bow mew moo quack boys	16 15 15 14 14	pigeons man many black elephant
7 7 7	Chittu dear girls	14	look

To find out more about patterns in the text and how the most frequent words are being used, corpus lines were pulled for the top 5 most frequent content words. Five examples from each word set were chosen to represent the different uses, occurrences and contexts (see Table 4).

Table 4. A sample of TN Government textbook corpus lines of the top 5 most frequent content words.

say	2 When grandpa gives you something, **Say** 'thank you'. 7 like Chittu, the elephant, we should also learn to **say** 'thank you'. 8 Come with joy or not at all **Say** 'Please' Please shut the door. 11 We shall **say** a rhyme. May I go out? May I go out? 14 When I pull your hair I **say**, 'sorry'. It makes you happy.
good	2 'Tick-tock, six o' clock **Good** Morning!' says the cock. 7 dear! **Good** afternoon, dear! **Good** evening, dear! **Good** night, dear! 12 father gives you something Say 'thank you'. Yes, **good** boys and girls 15 makes you happy When I say, 'sorry'. Yes, **good** boys and girls always 16 the dishes Ring the bell for tea Three good wishes, three **good** kisses
come	1 I am waiting for my friend in the moon, who will **come** and take me 2 We speak Tamil in the south. **Come** shake my hand, Together we must 5 The moon does shine as bright as day **Come** with a smile, some with a 8 It's so nice. 'May I **come** in?' 'May I **come** in?' 'May I come in?' 14 Rosy Boys Smiling girls, rosy boys, **Come** and buy my little toys;
go	1 Oh, my dear! What's your name? Shall we **go** and play a game? 5 A Merry Rhyme **Go**, **go**, **go** to school, **Go** to school on time; 8 say a rhyme. May I **go** out? May I **go** out? May I **go** out? 11 Mother Rabbit said, 'Come Baby let us **go** for a walk'. Baby Rabbit was 12 Mother, what is that? It is a crow, now let us **go**. Colour Talk I am in the
name	1 Brother Father Mother Sister What is your **name**? My name is Ravi. 5 What is your father's **name**? My father's **name** is Raja. What is your 10 My brother's **name** is Hari. What is your sister's **name**? My sister's 12 Pattu the elephant had a little baby. The baby's **name** was Chittu. One 13 Tell me your school's **name**, I will guide! It's Government Primary

The 5 most frequent content words from the TCT include:

- imperative verb forms (say, come, go)
- polite expressions of greetings and introduction (Good Morning, What is your name?)
- an adjective (good) often used to praise the students after using a polite expression like 'thank you' or 'I'm sorry'

These examples indicate a tendency in the text to use the imperative verb as a command; used by adults to tell, teach, or command the students to do something. Even though there are several pages in the TCT dedicated to learning expressions like 'please' 'thank you' and 'I'm sorry', these are not reused in conjunction with the imperative form or otherwise. Perhaps this is a trait particular to Indian English. With this in mind, the MBT corpus was checked and has several examples of 'please' and 'thank you' ('I'm sorry' is not used in the MBT) with imperative verbs in the text (see Table 5).

Table 5. Examples of polite expressions used in the MBT.

please	1 Polite Forms Can I borrow your pencil, **please**? Sure, you can. Take 2 May I come in, please ? Yes, you may. **Please** come in. Thank 4 Yes, it is. Thank you very much. **Please** may I keep my bag here? 6 Thanks. May I sit here? Sure, **please** sit here. Excuse me. 7 Teacher. 'Good morning children. **Please** sit down.' The children
thank you	1 Sure, you can. Take this. **Thank you**. May I come in, please? 2 Yes, you may. Please come in. **Thank you**. 3 Is this your pencil? Yes, it is. **Thank you** very much. Please may I 4 Is this your dog? Yes, it is. **Thank you**, bye. 27 A NEW FRIEND 5 the other side of the road. '**Thank you** Madam,' say Ben and Sam

While these forms are not explicitly taught, as they are in the TCT, they are used throughout the text and in context, not as a directive given by adults. In contrast, a visual example of language taken from the TCT can be seen in the Pictures 3 and 4. Without the use of the polite expressions, already taught earlier in the text but not reinforced here, these images disturbingly remind me of children begging on the street. Both of these pages are stand-alone themes; they are not part of a larger (identifiable) context or story. The use of the stand-alone imperative form is unique to the TCT.

Picture 3. I want (TCT: 57)

Picture 4. What do you want? (TCT: 70)

In comparison, the top 5 most frequent content words in the MBT (see Table 6) include four nouns and only one verb. Considering these examples, the MBT appears to have a completely different language and learning focus from the TCT.

Table 6. A sample of TN Matriculation textbook corpus lines of the top 5 most frequent content words.

children	1 are swimming in the water. Some **children** are playing in the water. 3 is in class one. There are thirty-four **children** in her class. Miss Sonia 7 Miss Sonia says, '**children**, you have a new friend. Come in Li Yen.' 13 noses and big hats. The **children** clapped their hands and laughed. 21 watch. She said, 'come on, **children**. It's four o'clock. Time to go.' 27 The bear was laughing. 5. The **children** thanked Miss Usha.
exercise	1 a chick a frog a duck a fish **Exercise** I. Write the names of the pictures 2 a ship an ice cream an ant **Exercise** I. Let's write a or an before the 3 This is a baby. This is a tree. **Exercise** I. Look at the pictures and 17 She is happy to be with her friends. **Exercise** I. Answer the following 18 'Thanks,' says Li Yen. **Exercise** I. Answer the following questions.
tree	1 I can see **Tree** and grass. The sun and sky. I can taste chocolate 8 It is a very big garden. There is a big **tree** in it. There is a monkey 14 The hunter saw the pigeons on the **tree**. He wanted to catch them. He 18 The monkey swung from **tree** to **tree** following the flying pigeons. 21 4. He ___ the cage under the **tree**. 5. He ___ away to catch more animals.

see	3 In a small moat. Wear your coat. Let us **see** it float. Can you see the 5 Come in Li Yen. The children **see** a small girl standing near the door. 9 They craned their necks to **see** the giraffe. It had such a long neck! 13 They shouted, 'we want to **see** the camels!' An ostrich was looking at 16 the big bear do? 6. What did the children **see** in the pond? II. Tick (Y)
days	3 names of the **days** of the week. There are seven **days** in a week. 4 Friday Saturday. The names of the **days** always begin with a capital 8 3 March - 31 **Days** 4 April - 30 **Days** 5 May - 31 **Days** 6 June - 30 14 September - 30 **Days** 10 October - 31 **Days** 11 November - 30 17 4. How many months have 31 **days**? 5. Find out the months that have

In summary, the top 5 most frequent content words from the MBT include:

- Several nouns: children, tree, days
- Instructional word: exercise
- Verb: see

First, the use of the word 'children' is used throughout the book to refer to groups of boys and girls. However, the TCT only uses that word once and thereafter says 'boys and girls' making clear the gender distinction. Secondly, activities, or exercises, in the book play an important role in the overall text, indicating that the students are being asked to engage with the text and manipulate words they have learned. Lastly, the one verb that is present in the MBT top 5, see, is primarily used in stories to describe the actions of others, and not used as a command. In comparison to the pictures from the TCT, below is a unit from the MBT, demonstrating the use of a story followed by exercises (see Pictures 5 and 6).

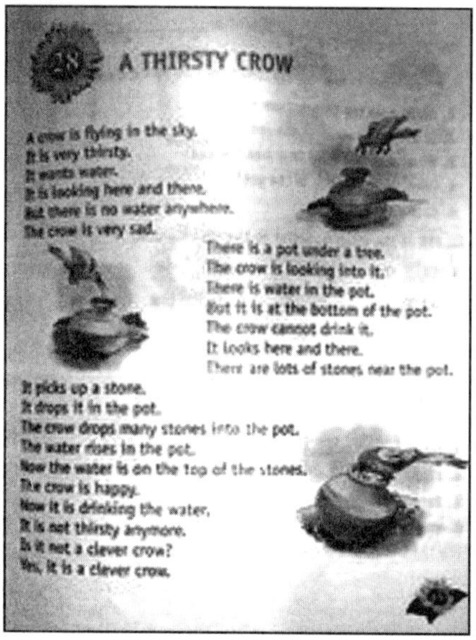

28 A THIRSTY CROW

A crow is flying in the sky.
It is very thirsty.
It wants water.
It is looking here and there.
But there is no water anywhere.
The crow is very sad.
There is a pot under a tree.
The crow is looking into it.
There is water in the pot.
But it is at the bottom of the pot.
The crow cannot drink it.
It looks here and there.
There are lots of stones near the pot.
It picks up a stone.
It drops it in the pot.
The crow drops many stones into the pot.
The water rises in the pot.
Now the water is on the top of the stones.
The crow is happy.
Now it is drinking the water.
It is not thirsty anymore.
Is it not a clever crow?
Yes, it is a clever crow.

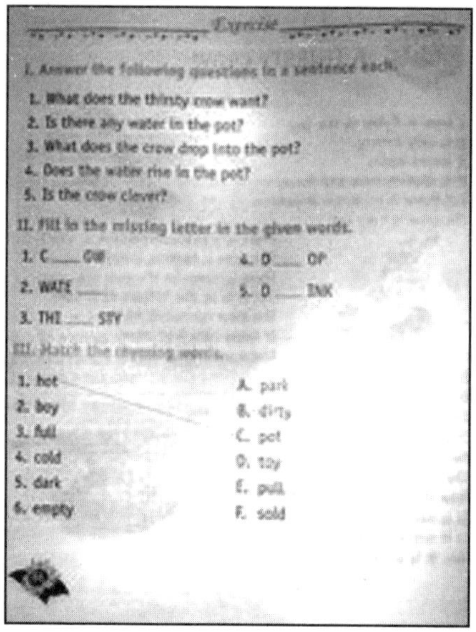

1. What does the thirsty crow want?
2. Is there any water in the pot?
3. What does the crow drop into the pot?
4. Does the water rise in the pot?
5. Is the crow clever?

1. hot
2. boy
3. full
4. cold
5. dark
6. empty

A. park
C. pot
D. toy
E. pull
F. sold

Pictures 5 and 6. A Thirsty Crow (MBT: 65-66)

Looking at the 5 most common non-grammatical words provides insight into the different structures, approaches and methodology being used in the two textbooks.

The Progression of Grammatical Structures

These textbooks do not use meta-discourse to explicitly teach grammar structures, except on one occasion at the end of the MTB. Both textbooks have essentially the same basic grammatical focus: present and past simple (see Table 7). However, the MTB builds on those structures by adding present continuous about halfway through the book and past continuous towards the end of the textbook. Many of the verbs used in these more advanced forms have already appeared in the book at least once. This places the focus on the new form of the verb, not on a new word. The continuous forms are not salient features of the TCT. In contrast, while only 17 verbs are used in the present tense in the TCT, 39 different verbs are used (at least once) in the imperative form. Of those 39 imperative verbs, 26 are only used once in the TCT. The imperative form tends to only exist in the activity instructions at the top of each page in the MTB, not in the text on the page. Many of these instructional verbs also only appear once in the textbook.

Table 7. A comparative list of verb tenses.

Verb Tenses	*TCT*		*MTB*	
	Verbs used	*Single use Verbs*	*Verbs used*	*Single use Verbs*
Simple Present	17	9	64	20
Simple Past	12	4	52	20
Simple Present Continuous	1	1	26	6
Simple Past Continuous	0	0	9	0
Imperative	39	26	16	9

Single use verbs are only used in the text in that tense, they are not represented in another form elsewhere. This is important because similar to the explicit vocabulary, the more times students are exposed to the same words, the more likely they are to recognize them and learn their meanings. However, if new words are used in combination with new tenses, students cannot build on what they already know. It requires learning something new, which may be difficult in the EYL context. However, this may be a mute point considering there is no built in programme to teaching children to learn to read at this level.

An added element of difficulty is the polysemous nature of many words found in the textbook. For example, in the TCT, the word 'like' is only used as a simple verb form once but appears five times in the textbook (see Box 3).

Box 3. TCT corpus lines for 'like'.

1 dear! Good night, dear! I like to have baby corn, For my breakfast in the morn.
2 morning, little rabbit! Would you like to have it? Good afternoon, my little one!
3 my little one! Would you like to have this bun? 'Good evening,' says the
4 says the parrot. Would you like to have a carrot? Good night! I am waiting for m
5 Chittu said, 'Thank you mother.' (Like Chittu, the elephant, we should also learn

A similar example with the same word, 'like', is also found in the MTB (see Box 4). The meaning of 'liked' in line 1 seems more intuitive for young children than the use of 'like' in line 2 and 3. Using more than one meaning in the text for a common and useful word occurs in both texts and may be challenging for young learners.

Box 4. MBT corpus lines for 'like'.

1 The children saw many animals at the zoo. They liked the giraffe and the elepha
2 I can hop. I can spin around like a top. I can dance, I can jump. I can fall and gent
3 What does his tail look like? 3. How does the squirrel scamper on the ground?

In addition, the textbooks use words in both their verb and adjective form. More corpus lines from the TCT show 'clean' as both an adjective and a verb (see Box 5). With only three appearances in the textbook, the meaning of 'clean' might be intuitive but how to use it would be confusing without an explicit explanation.

Box 5. TCT corpus lines for 'clean'.

1 It's 2, Gandhi Street, It is broad, clean and neat. Oh! My sweet boy, What's your
2 You are green My garden is clean. Your eyes and your hair you know, I am there
3 book. Close your book. Come here. Clean the blackboard. Stand up. Sit down.

Similarly, in the MBT, 'open' is used both as a verb (only in the past tense) and as an adjective (see Box 6).

Box 6. MBT corpus lines for 'open'.

1 He ___ (take) it in his hand. He ___ (open) the jar. Smoke ___ (come) out of the jar.
2 The hunter came back. He saw the open cage. It was empty. He could not find th
3 The pigeons landed in an open place. The monkey helped the trapped pigeon out
4 They couldn't see its feet. It opened its mouth and the children cried out, 'Ah!'
5 The monkey came down the tree and opened the cage. The parrots flew away, fre

These are just several examples of a common occurrence (or problem?) with both textbooks. If a standard word list exists for these textbooks, I did not come across it in my research. Considering, for example, the number of verbs only used once in both textbooks, a core verb list seems unlikely. For example, the verbs on the action verbs vocabulary list in the TCT, do not appear anywhere else in the text. They are unique to that page only and no example sentences are given. There seems to be a gap concerning related to a common word list (especially verbs), limited repetition of words, and mixed uses of words in both textbooks.

Explicit Vocabulary

Both textbooks have explicit vocabulary, or pages dedicated to new words in the form of labelled actions or objects. Presumably, these words are meant to be learned and provide a focus for the text. The TCT employed a much more traditional approach, labelling items on a page. However, the explicit vocabulary is less prominent in the MBT, as new words are often given in example sentences and highlighted. Other times new words are given on the top of the page and students were asked to match them to the corresponding picture. If students were asked to write the name of the object, without a list given, those items were not counted as explicit vocabulary because it assumes previous knowledge. Explicit vocabulary words make up almost 8% of the TCT and 2.5% of the MBT (see Table 8). However, perhaps somewhat shocking is the fact that 64% of the explicit vocabulary words in the TCT are not used anywhere else in the textbook versus 33.8% in the MBT. Which conversely, means that only 35.5% of the vocabulary words in the TCT are used more than once, but never more than nine times. In contrast, 65.3% of the vocabulary words in the MBT are used more than once and 4.8% are used 15 or more times in the text.

Table 8. Explicit vocabulary in the textbooks

Explicit Vocabulary	*TCT*	*MTB*
Total words in textbook	1817	4904
Total explicit vocabulary	145	124
% of text as explicit vocabulary	7.9%	2.5%
Explicit vocabulary **NOT used** in the text	**64% (93)**	**33.8% (42)**
# of different words listed on 2 or more lists	14 (31 or 21%)	4 (8 or 6%)
Explicit vocabulary used 1-4 times in the text*	30% (44)	36% (45)
Explicit vocabulary used 5-10 times	5.5% (8)	14.5% (18)
Explicit vocabulary used 11-15 times	0%	10% (13)
Explicit vocabulary used 15+ times	0%	4.8% (6)
Total explicit vocabulary **USED** in the text	**35.5%**	**65.3%**

As shown in Table 8, the MBT reuses the explicit vocabulary throughout the text more than the TCT.

Errors, Inconsistencies and Oddities

In addition to the textbook comparisons discussed in this chapter, textual errors were documented during the research process (see Appendix 1). While some errors are permissible in a printed document, these textbooks have errors, inconsistencies, and oddities beyond simple typos. However, there are more punctuation and capitalization errors in the TCT, implying a poor writing and editing process. If textbooks are supposed to model the correct use of the language, grammar and punctuation, we cannot expect children to learn without a good model to follow.

Discussion

Different Linguistic Content

The differences between the textbooks are evident at the linguistic level. Not only is there much more linguistic information in the MBT but it is presented and used very differently. The vocabulary tends to be more extensive and there is a clearer progression of grammar. In addition, there seems to be more emphasis placed on using the explicit vocabulary words throughout the text to reinforce the learning. The TCT, on the other hand, has pages of explicit vocabulary words that are meaningless without repetition and follow-up examples in the textbook. If young learners need repeated exposure to new words and structures, the TCT is setting up the students for failure. Without L1 or L2 literacy, young learners cannot be expected to learn without repeated exposure to individual words, especially explicit vocabulary words.

While the content words of the top 50 most frequent words were entirely different in this two textbooks, beyond the level of the individual word, the sentence is also significant in this comparison. The top 5 most frequent lexical words provided a look into the common types of sentences, structures and overall attitude of the text. The TCT examples present a hierarchical (actually matriarchal) situation placing the female teacher in the role of 'telling' the students how to act and behave, but not necessarily by setting an example. In contrast, the MBT is primarily describing situations as part of a story, followed by an exercise or comprehension questions. The dichotomy presented is perhaps indicative of the overall methodological differences: drill and repeat versus a more interactive style. That being said, the Indian education system across the board is known for its focus on memorization but not always comprehension. While the textbook might present one image, what happens in the classroom is beyond the scope of this research.

Implications

Regardless of enrolment numbers, are the resources available capable of providing a quality education if India achieves UEE by 2010 or even 2015, as set forth by the MDGs? Having only looked at two English textbooks, no broad generalizations can be made. However, after paging through these two textbooks for months, counting and categorizing images (research not included here) and comparing results from the corpus, it is my conclusion that the TNGBE, in particular, is doing a disservice to the students at TM schools. The TNGBE seems to have good intentions to provide equal access as well as a quality education, especially with the recent introduction of Action-based learning (ABL). However, the national and local governments also seem focused primarily on enrolment and achieving UEE. While this may be improving, without quality materials such as textbooks, and without teachers trained to use them (Duraisamy et al., 1997), primary education in India will continue to perpetuate social and inequalities, instead of giving the students the educational tools they need to succeed in life.

Unfortunately, for the disadvantaged yet highly motivated students, language schools are often out of reach and provide another example of the educational inequality that exists for students. This means they have to supplement their education with the help of local organizations, tuition centres and/or self-study. To balance the effects of the linguistic and cultural gap between the EM and VM schools, some NGOs are trying to provide additional educational opportunities to sustain a comparable level of education between the EM and VM schools. Acknowledgement and identification of the socio-educational gap in the textbook industry in India could be used to inform these NGOs in order to enrich their supplemental curriculum.

Recommendations

On a positive but slightly skeptical note, according to two newspaper articles written in the last year, the government of TN is working on 'bringing out new textbooks with a common syllabus' (*The Hindu*, 25 April 2008) that 'will be applicable to all State boards, Oriental, Anglo-Indian and Matriculation stream schools' (Indiaedunews.net, 4 November 2007). While these articles were not specific about how these changes will impact the current English syllabus and textbooks (or the ABL programme), it seems the government is cognizant of the disparities and is attempting to equalize the quality of public and private education. While it might be a step in the right direction, implementation including but not limited to textbook writing and teacher training would need close monitoring, especially considering the new ABL approach in TN. Even if new methodological practices like ABL are gaining ground in India, the assessment practices continue to remain the same. The public written exams are based on the textbook, therefore the washback effect, or teaching to the test, is a popular and dominant methodology in many classrooms, regardless of the textbook and its implied methodology (Watts, 2003-2004: para. 13). In addition, specific mention was made in *The Hindu* that the state will begin 'introducing English lessons for students through radio and improving schools' infrastructure' in the coming academic year. (*The Hindu*, 25 April 2008). Again these ideas and plans are met with skepticism until the implementation process has been thoroughly worked out. The basic discrepancy remains unchangeable; India has a dual education system that operates at different levels of society. The language of instruction, and all its complexities, is perhaps one key to unlocking the doors that divide Indian society.

Reduce, Reuse, Recycle

Without additional classroom observation it is difficult to make recommendations-based on this limited corpus-based comparative analysis. However, borrowing from the environmentalists' motto, it seems textbook writers and publishers need to consider three things in terms of content: Reduce, Reuse, and Recycle.

Reduce

Although appropriateness was not a focal aspect of this research, both textbooks placed a large focus on reading and the MBT on writing and comprehension. Given the age and assumed needs it seems that the focus should be on basic literacy: teaching skills necessary to read and begin to write, especially in the case of the TCT but also with the MBT. It is currently unclear where or how students learn these skills if they are not presented at the beginning of their language education. Essentially, the amount of written text on one page needs to be reduced to a manageable amount that is not overwhelming and frustrating for young learners and only after they have started learning how to read the text on the page.

Reuse

Assuming students learn best from repetition through a variety of seeing, hearing, and using the same words over and over again, the textbooks need to reuse an identified and standardized word list throughout the text. This word list would need to be visible to both teachers and students providing clear learning goals and objectives. Reusing words would help increase the speed and confidence while reinforcing those words in their memory.

Recycle

Both textbooks introduce topics or themes that were often not seen again in the textbook. If these topics/themes in conjunction with the related vocabulary or grammar structure were recycled in new and creative ways throughout the textbook it may also help to reinforce the overall learning objectives.

Conclusion

As a non-Indian from the United States, studying at a British University and researching textbooks from Tamil Nadu, I recognize and admit that my understanding of the context, the analysis of the textbooks, and my reflections of that analysis may reflect my cultural bias as an outside observer and researcher from the West. While my previous experience and knowledge of India has informed this research, this dissertation lacks an Indian perspective and is thus undoubtedly incomplete. However, this research has been my personal attempt to understand the complex educational context through the minute cultural and linguistic details of two textbooks with the hopes that it will inform my projects as an American India Foundation Service Corps Fellow working with AID India, a non-governmental organization (NGO) seeking to improve English education in Tamil Nadu.

To narrow the scope of the research questions, this paper was limited to the information provided in the textbooks. Unfortunately, this research did not have access to classrooms, teachers and students using these textbooks. It was unable to adequately judge the age and appropriateness level of the content, exercises, lexis, grammar and readings of the textbooks. This research was also unable to take into account the teachers' interpretation of the textbook or how they use it in their classrooms. It is possible that creative and/or trained teachers adapt and use the texts to suit the needs of the learners (H. Ramanathan, 2008: 118). Lastly, this research would have benefited from students' opinions and comment on the textbooks. Nevertheless, the textbook is only one small piece of learning that is necessary for the classroom. To adequately measure the quality of education, lesson observation is necessary (O'Sullivan, 2006). All of these additional research questions, to discover exactly what is happening instead of hypothesizing about what *might* be happening, would require access to classrooms, teachers and the students. Only by understanding each angle and perspective can education policies, curriculums, syllabi and textbooks be changed to positively influence the educational system.

Recognizing the limited scope of this research, the results and analysis confirm that there is a substantial socio-linguistic gap. Concerns and questions regarding the linguistic as well as cultural content demand that issues of quality and equality be at the forefront of future language education policies. While India is inching toward ensuring that UEE, as set forth by international and domestic policies, these documents do not enforce equality or ensure a standard level of quality – a monumental task. It remains the work of subsequent researchers to further qualify the task at hand.

Appendix 1

List of Textbook Errors, Inconsistencies and Oddities

Errors	*Page*	*Textbook 1*	*Page*	*Textbook 2*
		English Coursebook 1 (TN Textbook Corporation)		English Main Course Book 1 (TN Matriculation Board)
Spelling	29 29	• icecream • 'marble' should be 'marbles'	26, 50	• icecream (correct spelling pg. 2,7)
Punctuation	14 15 19 20 21 33-34 35 44-45 50 51 52 57	• Missing punctuation • Use of double vs. single quotes is inconsistent • Use of double vs. single quotes is inconsistent • Inconsistent punctuation • Use of double vs. single quotes is inconsistent • No use of quotes for speech • No use of quotes for speech • Mis-punctuation • No closing punctuation • Missing punctuation • Unnecessary semicolons • Missing punctuation • Missing punctuation • Missing punctuation	30 53 74	• Missing punctuation • Mis-punctuation • No closing punctuation
Capitalization	7 14-15 22 26 30 39 41 50 62 63	• Nouns unnecessarily capitalized • Inconsistent capitalization • Inconsistent capitalization • Inconsistent capitalization • Noun unnecessarily capitalized • Noun unnecessarily capitalized • Inconsistent capitalization • Inconsistent capitalization • Inconsistent capitalization • Inconsistent capitalization • Inconsistent capitalization	17 62	• Proper noun not capitalized • Noun unnecessarily capitalized
Incorrect Grammar	62	Say after me		Is Mrs Gopal's sandals white?
Fragment Sentence	23 35	Now it's your turn say after me. Today is Sunday, Why to school?	62	They wish her.

Inconsistency	 vi vii 1 26 35-36 61 70 71-72	• Unit titles are inconsistent Goodmorning, Children! GOOD MORNING CHILDREN Good morning, children! • Inconsistent use of articles • Images are inconsistent: barefoot boy without shoes, next page he is wearing shoes • Use of imperative without polite form • Question and answer don't match: What do you want? Give me a _____ • Phonics practice that doesn't use the same sounds, unrelated/ random	59 62-63 64 78	• Inconsistent use of contractions • Inconsistent use of titles for the same person: Ms & Miss • Inconsistent labeling: 'class one' or 'class 1' • Inconsistent use of titles for the same person: Ms & Miss
No Explanation			74	• Verb conjugation exercise using new irregular verbs: take, catch, try
Something Odd	12 18 23 37 57 13, 19, 50, 57, 67, 70	• Non-Indian reference in text and image: 'eyes so blue' • Poem asking children to come to play at night. • ABC = ABCs (needs plural) • Repeat 5 times: 'May I take this?' No vocab substitution. • Image looks like stealing. • Image looks similar to begging. There is no context for the conversation, no polite language. Children are barefoot. • Pictures of barefoot children		
Confusing	14 42-43	• New words introduced in the text that are not in the picture. • Bubble conversation reads from right to left, it is easy to read the answer first and then the question.	64	• Instructions for activity do not match activity.
Unknown Word			74	• jinn: the text seems to refer to a demon or spirit. Apparently it comes from Islamic mythology (*Dictionary.com* Accessed 29 June 2008)

REFERENCES

AID India Chennai, (n.d.), 15 June 2008, <http://www.chennai.aidindia.org/education.html>.

Baik M. and Shim R., 'Language, culture, and ideology in the English Textbooks of two Koreas', In M. Tickoo ed., Singapore: Sherson Publishing House Pvt. Ltd., 1995, pp. 122-138.

Bellarmine R., 'Issues of Experimenting with TED', In Nagaraja & Nagaraja ed., Bangalore: *Regional Institute of English South Asia*, Vol. 3 & 4, No. 1 & 2, 1993-1994, pp. 16-22.

Bhan Prasad C., *Dalit Phobia: Why Do They Hate Us?*, New Delhi: Vitasta Publishing Pvt. Ltd., 2006.

Brass R.R., 'Elite Interests, Popular Passions, and Social Power in the Language Politics of India', In *Ethnic and Racial Studies*, Vol. 27: 3, 2004, pp. 353-375.

Cameron L., *Teaching Languages to Young Learners*, Cambridge: Cambridge University Press, 2001.

Constitution of India, (n.d.), 'Article 45: Provision for Free and Compulsory Education for Children', 28 June 2008, <http://www.indiacode.nic.in/coiweb/welcome.html>.

Crystal D., *English as a Global Language*, Cambridge: Cambridge University Press, 2003.

Duraisamy P., James E., Lane J. & Tan J.P., 'Is there a Quantity-Quality Tradeoff as Enrolment Increase? Evidence from Tamil Nadu, India', World Bank Policy Research Working Paper No. 1768, 5 August 2008, <http://www.ssrn.com/abstract=604926>.

Dyer C., *Operation Blackboard: Policy Implementation in Indian Elementary Education*, Oxford: Symposium Books, 2000.

Government of Tamil Nadu, (n.d.), April-August 2008, <http://www.tn.gov.in/>.

'Department of School Education', Government of Tamil Nadu, (n.d.), 16 June 2008, <http://www.tn.gov.in/schooleducation/default.htm>.

'Framing of Curriculum/Syllabus', Government of Tamil Nadu, (n.d.), 15 August 2008, <http://www.tn.gov.in/dee/mainaspect.pdf>.

'Matriculation Syllabus, Class 1 English', Government of Tamil Nadu, (n.d.), 4 August 2008, < http://www.dge.tn.gov.in/matricsyllabus/class01/class01EN.pdf>.

'Textbooks Online, Std. 1', Government of Tamil Nadu, (n.d.), 1 April 2008, <http://www.textbooksonline.tn.nic.in/Std.1.htm>.

'School Education Department, Policy Note 2004-2005, Demand No. 41', Goverment of Tamil Nadu, (2004-2008), 27 June 2008, <http://www.tn.gov.in/policynotes/archives/policy2004-05/sedu/edu2004-5-4.htm>.

Hoffer C., 'Better Teaching of Languages', In Mialaret, G., ed., Paris: UNESCO, 1979, pp. 203-215.

'Common Syllabus for Tamil Nadu Schools Soon', Indiaedunews.net (2008), 4 November 2007, 21 August 2008, < http://indiaedunews.net/Tamil_Nadu/Common_syllabus_for_Tamil_Nadu_school s_soon_2385/>.

Dictionary.com Unabridged (v 1.1), Random House, Inc., jinn. (n.d.), 29 June 2008, <http://www.dictionary.reference.com/browse/jinn>.

Laurence A., (2008), 'AntConc 3.2.1w 2007', 8 August 2008, <http://www.antlab.sci.waseda.ac.jp/software.html>.

Littlejohn A., 'The Analysis of Language Teaching Materials: Inside the Trojan Horse', In Tomlinson B., ed., Cambridge: Cambridge University Press, 1998, pp. 190 216.

Maley A., 'The Teaching of English in Difficult Circumstances: Who Needs a Health Farm When They're Starving?', In *Humanising Language Teaching*, Vol. 3: 6. Pilgrims Ltd., 2001, 5 August 2008, <http://www.hltmag.co.uk/nov01/mart4.htm>.

Mathew R., 'English in India: A Response to Mark Tully', In *ELT Journal*, Vol. 51: 2, 1997, pp. 165-168.

Mazaba J.M. and Nthépé É., 'The Mother Tongue and the Teaching Language', In Mialaret G., ed., Paris: UNESCO, 1979, pp. 161-169.

Mehrotra S., 'Reforming Elementary Education in India: A Menu of Options', In *International Journal of Educational Development*, Vol. 26, 2006, pp. 261-277.

Mehrotra S. and Panchamukhi P., 'Private Provision of Elementary Education in India: Findings of a Survey of Eight States', In *Compare*, Vol. 36, 2006, 4, pp. 421 442.

Mialaret G., ed., *The Child's Right to Education*, Paris: UNESCO, 1979.

Mishra R.C., 'Research on Education in India', In *Prospects*, Vol. 29: 3, 1999, pp. 335-347.

Naik J.P., 'Equality, Quality and Quantity: The Elusive Triangle in Indian Education', In *International Review of Education*, Vol. 25: 2/3, 1979a, pp. 167-185.

Naik J.P., 'The Economic, Social and Family Context', In Mialaret G. ed., Paris: UNESCO, 1979b, pp. 77-82.

'Enrolment in Schools', NCERT (2008), In 7th All India Survey Report, 14 June 2008, <http://www.ncert.nic.in/html/pdf/Publication/Journal2008/Survey_reports2007/En rolment_Schools/Enrolment_in_school.pdf>.

O'Sullivan M., 'Lesson Observation and Quality in Primary Education as Contextual Teaching and Learning Processes', In *International Journal of Educational Development*, Vol. 26, 2006, pp. 246-260.

Pinter A., *Teaching Young Language Learners*, Oxford: Oxford University Press, 2006.

Ramanathan H., 'Testing of English in India: A Developing Concept', In *Language Testing*, Vol. 25, 2008, 111-126, 30 June 2008, <http://ltj.sagepub.com/cgi/content/abstract/25/1/111>.

Ramanathan V., 'English Is Here to Stay': A Critical Look at Institutional and Educational Practices in India, In *TESOL Quarterly*, Vol. 33: 2, 1999, pp. 211-231.

Ramanathan V., *The English-Vernacular Divide: Postcolonial Language Politics and Practice*. Hyderabad: Orient Longman Pvt. Ltd., 2005.

Richards J. and Schimdt R., *Longman Dictionary of Language Teaching & Applied Linguistics*, London: Pearson Education Limited, 2002.

Schmitt N. and McCarthy M., eds., *Vocabulary: Description, Acquisition and Pedagogy*, Cambridge: Cambridge University Press, 1997.

Sarva Shiksha Abhiyan, (n.d.), 30 September 2008, <http://ssa.nic.in/>.

Sheorey R., *Learning and Teaching English in India*, New Delhi: Sage Publications, 2006.

Skutnabb-Kangas T., Phillipson R. and Rannut M., ed., *Linguistic Human Rights: Overcoming Linguistic Discrimination*, Berlin: Mouton de Gruyter, 1995.

Skutnabb-Kangas T. and Phillipson R., 'Linguistic Human Rights, Past and Present', In Skutnabb-Kangas, Phillipson and Rannut ed., Berlin: Mouton de Gruyter, 1995, pp. 71-110.

Swan M., 'The Influence of the Mother Tongue on Second Language Vocabulary Acquisition and use', In Schmitt & McCarthy ed., Cambridge: Cambridge University Press, 1997, pp. 156-180.

English Course Book 1, 2 edn, Tamil Nadu Textbook Corporation (2007), Chennai: Tamil Nadu Textbook Corporation, 1 April 2008, <http://www.textbooksonline.tn.nic.in/>.

TED Initiative, 'A Working Draft: About the Teaching English to the Disadvantaged (TED) Initiative', Madras: British Council Divison, (Workshop 3-8 October 1994).

'Work on Uniform Syllabus to Begin Soon: Minister', *The Hindu* (2008), In The Hindu, Friday, 25 April, 2008, 21 August 2008, <http://www.hindu.com/2008/04/25/stories/2008042553640400.htm>.

Tollefson J. and Tsui A., ed., *Medium of Instructions Policies: Which Agenda? Whose Agenda?* Mahwah, NJ: Lawrence Erlbaum Associates, 2004.

Tomlinson B., ed., *Materials Development in Language Teaching*, Cambridge: Cambridge University Press, 1998.

Tsui A. and Tollefson J., 'The Centrality of Medium-of-Instruction Policy in Sociopolitical Processes', In Tollefson and Tsui ed., Mahwah, NJ: Lawrence Erlbaum Associates, 2004, pp. 1-18.

'The Declaration of the Rights of the Child', UN Human Rights Commission, (n.d.), 23 June 2008, <http://www.unhchr.ch/html/menu3/b/25.htm>.

'Education', UN Millennium Goals, (n.d.), 25 September 2008, <http://www.un.org/millenniumgoals/education.shtml>.

Vaish V., *Biliteracy and Globalization: English Language Education in India*, Clevedon: Multilingual Matters, 2008.

Visweswaran L., *English Main Course Book 1*, New Delhi: Tata McGraw-Hill Publishing Company Ltd., 2007, <http://www.tatamcgraw-hill.com>.

Volio F., 'The Child's Right to Education: A Survey'. In Mialaret G., ed., Paris: UNESCO, 1979, pp. 19-33.

Watts E., 'Cocking a Snook at the Communicative Approach', In *IATEFL Issues*, Vol. 176, (2003-2004).

11

A Profile of the Disadvantaged Learners in the Context of Teaching English to the Disadvantaged

A. Joseph Dorairaj

Prelude

Indian society is hierarchical, stratified and inegalitarian. It is divided on the lines of caste and religion, occupation and class, language and religion and a host of other determinants. It is a stark fact that a majority of the Indians are disadvantaged in multifarious ways. In the realm of education, there are hundreds of thousands of students from socially marginalized and economically vulnerable sections and there are those who live in remote rural areas where education is grossly neglected, for even today when the Government of India has launched SSA (*Sarva Shiksha Abhiyan*) on a massive scale there are rural pockets without schools and even the few schools that exist in these areas lack adequate infrastructure.

It has to be noted that structural imbalances and inequalities which characterize the Indian society have led to headstarts in the case of the privileged sections of our society and handicaps in the case of the disadvantaged. And these headstarts and handicaps have a cumulative and synergistic effect for they are the outcome of centuries of dominance or subjugation—whatever may be the case. In the context of headstarts and handicaps, Girod (1990: 35) in *Problems of Sociology in Education* writes that 'the motivation, means and opportunities to learn are not equally distributed among all social classes. The same is true of factors which affect knowledge negatively, which stifle the desire to learn, hinder its realization or favour the forgetting of what has been learned.'

From a historical perspective, headstart in the case of the privileged sections is the result of easy, sometimes exclusive and esoteric, access to social status and power, economic stability and political authority, and education. In the case of the disadvantaged, the systematic denial of access and opportunity to social mobility, economic growth and educational advancement—sometimes backed by religious sanction and even legitimization—has pushed them to the fringes of our society. Unfortunately, the disadvantaged are caught in a vicious circle because their disadvantage breeds further disadvantage thus perpetuating the cycle and system. Okun's (1975: 77) insightful comment captures this idea quite crisply: 'Unequal opportunity at one point in time generates unequal opportunity over time' (*Equality and Deficiency: The Big Tradeoff*).

Who are the disadvantaged pupils? What are the yardsticks used to designate a group/groups as disadvantaged? Notwithstanding the fact that the bulk of our learners are disadvantaged in one way or the other, for the term or label 'disadvantage' itself is a relative one, we focus our attention on those learners who suffer from multiple handicaps or disadvantages which stem primarily from gross 'inequality of opportunities'. In other words, the disadvantaged learners are those who are socially, culturally, economically, psychologically, locationally, environmentally and educationally backward, and empirical studies corroborate this standpoint. We have to be careful to exclude those who suffer from physical disabilities and/or neurological disorders and other psycho-pathological abnormalities from our target group.

While some educationists under the banner of meritocracy cite the examples of scores of Indian men and women who overcame their socio-economic handicaps and achieved eminence in different walks of life, including the educational sector, to contest any causal connection between socio-economic disadvantagedness and academic backwardness, others assert that there is a strong link between the two. Sociologists, educationists and language experts contend that socio-economic backwardness hampers academic growth for there is a nexus between the two. They argue that socio-economic backwardness is the distant cause, if not the immediate or proximate cause, of academic backwardness. Against this backdrop, they suggest a two-pronged strategy: one, working towards their academic growth and language (English) development and two, working with them for their empowerment, which is considered a long-term goal. Therefore, any academic enrichment programme in this sector should pay attention to both the short and the long-term goals.

Almost all these disadvantaged students have a poor command over English. Studying the causes of their linguistic backwardness, educationists have ascribed various reasons ranging from restricted to practically no exposure to English, especially the spoken medium. In this context it needs to be recorded that quite a few approaches to English language teaching, specially designed for these disadvantaged learners, have been launched and some quite successfully too. TED (Teaching of English to the Disadvantaged) is a veritable case in point.

How do we conjoin the disadvantaged and ELT? In other words what is TED? Any successful ELT programme is founded on four pillars: the teachers and the taught, materials, methodology and evaluation/testing (otherwise known as 4 Ms: men (no gender bias implied here), materials, methodology and monitoring). Of these four, the learners constitute the most important category, for it is the target group that influences and determines all other factors. In any ELT programme, we first identify our clientele and then on the basis of a needs analysis design, develop a package suitable to their behaviour and needs, and not the other way round which amounts to putting the cart before the horse. Therefore, before venturing into TED programmes it is mandatory that we first identify our clientele, i.e. the disadvantaged learner, and spell out their characteristics within the framework of TED with a view to gaining a better understanding of the target group and its ethos.

Characteristics of the Disadvantaged Learners

Socially Backward

Even though casteism seems to be on the decline in urban centres despite the unpalatable fact that our politicians joining hands with fundamentalists stoke it periodically with a great measure of success, it still has its vice-like grip in rural and semi-rural areas from where most of the disadvantaged learners come. These pupils who generally belong to the lower rungs of the social ladder—scheduled castes and scheduled tribes and most backward castes—cannot slough off their millennia-old oppression and segregation, for the whole idea of untouchability is based on the notion of ritual purity and pollution which has eroded their basic humanity and self-worth. Here it has to be noted that even though education ('Sanskritization' in the words of M.N. Srinivas) enables them to attain economic growth it does not help them much in terms of social mobility for the interfacing of caste and class is kept to the minimum.

The behaviour-pattern of these socially marginalized pupils in our classrooms needs to be analysed. While a handful of them somehow fit into the mainstream culture which basically upholds the upper and middleclass norms and values, many of them continue to feel alienated. Their withdrawn behaviour, inadequate socialization, a low self-image and a lack of initiative and leadership could be imputed to their caste-based subjugation.

Economically Backward

The bulk of the disadvantaged learners come from economically backward families. Most of their parents are either small-scale or tenant farmers or unskilled or semi-skilled labourers, and their economic condition is pathetic, for many of them live below the poverty line. A small percentage of them hold government or quasi-government jobs. Agricultural off-season and monsoon failures aggravate their condition. The large size of their families which means 'less resources but more mouths to feed' adds to their cup of sorrows. Highlighting the 'many faces' of poverty, Speth in his Foreword to the *Human Development Report* (1997: iii) writes: 'Poverty . . . is much more than low income. It also reflects poor health and education, deprivation in knowledge and communication . . . the absence of dignity, confidence and self-respect.'

Students who come from such poverty-ridden and undernourished families face a lot of hardships. Firstly, their families cannot provide them with decent education. Private, exorbitant-fee-collecting English medium schools are beyond their reach. Almost all of them take refuge in panchayat or union schools which woefully lack educational infrastructure and are run by mediocre teachers where education, English in particular, is a casualty. At the tertiary-level, these pupils cannot dream of entering elite institutions such as the IITs, IIMs and NITs. Even the OBC reservation may not drastically alter the situation for not many from socio-economically disadvantaged families enter the portals of prestigious colleges and universities, especially premiere institutions. Most of them are happy joining run-of-the-mill institutions and settle for courses in humanities like History and Politics whose market value is minimal as against the much sought after courses like IT and Management. Secondly, some of them even after joining colleges have to work to augment their family's meagre income. Thirdly, weighed down by peer-group competition where they are forced to compete with some of their better placed counterparts in terms of fashionable social habits, they develop a complex which eats into their already low self-image. For instance, flashy bikes and trendy iPods are beyond even their wildest dreams.

Educationally Backward

A good majority of the disadvantaged learners come from educationally backward families. Empirical studies point to the fact that the parental education of these disadvantaged pupils is appalling. Most of their parents are either illiterates or neo-literates who have received paltry education. Even their siblings' educational attainment is just mediocre. The reasons for this dismal scenario are manifold: lack of educational infrastructure in rural areas, girl students being forced to drop-out either due to marriage or because of sheer gender bias, the missing link between education, employment and economic success which compels many parents to terminate their wards' education abruptly and force them to take up even menial jobs in the unorganized sector, a strong belief in traditional and family occupations (an insidious manifestation of casteism), and the impact of the myth in some rural sectors that education will make their children, particularly girls, headstrong and rebellious.

This lack of educational back-up system at home greatly handicaps the already disadvantaged learners, who are quite often first generation learners. These students receive little guidance and counselling in terms of the choice of schools, programmes and method of study. At the tertiary-level, most of them drift in and out of colleges which is in sharp contrast to their privileged counterparts whose education and career are planned meticulously by their parents. Foucault's theory of knowledge and power and the complicitous relationship between the two needs to be underscored here. Foucault argues that what counts as knowledge is determined preponderantly by those who have power and conversely the 'dominant castes' and classes play a decisive role in discursive formation. Discourse and politics are intimately intertwined. He writes: 'Power and knowledge directly imply one another . . . there is no power relation without the correlative constitution of a field of knowledge, nor any knowledge that does not presuppose and constitute at the same time power relations' (cited in Simons 2004: 190). Secondly, these students receive little educational assistance from their parents and siblings, particularly when it comes to learning English. Thirdly, the poor educational climate at home in terms of discussions and debates, reading habits and materials, bed time stories and media exposure minimizes their chances of acquiring (English) language and knowledge.

Environmentally Backward

A high percentage of our target group comes from locationally and environmentally remote and backward areas. They come from rural and semi-rural pockets which lack adequate educational facilities, among other things. The print medium (in terms of newspapers and magazines in the vernacular and English) has not really invaded these far-flung places in any significant manner. This is in sharp contrast to urban pockets and metros where English is in the air and where information just about everything is available around the corner and at the click of the mouse.

These factors, viz. physical inaccessibility to sources of information and knowledge, lack of educational infrastructure and limited interaction with the media are largely responsible for their stunted growth in terms of English language development and education in general.

Psychologically Backward

Our clientele is not only socially, economically, educationally and locationally/environmentally backward but also psychologically disadvantaged (not psychogenic) in the sense that they have a low self-image and nurse very modest ambitions in life. Because of their humble origin and the many deprivations experienced, they have developed a poor self-image which is reinforced by the present-day educational system which is tailored to suit the culture of the upper and middle classes. The spectre of academic failure and retardation haunts them and makes a dent in their already low self-image. Most of these pupils occupy innocuous places in the classroom to escape their teachers' reach and attention which is symptomatic of their withdrawn behaviour.

Incidentally, a majority of these pupils have very modest educational and occupational ambitions and aspirations in life. Very few aspire to become executives and professionals in corporate sectors and MNCs and move into the top echelons of society. This is in striking contrast to a sizable section of the privileged pupils' drive to occupy influential and plum postings especially in bureaucratic circles and also have the wherewithal to transform most of their dreams and aspirations into concrete realities. This brings to light the disadvantaged pupils' lack of awareness of educational and employment openings and opportunities and their inability and even reluctance to dream big. Even if some of them think big they are unable to translate their dreams into realities. May be they blame it all on the *karma* theory of fatalism and are resigned to it!

Linguistically Backward

Many of the disadvantaged pupils are enveloped in a culture of silence. They are poor articulators which reflect in large measures their linguistic impoverishment, among other things. Surprisingly, their articulation inside the classroom even in their vernacular is minimal. And this brings to light their cognitive and affective barriers to communication. Yet another reason for their limited articulation, especially inside the classroom, is the effect of our present-day educational system which is preponderantly writing-based.

Bernstein, a British sociologist, researched the association between language and socialization and came up with startling evidence of 'the quite different types of language that different social groups employ' (Wardhaugh 1992: 328). Bernstein's 'code analysis' sheds light on the linguistic impoverishment of the disadvantaged learners. The 'restricted code' of this group contrasts sharply with the 'elaborated code' of the upper and middle classes. The 'restricted code' which is embedded in local contexts and is linguistically implicit has particularistic meanings and accounts for the linguistic inadequacy of the disadvantaged with reference to both L1 and L2. On the other hand, 'elaborated code' which is linguistically explicit and 'is less tied to a specific social context' tends 'to promote universalistic meaning' (Bernstein 1977: 64).

Bernstein's coupling of 'restricted code' with 'position-oriented' families where authority stems from position and hierarchy and 'elaborated code' with 'person-oriented' families throws up a host of issues for discussion. The disadvantaged pupils invariably come from 'position-oriented' families where authority stems from position and hierarchy demanding implicit and uncritical obedience which is opposed to 'person-oriented' families where authority flows from personal dynamism and charisma. Drawing room chats, debates and discussions, table-talks and bed-time stories are outside the purview of such a person-oriented system. This accounts for the linguistic inadequacy of these disadvantaged learners both in L1 and L2 for they are heavily influenced by role models who devalue the use of language and resort to non-verbal communication. On the other hand, 'person-oriented families . . . facilitate the verbal exploration of individual differences, orientations and motives' (Bernstein: 63-64). McQail (1975:74) provides the peroration. He notes that Bernstein is 'primarily concerned with a difference between what he terms a middle class and a lower working class, and a difference between two forms of speech use, two languages or codes'.

A disadvantaged student perceives the teacher as an authority figure who has to be implicitly obeyed. In other words, he/she sees the classroom as an extension of his/her house which is controlled by an authority figure who would brook no dialogue, discussion and questioning. This underscores the reasons for his/her poor articulation both in L1 and L2 in the class which is a veritable microcosm reflecting real life socio-economic and even linguistic differences, though not glaringly. Lawton (1969: 31) argues that 'it seems entirely possible that subjects from the least favoured socio-economic categories can find themselves at a disadvantage in schools where the verbal linguistic skills of the middle class prevail' (*Social Class, Language and Education*).

Aesthetically Backward

The myth that the disadvantaged are culturally and aesthetically backward has to be exploded for it smacks of cultural imperialism and ethnocentrism. Even though the disadvantaged are not aesthetically backward *per se*, the dominant classes/castes and ideologies ignore their aesthetics or at best give it a patronizing treatment. M.N. Srinivas (1987:114) contends that 'numerical strength, economic and political power, ritual status, and Western education and occupations are the most important elements of dominance' (*The Dominant Caste and Other Essays*). Because the aesthetics of the disadvantaged is at variance with that of the mainstream culture and aesthetics, it is either stamped out or given a step-motherly treatment.

Our educational system duly reflects this cultural imperialism and ethnocentrism for it upholds and propagates the upper and middle class culture and values. Karabel and Halsey's (1977: 67) comment is quite pertinent against this backdrop: 'If dominant social groups have the power to determine what is valued in the educational system at a particular juncture, it should not be surprising to find that subordinate social groups are deficient in terms of criteria set by the powerful' (*Power and Ideology in Education*). It was Marx who argued that the ideology and/or values of the dominant classes (and castes) are valorized and projected as the ideology and/or values of the whole society as such which are, in the long run, 'naturalized'. Examining the nature of ideology, Eagleton (2007: 30) argues that 'ideology signifies ideas and beliefs which help to legitimate the interests of a ruling group or class specifically by distortion and dissimulation' (*Ideology: An Introduction*).

Looking Ahead

Wiping out structural inequalities and imbalances and creating an egalitarian society is the cherished dream and ideal of all committed men and women. Conscientization and empowerment of the disadvantaged and the creation of a just and equitable society are wrought with political and sociological ramifications and are outside the direct purview of TED thinkers and practitioners. But all the same conscientization has to constitute a vital component of all educational programmes, especially language programmes, for a language like English in the Indian context is vested with power and status.

Our task and responsibility as TED thinkers and practitioners would be to study the characteristics of the disadvantaged and their ramifications when launching programmes in TED rather than enquiring into the causal factors of structural inequalities and imbalances. In other words, we have to shift our focus to the crystallization of these multiple disadvantages in the cognitive (related to vital skills which include inferencing, deducing, hypothesizing, summarizing, validating, etc.), meta-cognitive (crucial skills like planning, management, evaluation, etc.) and affective (key factors like socialization, interaction, self-enhancement, etc.) domains and relate it to TED.

Works Cited

Bernstein Basil, 'Social Class, Language and Socialization', *Power and Ideology in Education*, ed. Jerome Karabel and A.H. Halsey, New York: OUP, 1977, pp. 473-486.

Eagleton Terry, *Ideology: An Introduction*. London: Verso, 2007.

Girod Roger, *Problems of Sociology in Education,* London: Jessica Kingsley, 1990.

Karabel Jerome and A.H. Halsey, 'Basil Bernstein: Harbinger of a New Synthesis', *Power and Ideology in Education*, New York: OUP, 1977, pp. 62-71.

Lawton Denis, *Social Class, Language and Education*, London: Routledge and Kegan Paul, 1968.

McQuail Denis, *Communication*, 2nd edn, London and New York: Longman, 1975.

Okun Arthur M., *Equality and Efficiency: The Big Tradeoff*, New Delhi: Oxford and IBH Publishing Co., 1975.

Simons Jon., ed., *Contemporary Critical Theorists: From Lacan to Said*, Edinburgh: The Edinburgh Press, 2004.

Speth James Gustave, Foreword to *Human Development Report* 1997, New York: OUP, 1997.

Srinivas M.N., *The Dominant Caste and Other Essays*, Delhi: OUP, 1987.

Wardhaugh Ronald, *An Introduction to Sociolinguistics*, 2nd edn, Oxford and Cambridge: Blackwell, 1992.

12

Towards Understanding Rural ELT

Amol Padwad

Teaching and learning English is fast growing into a national mission all over our country, thanks to the political and social enthusiasm about the promises of bright future English is supposed to hold. Our country is now facing a new kind of divide – between the English-haves and English-have-nots. There is a growing feeling among some underprivileged sections of the society that one important reason of their being underprivileged is their lack of English. Some even go to the extent of a conspiracy theory behind keeping them away from English. Many states, which have recently introduced English early in the primary classes, claim that they have heralded a social revolution whereby they hope to ensure equal opportunities of progress for their people. In short, English is viewed as a panacea for all problems! How well-founded is this belief is another question. But in the present world access to English can certainly and significantly contribute to the uplift and growth of the disadvantaged sections.

It is often customary to count the rural population as a whole among the disadvantaged sections of our country. There are many arguments in favour of doing so. The common ones among them are related to the overall poverty, lack of development, lack of access to modern amenities, low standards of education and health and peripheral status in the socio-political structure. It is not difficult to see that the urban and the rural situations in our country are poles apart. That is why usually different approaches are adopted for the rural and for the urban in our policies, programmes, planning and implementation in the domains of politics and governance.

There is often an analogous demand in educational sector of adopting different approaches to educating the rural and the urban. Several states in India have uniform syllabuses, course structures, materials, evaluation systems and policies for the entire state, common to both the urban and the rural. Many educationists are against this practice and argue that the courses, materials, etc. designed for urban learners will not be appropriate for the rural learners and vice versa. For many of us teachers our experience and teacher like intuitions support this argument. We often find that the needs and interests of learners, the objectives of teaching and learning English, the content of the course materials, and even recommended methods and evaluation patterns tend to be decided with urban learners in mind. Many believe that this urban focus of our educational design is an important reason why rural learners do not benefit from education and remain poor achievers.

However, instincts, personal experience and observations are not enough to diagnose and analyse a situation which they point out. It is necessary to try to describe as many aspects of a problem as possible and to define it as precisely as possible so that we can then hope to devise more effective strategies of addressing it. If our intuitions and experiences suggest that there is a significant difference between urban and rural educational contexts, warranting separate approaches, then it is essential first to try to understand what characterizes a rural context. It is a complex issue and will need a lot of time and effort. In this paper I wish only to make a hesitant attempt to scratch the surface of this deep-rooted and complicated matter of what constitutes 'rural' with specific reference to teaching and learning English. The purpose here is to raise some questions and suggest some areas where research needs to be carried out, rather than suggesting any solutions or strategies to handle ELT in rural areas. This article will have served its purpose if it convinces some of the need to undertake an in-depth research in this area and suggests some issues and areas to research on.

What is Rural and Urban Education?

Any attempt to understand the dimensions of rural ELT should begin with trying to understand what is rural and what is urban. Since there seem to be no specific parameters, descriptions or definitions of the rural or urban in educational terms we can start by looking at how these two are differentiated in economic, social and political aspects. A cursory look at the world scenario is enough to convince us that the term rural and urban connote very different things in different countries. Population density is the most common parameter of defining urbanity used in many countries. The statistical figures used to define urbanity, based on the various kinds of census, also vary from country to country. For example, in Australia, urban areas are population clusters with a minimum density of 200 people per square kilometer, while for Japan they are units with a density of 4,000 people per square kilometer. For the USA an urban area has a population density of at least 1,000 people per square mile (386 per square kilometer). European countries define urbanized areas on the basis of type land use, they speak of a cluster of buildings with gaps not larger than 200 meters, and use satellite photos to determine, using this criterion as the boundaries of urban areas. In less developed countries, in addition to land use and density requirements another parameter is considered – that a majority of the population, typically 75%, is not engaged in occupations considered typically rural such as agriculture and fishing. In India population density and major occupations are considered while determining rural and urban population.

Rural areas reveal a marked difference from urban in terms of population size, density and land use. A settlement in a rural area (in India) is quite small ranging from a handful of people to several hundreds with low population density. The typical occupations are agriculture and fishing related, collecting and selling forest and non-forest produce and localized support services based on these. But this is not all. The rural areas also differ in the lifestyle of their people, mainly because services, especially public services, are not available in many cases or are very limited where they are available. Governmental services like police, education, health, fire stations, and libraries are also usually limited in scope, or just not available in remote communities. Necessities like water, sewerage, street lighting, and public waste management are generally less developed, while public transport is limited or absent. Access to the urban or nodal centre in terms of transport and distance is also an important consideration. All these have an impact on the amount of exposure to the wider world that the rural inhabitants get, the time that the developments in the other parts of the country or world take to reach them and the rate at which development takes place in the locality.

How Big is the Rural Sector in Education?

It is in this context that we may have to start our efforts to understand and adequately describe 'the rural' in ELT. But one basic question is – does 'rural sector' warrant separate attention and is it so significant that it needs to be taken up for study? The answer, tentatively, is 'yes'. Yes, because we have some preliminary data from education that supports treating the rural apart, and 'tentatively', because this data is preliminary and needs to be further supplemented by more data and studies.

In India, according to the 2001 census data, 72.2% population is in rural area while only 27.8% live in urban areas. Even the state with the highest proportion of urban population (Goa) has less than half (49.76%) the people in urban areas. In the education sector, the preliminary data from the 7th Educational Survey 2006 conducted by NCERT shows the following figures in the three states of Maharashtra, Tamil Nadu and Uttar Pradesh. These states are relatively higher up in the rank of the states in the country in terms of industrialization, urbanization, transport networks, political influence, literacy ratio and educational infrastructure. So we can safely assume that the proportion of rural teachers and students is likely to be higher in other states of India.

Full-time Teachers	*Maharashtra*	*Tamil Nadu*	*Uttar Pradesh*	*Total*
Rural	327,020	163,042	441,941	932,003
Urban	213,613	188,377	220,277	622,267
Total	540,633	351,419	662,218	1,554,270

Enrolment (Std. I to XII)	*Maharashtra*	*Tamil Nadu*	*Uttar Pradesh*	*Total*
Rural	11,776,140	6,219,332	26,355,850	44,351,322
Urban	9,493,992	6,431,227	8,388,717	24,316,936
Total	21,270,132	12,650,559	34,744,567	68,668,258

The ratio of teachers and students in rural and urban sectors is as below:

Particulars		*Maharashtra*	*Tamil Nadu*	*Uttar Pradesh*	*Total*
Full-time Teachers	Rural	60.49%	46.40%	66.74%	59.96%
	Urban	39.51%	53.60%	33.26%	40.04%
Student Enrolment	Rural	55.37%	49.16%	75.86%	64.59%
	Urban	44.63%	50.84%	24.14%	35.41%

This data of students and teachers at school level shows that at least more than half of the teacher and student population are in the rural area. This is reason enough to give a separate treatment in ELT to the rural sector.

Features of Rural ELT Context

It is urgently necessary to undertake systematic studies to describe features of rural ELT at least for two reasons. Firstly, such a description will help us understand how far the demand for separate (ELT) courses, materials, methods and policies for the rural areas is justified, and if it is, then how to devise these. Secondly, it will also help us understand how far the rural population is 'disadvantaged' (especially with reference to ELT) as claimed and what measures might be undertaken to correct the imbalance.

On the basis of the personal experience of living and working in a rural area, the formal and informal feedback collected from numerous teachers and parents from rural areas, and the experience of the English Teachers' Clubs experiment for rural teachers that I have been associated with, I find that the following features are commonly presented as typical of a rural ELT context:

- A rural teaching (especially ELT) context is marked by the lack or shortage of resources. Sometimes just the bare minimum of these are available.
- Both teachers and students in rural areas do not get as much exposure to the wider world and recent developments as their urban counterparts do.
- There is low general awareness in the society as a whole about the happenings in the world around them. There is a significant time lag between the urban areas and the rural areas.
- There is an overall disinterest in/apathy towards education. Getting educated is not a priority; children as working hands or earning support gain more premium. Most state governments in India have several incentives-and-support schemes to persuade rural parents to send their children to school.
- Even when children are sent to school, the priorities may be different. Educating the child is often seen as a formality undertaken for various extrinsic reasons, without great expectation from it.
- Since rural settlements are usually small in size there is greater social cohesion. Most people know each other; social issues and relations are more important for the rural people. Community festivals, marriages and deaths are some occasions when social relations are prioritized over everything else. A teacher in a rural school is also expected to be a part of this social fabric.

Profile of a Rural Learner

Another area in ELT that demands a series of in-depth studies is the profile of a rural learner. We do not have any significant and comprehensive data on this matter. In many instances, the textbook production bodies, syllabus design committees and similar other academic agencies do talk about keeping the rural learner in focus. Often the rural learner is the touchstone deciding the choice of texts, course structures, evaluation schemes, etc. But such decisions sadly are based on an assumed profile of a typical rural learner based on limited personal experience and subjective generalizations. Systematic studies may yield a more reliable picture of a rural learner that will help better decision-making.

By way of suggesting some parameters to differentiate a rural learner from an urban, we may begin with a tentative list like the following:

- A general impression – especially frequently mentioned by teachers – is that rural learners are intellectually poor, low ability learners as compared with urban learners. Educationists and psychologists will object to such an impression, because there is still no convincing proof for this. It will be more realistic and fruitful to start with an assumption that rural learners are 'differently abled'. They have skills and talents, which may be neither better nor worse than those of urban learners.

- A rural learner usually lives in less supportive (for education) family and social atmosphere in material, emotional and financial terms.
- A large number of learners may be first/second generation learners. This can be a handicap in comparison with urban learners, because a family with a long tradition of learning offers a lot of (implicit) learning support in terms of models of learning, supplementary materials, help in trouble, recognition of the importance of learning and so on.
- The needs, interests and priorities of a rural learner are likely to be quite different from those of an urban learner.

Profile of a Rural Teacher

As in the case of learners, in-depth studies are also necessary to arrive at some description of a typical rural teacher. While working with rural teachers in my region, I found that a large number of rural teachers showed the following features:

- There was overall very little job satisfaction. Most teachers looked at their work as a burden, did not seem to take any more interest than what is mandatory; were engaged in lots of activities other than teaching and did not seem to be occupied with their learners, school or work (apart from the school politics).
- Most teachers had lower qualifications, usually just the bare minimum prescribed for the job. Most of them came with very limited or no pre-service training at all and had undergone hardly any in-service training.
- Most teachers' own language (English) competence was very low. Many of them were conscious of it and hence seemed to suffer from low self-esteem.
- However, many of them, particularly those living in smaller places, seemed to enjoy social prestige. The teachers were seen as important members of the local society.
- Most of the teachers were required to shoulder many out-of-the-school roles and responsibilities which had no or very indirect relation to their teaching job.
- Since they had relatively high social standing and were considered important members of the society, they had some potential to influence the community.

Do We Need Rural Specific ELT?

In view of the foregoing discussion, we can assume a prima facie case for treating rural as a distinct context from the urban one and for demanding separate courses, syllabuses, policies, approaches, methods, evaluation systems and so on designed specifically for them. Such demands have been made in the past, mostly informally, at various forums and events.

It is, however, not a straightforward case, as there are quite a few arguments put forward to oppose any demand for treating rural ELT separately. Some of these arguments point out some crucial issues involved in setting up a separate entity called rural ELT. The more common arguments raised against a separate rural ELT are summarized below.

Arguments against:

- Separate syllabuses, materials, courses, etc. will perpetuate the status quo, continuing the separate identity and status (intellectual, social, pedagogic, etc.) of rural learners, instead of promoting their uplift.
- If rural learners are disadvantaged, then they need to be brought into the 'mainstream'. Integration of the rural learners in the mainstream will be hampered if they are treated separately.
- There is no point in considering ELT differently for rural or urban learners, since the instrumental needs are the same.
- Separation into rural/urban may 'brand' rural learners as inferior resulting in low self-esteem and a feeling of discrimination.
- Evolving separate rural ELT will entail a huge additional burden on staff, resources, administration and finances.

In short, there are some valid points on both the sides, but as yet no conclusive evidence to settle the case one way. What we need now is systematic research aimed at describing the rural ELT sector, including the learner, the teacher, the context and the milieu. Whether or not we arrive at a consensus on the need for a separate 'rural ELT' is a different question. But one thing is sure—with the increasing amount of such research we will gain richer understanding of the rural context, and we will at least be in a position to fine-tune, adapt and re-orientate our thinking and planning more effectively.

A 'Minimum Agenda' for Research and Experimentation

There are several, though isolated, examples of experimentation and initiatives in this direction. It is not difficult to find many innovative schools, agencies and persons who are trying to adapt or re-design the 'mainstream' education to suit the rural, tribal and other disadvantaged sections of the society. These are often experiments in overall literacy and not specifically for teaching/learning of English, but still there is lot we can learn from them. About two decades ago, a noted social worker in Maharashtra, Datta Sable, worked innovatively with tribal children in Thane district to teach them basic literacy by using content, language and experiences from their shepherding lifestyle. An NGO is working on informal and innovative means of educating the children of sex-workers in Kolkata's Sonagachchi red-light area. A devoted old couple in the hilly area of tea-plantations near Ooty has been running an unusual 'school' for the tribal children for several years, where the children pick up not just literacy, but leadership, management and life skills too. Andhra Pradesh has tried an experiment of publishing different versions of primary textbooks in various tribal dialects and minor languages in the state. The need is to gather insights from all such initiatives, to back these with systematic data collection and to begin to construct an outline of 'rural ELT'. This is perhaps a very long-term and ambitious plan. But we can begin with something more immediate and manageable. By way of a 'minimum agenda' of studies in rural ELT, I suggest we may start by trying to address the following questions:

- How to understand the contexts, needs, interests and opportunities in rural ELT better?
- Assuming that no immediate separation of syllabuses, courses, materials, etc. is possible, how to put the 'uniform'/'common' materials, courses, etc. to best use?
- What seem to be very obvious and easily identifiable special requirements of rural ELT? In what ways can these be accommodated in the current centralized system?

Beginning with this we can gradually expand the agenda to include the emerging needs. The work we undertake may not remain restricted to rural people alone; hopefully it will gradually grow into a much broader and more relevant field of 'English for the Disadvantaged'.

13

The Power of Context

Alan Maley

Learning involves a 'something' to be learned and a context of circumstances in which it takes place. It is this rich texture of factors, ranging from the material to the ethereal, that I want to reflect on in this article. Clearly these factors intersect and overlap in complex and not always predictable ways, but I shall nonetheless attempt to separate out the following six strands for discussion:

- Physical, material, economic factors.
- Socio-political and religious factors.
- Linguistic factors.
- Philosophical/educational factors.
- Family and peer group factors.
- Psychological, relational, affective factors.

Physical, Material and Economic Factors

On the face of it, it appears obvious that material circumstances have a massive influence on the effectiveness of learning. In the 1960's I worked with primary schools in Ghana. Many of them, particularly in rural areas, lacked even the most basic facilities: no desks or chairs, few books, blackboards pitted like battlefields... Classes were crowded into classrooms as hot as ovens. Children had sometimes to walk long distances to school after performing early morning chores such as foraging for wood and collecting water. Many were under-nourished or suffering from malnutrition.

Poverty, disease and malnutrition are the daily reality in many educational settings worldwide. They are certainly not confined to West Africa. Neither are they the exclusive reserve of rural communities. However, I want to suggest that such deprived material settings can sometimes—all too rarely but sometimes—be overcome by affective and relational factors. I have seen some of the most joyful and creative educational moments of my career in just these kinds of classrooms: an improvised puppet show using old newspapers to make the puppets and a table on its side as a stage, with the kids performing a play they had themselves written; an art exhibition of collages made from the clippings of the seamstresses stalls in the market... I do not suggest for a moment that such deprived environments are in any way desirable, but we should not assume that material circumstances are everything. I have seen some of the most lacklustre, deadening lessons given in classrooms with ergonomic furnishings, designer lighting and with the entire technical equipment one could desire. The material circumstances are important but not always decisive.

Socio-political and Religious Factors

These factors can exercise a negative influence on learning when, for example, the belief systems in some places exclude (or downgrade the importance of) women in education. There are also cases where certain sections of the population are given privileged access to education to the detriment of other sections, as, for example in Malaysia or India. Or the system may take a non-scientific stance towards science, as in the Creationist approach in the US, or view science as a fixed body of expertise to be used for political objectives rather than as an open-ended practice of inquiry. They clearly affect the way geography or history is taught. Even the Mercator projection, which forms the basis for many maps, has a lot to answer for. Politics can affect language learning too, as in cases of post-colonial resistance to the language of the colonizers, or in views of one's own language as being inherently superior to the one being learned. Factors such as these are more influential and more stubborn than even material factors, partly because those who hold such views are often unaware that they do so.

Linguistic Factors

The linguistic environment can have significant effects on language learning in particular. Is the society monolingual (the exception), or plurilingual, where it is common for people to switch between several languages, and not to regard learning another language as difficult? Is the target language being learned in a country where it is in use outside the classroom, or not? How distant are the mother tongue and the target language, and what effect does this have? (Curiously, languages which are close to one's own are not always the easiest to learn.) What difference does it make if the language being learned is high prestige or low prestige? Because English is the major international language, are native speakers of English disadvantaged in their learning of other languages? How do folk beliefs about language impact on learning? ('French is the language of culture',

'Italian is so musical', 'German sounds harsh', 'Greek sounds really masculine', etc.). And how do attitudes toward the target language affect the learning of it? Do I resent having to learn this language, or do I embrace the opportunity? Are my most cherished values put at risk when I acquire this language?

Philosophical and Educational Factors

Some societies accord greater prestige to education than others and this clearly affects the educational environment. Of course, it may also have a negative impact on some members of the society, who may be excluded or who simply drop-out of a race they feel certain they can never win. There are also clear differences between broadly elitist systems and 'democratic' ones. Sadly, it is often the case that equality of access to education may not guarantee equal quality of provision however. But there are winners and losers in all societies, and to teach or learn in an environment of 'losers' is all too often a guarantee of failure, leading to more failure in a downward and irreversible spiral.

Other factors include the overall beliefs about how learning should be conducted. Broadly conservative or traditional beliefs place high value on discipline, effort, competition, memorization and testing, and tend to view learning as something difficult and painful. By contrast, more liberal or exploratory approaches view learning as a pleasurable, creative and cooperative enterprise where the emphasis is on the quality of the process rather than the short-term product in the form of examination results. I am aware of the dangers of stereotypes, of course, but it is nonetheless true that generalizations can sometimes usefully be made. There are societies where the form is more important than the substance, the word than the deed. It is important however to avoid attributing such beliefs to whole societies (the Chinese are all influenced by Confucian values). There is often more variation within societies than between them. Things change, and one complaint increasingly heard about young 'nouveau riche' Chinese students abroad is precisely that they do not conform to the expected disciplined and obedient model!

Family and Peer Group Factors

The family, and in particular parental influence, is still paramount in the environment of most learners. Parents can exert positive influence through active involvement in their children's education, by non-coercive encouragement, by supporting them in moments of crisis and through their example as role-models. This is perhaps nowhere so apparent as in the development of literacy. Those children whose parents read to them at night, who provide reading material of compelling interest to their kids, who show themselves to be avid readers themselves – those children become readers, and reading is the best predictor of academic success that we have. Children whose parents are not like that will have a struggle ahead to achieve even minimal standards of literacy. Most people learn more from their parents – for better or worse – than they ever do from their teachers.

Arguably, they also learn far more from their peers, both positively and negatively. The pressure to conform to group norms has never been stronger, supported as it is by an aggressively consumerist ethos. How they look, what they own, how they speak, how quickly they can adjust to the latest change of fashion – all are subject to the unforgiving judgments of their peers. But they also learn how to be with other people, to respect and be respected by them, to give and receive understanding... and much else. We sometimes forget just how much kids learn outside school: arguably more than they ever learn inside it. And this too is part of the wider learning environment, especially when so much information is so readily available on the Internet.

Psychological, Relational, Affective Factors

An article of this length can scarcely do justice to the multitude of personal factors which pervade the learning environment. All I can do is remind myself, and you, of some of the stronger currents running beneath the surface of the learning-teaching surface. Hormones, hangovers and hyper-activity can cause havoc in any learning group. The moods, expectations, aspirations and attitudes of both teachers and learners also form an important part of the learning environment. Just how the skilful teacher manages to harness and orchestrate the energies and tensions of a group, and direct them in productive directions remains one of the greatest pedagogical mysteries. As teachers, we have all experienced classes which went like a dream and those which felt like endless nightmares. How to achieve the 'flow' experiences of the former, where both teacher and class are lost in the 'effortless effort' of the moment is elusive, though Jill Hadfield's book, *Classroom Dynamics* gives valuable signposts. Nancie Atwell, in *The Reading Zone*, also gives some guidance in how to harness the energy of a group in the shared and powerful experience of reading. And the 'flow' Bible is, I guess, still *The Inner Game of Tennis* by Timothy Gallwey. As teachers we need to be 'present' in the fullest sense, yet simultaneously absent, so that we leave space for the individuals and the group to enact their learning. I have a particular conviction that it is the teacher's voice quality which is a key to this, though I have only anecdotal evidence to support my case (Maley, 2000). But it is certain that teachers' voices remain with us for good or ill throughout our lives. The immediate chemistry of a class, requiring split-second decisions by the teacher is unlikely ever to be completely anatomized, yet it is this which ultimately overrides virtually every other factor I have discussed.

Good luck!

Works Cited

Atwell Nancie, *The Reading Zone*, New York: Scholastic, 2007.

Gallwey Timothy, *The Inner Game of Tennis*, London: Pan Books, 1974.

Hadfield Jill, *Classroom Dynamics*, Oxford: Oxford University Press, 1992.

Maley Alan, *The Language Teacher's Voice*, Oxford: Macmillan/Heinemann, 2000.

14

Teaching English to the 'Disadvantaged' (TED): Towards a Socio-cultural Perspective

T.S. Arul Kumar

Between the idea
And the reality
Between the motion
And the act
Falls the shadow
— T.S. Eliot

We live in a knowledge society, where lifelong learning is no longer an option but the key to our survival and success. The implication for a country like India, where millions of people are still poor and illiterate and struggling to make sense of the world around them, is that it is not enough if a few elite institutions like the IIT and the IIM succeed in providing cutting edge skills to their students; it is equally important that our Government schools and colleges, particularly those in rural areas, where more than 90% of the students are from poor and illiterate families, should succeed in providing quality education.

Obviously, this has not happened. Even after 50 years of independence, many five-year plans and our so-called thrust towards modernization, academic failure and, more particularly, under-achievement in English continue to persist among learners from these 'disadvantaged' sections of society. A facile response would be to blame the learner. But then all learning involves an interplay of factors, both external and internal to the learner and so when learning is not happening , we need to heed Spolsky's caution (op.cit Cloud, 1994:247-59) and look critically at all the external factors that may be causing the problem. In our context, there is all the more reason to exercise such caution, given the fact that these sections were brought into the educational mainstream only through Governmental intervention in the 1950s. I am referring to the historical decision taken by the central Government at the time of our independence to provide educational opportunity to sections of society that had been marginalized for centuries (Art. 45 & 46, Constitution of India.); but for that decision, even access to schools would not have become possible for children from these sections.

The point I am trying to make is that the problem of under-achievement cannot and should not be seen in isolation from the context and conditions in which learning takes place. In fact, critical theorists ask the question as to why key issues like discrimination and lack of social justice are not even mentioned in the educational literature, while lack of 'competence' among certain social groups is given such prominence (Blackledge, *Journal of Multilingual and Multicultural Development* 0200179: 182).

Cummins calls these underachieving groups 'curriculum casualties' (in Genesee, 1994: 34). Bearing in mind the distinction between the narrow, technical implications of a 'problem' and the broader socio-political implications of an 'issue', I strongly feel that academic failure among these 'disadvantaged' groups can be understood rightly only if it is seen within the broader context of the Government's attempts to 'universalize' educational opportunity (CABE Report, 2005; Louis, 2001) and, more importantly, the curricular and pedagogical aspects of these attempts (Dighe, 2003:.11-21).

On the positive side, it should be mentioned that we have succeeded in making education free and compulsory for all, because of which education has been brought for the first time in recorded history within the reach of people who had been denied such opportunity for centuries. This is no small achievement, given the state of affairs at the time of independence. But then providing educational access and opportunity to these learners is one thing; helping them succeed in exploiting the opportunity effectively, which includes among other things learning to become literate in English, is quite another thing (Louis; Rajabalasubramanian Aruna, 1997). At the very least, it implies a pedagogical strategy to help these learners turn opportunity into achievement.

Today, instead of becoming a tool of empowerment, as visualized in our educational policy, English has become a major source of disadvantage to these learners; what should cause concern is that the social implications of this situation are quite serious. Given the fact that English will continue to be the language of opportunity for many years to come, our continued failure to address the issue would only make access to high-paid jobs and career opportunities that much more difficult for these sections vis- a-vis their relatively more privileged peers in matriculation and central board schools. Peace, they say, is indivisible, but so is the right to quality education, if participatory democracy is to become a reality in India.

Why is it then that in spite of our constitutional commitment to use education to empower the masses, despite the good intentions and social activism of successive governments in the crucial fifties and sixties, this has happened, or to own our share of the responsibility, been allowed to happen? As responsible teachers, we need to ask the question as to why under-achievement is systematic and persistent among these sections; for, questions, as Derrida seems to suggest ('On Love and Being' 2008), have the power to contextualize debate and focus critical attention on issues that do not otherwise become easily manifest.

Institutional Inertia: Mismatch between Macro-policy and Micro-practices

The Default Potential of Education

Education has a double potential- the reproductive and the 'emancipatory' (Avermaet, 2006). It can be used to transmit and thus legitimate the dominant cultural patterns of the past; it can also be used, though extremely difficult, to critique practices of the past and thereby make possible a more egalitarian social order. The reason this is difficult is that education, like any other man-made system, is designed to be in a state of inertia. That is, educational systems are orthodox creatures- they are reproductive by default (Thomas, 2002:1-15). This does not mean that education cannot be used to transform society. The point made is that education cannot become 'emancipatory' by accident- it can become so only by deliberate design and strategic intervention. Even then, the process has to be constantly monitored and fine tuned or else the system would go back to the reproductive mode, though more covertly than overtly. In fact, this is what has happened in India. Education continues to be 'commissioned rather than practised'.

Missed opportunities

When India became independent, our leaders took the right decision—to use education effectively to transform society; naturally, we opted for the emancipatory model of education. But then visualizing a change is easy, relatively speaking; not so easy is the process of making it happen. Innovation is a dynamic process-more so, educational innovations. When the decision to 'universalize' educational opportunity was taken, it implied clarity at two levels:

(a) at the design level, a clear understanding of the curricular and pedagogical implications of providing educational opportunity, and more particularly, the opportunity of becoming literate in English to millions of children from poor and illiterate families;

(b) at the implementation level, a clear grasp of local realities at the classroom level and a pedagogical strategy for effectively implementing macro objectives within the constraints of the local environment.

To elaborate in little more detail, there was a three-fold need at the time we took the decision to bring education within the reach of these learners: the need for

- an educational programme that focused on the 'disadvantaged' learner, her socio-cultural background and needs, both in terms of curricular content and learning processes;
- an implementational strategy that could anticipate and effectively address the kind of problems likely to occur in the process of implementing such a large-scale educational innovation;
- an effective system of monitoring both the processes of implementation in schools and the actual instructional and evaluative practices in classrooms to make sure that appropriate and effective systems and strategies were in place to make education, and, more particularly, ESL (English as a Second Language) teaching, meaningful and relevant to these students .

But, to cut a long story short, apart from providing access to (ill-equipped) Government schools, none of these needs was effectively addressed; access becomes meaningful only when it helps the learner to actively participate in the learning process; in the absence of a meaningful, interactive teaching-learning process and an effective support system at the institutional and Governmental level, the needs could not be effectively addressed (Dighe, 2003:1-11; Louis, 2001). Any way, given the lack of a socio-cultural perspective, the needs could never have been effectively addressed, for literacy is in an important sense, a trans-generational issue, a socio-cultural process (Feuverstein, 1980; Kozulin,2003; Tores. ADEA, 2006). The upshot of it all is that educational processes have failed to engage these students' under-achievement in English. It continues to persist and the chances of these learners making the grade in institutions of higher learning, like the IIT, continue to be slim.

Naïve Assumptions

The pity is that even at this point the problem continues to be conceptualized narrowly in terms of language and learning deficits in the learner. No genuine attempt has been made to assess the effectiveness of the materials or the instructional processes in these schools. In line with the deficit perspective, there have been some remedial teaching programmes focusing on a few discrete items of vocabulary and grammar, and tutorials or 'special coaching classes' for these students. But given the naïve assumption underlying these efforts that language competence is the ability to manipulate a few pre-selected words and structures, it is not surprising that these tutorials have not been effective in any worthwhile sense. Apart from giving these learners more and more of the same thing, that is, helping them to focus on these words and structures without any attempt at contextualizing them and to regurgitate the instructional content, nothing tangible has been done to understand the socio-cultural background of these learners, to identify their learning needs, to evolve materials that could effectively engage their attention or to modify the instructional processes to effectively cater to those needs.

Even today, the assumption underlying key classroom concepts and processes continues to be simplistic and naïve. Learners are seen as pitchers waiting to be filled with information given in the text, learning, as the successful regurgitation of this content, and, pedagogy, as the transmission of textbook content through lectures. I am not exaggerating or trying to pile it on, this is precisely what is happening even today in Government and even some aided schools and colleges in rural India. Officials may try to deny all this pointing to statistics about percentage of passes and marks scored by students in government examinations, but as experienced teachers and researchers we know what these marks and grades really mean in terms of actual, achieved competence.

In short, while 'emancipatory' education remains our espoused goal, we have woefully failed to make it an integral part of our micro processes in schools and classrooms, which constitute the immediate learning environment for these students (Louis). Three points are worth keeping in mind when we talk about emancipatory processes in the present context of educating these learners: a) emancipation is the end point of a process of empowerment, by which I mean that instructional processes need to empower before they can become emancipatory; b) empowerment is possible only when the learner is actively involved in the learning process; c) given that these learners come from poor and illiterate families and have only a minimal exposure to English, empowerment cannot mean non-intervention, as in the west. On the contrary, in our context, it would necessarily mean proactive and strategic intervention on the part of the teacher.

Towards an Alternative

The way forward then is not to continue to be language-centric or teacher-centric but to become learner and even more importantly learning-centric in the positive sense, by which I mean a refusal to play a non-interventionist role in the name of learner autonomy; but rather use all possible resources and strategies to help these learners build on their strengths and overcome their limitations and thus enable them to cope effectively with the demands of education.

But how can this be done? What does all this mean in terms of actual practices in classrooms? What can we learn from work done in similar situations across the world? Teaching ESL to first-generation learners, more particularly, those from sections of society that have been marginalized in the past is a complex situation that does not respond to readymade, mainstream educational programmes (Genesee 1994; Kozulin,

2003; 'Critical Pedagogy on the Web: Key Terms and Concepts Related to Critical Pedagogy' http://mingo.info-science.uiowa.edu/~stevens/critped/terms.htm)

The 'one-cap-fits-all' approach has failed to produce results in today's multi-cultural classrooms across the world and this accounts for the sudden explosion of interest even in the west in the socio-cultural theories of Vygotsky and Bruner. As Kozulin (2003) says there has been in recent years a growing realization that learning is more a socio-cultural than an individual phenomenon; there has been a turning away from what Paulo Freire calls the banking model to a problem-posing model of education (Shor & Freire, 1987), a shift from an objectivist to a constructivist approach to curriculum (Moore, 2000:44-45), and, from teaching as telling (Moje & Brien, 2004:34) to teaching as scaffolding. In the absence of such a response, education would only become a reductive process of assimilation. This would alienate them not only from educational processes at school, but also from their own cultural processes, which as Feuverstein (1980:36-40) says is the worst form of deprivation that can happen to a child. One of the important needs of these learners is for what Freire calls 'conscientization' (Freire, 1970), the need to become aware of the sources of oppression both in the society outside them and in the way these practices have become internalized in their own cognitive processes- this would mean becoming aware of how language is typically used to reproduce social power and how it could possibly be used to critique and challenge such power. The implication of all this is that an effective educational programme for these children will necessarily have to be underpinned by:

- a theory of learning that acknowledges the centrality and active involvement of the learner in the learning processes,
- a social theory of language that shows how language is not an alien object but an accessible resource for generating personal meanings,
- a theory of pedagogy that helps learners become aware of how language is used to construct world views, practices and discourse structures and, how some of these discursive practices have the potential to disempower them- in short, a pedagogy that emphasizes problem-posing.

These have been some of the premises underlying successful ESL programmes designed in similar situations in other parts of the world. Later, however, because of the impetus given by ELT theorists like Cummins, Kangas and a few others, these programmes have evolved into broader 'anti-racist' or 'multi-racial/ethnic' education programmes.

In the Indian context, developing and implementing such empowerment programmes on a large scale may sound too radical and political at this point. Of course, the *Sarva Siksha Abhiyan* schemes offer some hope that quality education could soon become available to students from 'disadvantaged' sections. But that is a different story –As a committed professional, I feel we need to intervene in the situation at least at this point of time and radicalize the debate so that teachers and academicians become more critically aware of the issue and initiate discussion and dialogue. This would help more effective curricular and pedagogical practices to become possible in classrooms. After all, teaching is in an important sense 'the patient pursuit of the possible'.

Reconceptualizing ELT

If emancipatory education is then our objective, it should mean in the first place helping these learners become critically aware of themselves, their environment and of issues that are likely to impact on their lives. In other words, there is a need to address the 'retrospective' as well as the 'prospective' identities of these students (Moore, 2000: 42-43;) and a more urgent need to incorporate the personal and cultural funds of knowledge these learners bring to school (Moll, 1988). As Cummins says (Genesee, 1994: 34-56.), any ESL programme for these learners has to inevitably address issues of identity, power and discourse so as to be effective. We need to move away from our present focus on English as information towards a process of focusing on English as social activity (NSW Syllabus support document 1972 in Watson 1994:40). As Shor (1987:8) points out, schools can and should no longer remain mere delivery systems to market official ideas but have to become social sites where students learn to develop critical thinking. None of this can happen within the present transmission style of ELT; within the present way of looking at language as an object to be manipulated.

There is a need, therefore, to foreground the socio-cultural background and life experiences of these learners, that is, to reconceptualize ELT as TED (Teaching English to the 'Disadvantaged'). This would mean designing programmes that focus critical attention on 'disadvantage', both as a socially constructed process and as a psycho-linguistic mind set internalized by the learner. It would also mean focusing on cognitive and linguistic skills needed to understand, critique and overcome the disadvantage. The implication is thus twofold – in terms of content, this would mean situating ELT within a broader critical literacy programme (Morgan, 1998); more importantly, in terms of processes and procedure, this would involve facilitating dialogic (Freire, 1987:8) and dialectical processes in the classroom through which the teacher scaffolds learning tasks and processes to help learners actualize their potential. In short, language learning has to become a teacher-mediated, tool-mediated, developmental learning experience for these students, similar to what Feuverstein calls 'Mediated Learning Experience' -MLE (Feuverstein et al., 1980, pp. 13-36).

TED as Teacher-Mediation

Learning as a Socio-culturally Mediated Process

What do we mean by all this? What is MLE? What is 'mediation' in the first place? 'Mediated Learning' is actually a basic form of human experience, what differentiates human beings from animals. Human learning, at least in the early formative years, would become ineffective in the absence of such mediation. It also implies that when learning is not happening in spite of intervention, there is a possibility that learning is not being effectively mediated.

Unlike animals, who it is said learn only by responding directly to stimuli, human beings learn to respond to stimuli not only directly but also indirectly, that is through other more experienced human beings. To put it differently adult human beings, like parents and other elders help the child during its formative years to select and respond in a certain way to stimuli; they intervene as it were in the child's encounter with the natural and the human world and help structure the experience for the child. This act of intervening and structuring the child's experience is called 'mediation' (Feuverstein et al., 1980, p. 16). To give an example, children usually learn to avoid putting their hand in the fire without directly experiencing its heat, unlike animals, which learn to avoid such things through trial and error. This is because parents and other elders at home pass on this knowledge and experience effectively to children through gestures or words or in some other culturally meaningful way.

Normally, this is the way every child learns; there is always this human factor intervening between the stimulus in the external world and the child's response. This H factor and the intergenerational knowledge that makes possible such human mediation and constitutes the content of such mediation is what we call culture. That is, in addition to nature, the primary modality of learning, human beings learn through culture, called the secondary modality of learning (Feuverstein 1980). During the formative years, sometimes extending into adulthood, we learn primarily from others-parents, elders, and teachers, in short from more mature, knowledgeable adults, who become the agents of our culture. In other words, culture and its mediation through others is what makes learning possible in the first place; it is what makes intergenerational knowledge assimilable.

Feuverstein (1980) calls this 'mediated learning experience' (MLE), which he says is the paradigmatic learning experience, the platform on which all subsequent learning is built. It is what enables the child to learn directly from stimuli in later life. Learning is thus always embedded in a socio-cultural situation; it is an interactive process through which the social becomes the individual, the interpersonal becomes the intrapersonal (Vygotsky, 1978). What makes learning complex is that this knowledge cannot be transferred from one human being to another, from the teacher to the learner; it has to be actively constructed by the learner. In other words, knowledge is a process of co-construction negotiated in interaction between a novice and a more knowledgeable elder or expert. It is true that learning is essentially a process of self-regulation but as Vygotsky says it has to be other-regulated before it becomes self-regulating. It is a process of helping the learner understand and construct the experience in her mind that is, helping her to internalize the use of cultural tools like language so that the external, communicative tool of society becomes transformed into the internal, conceptual tool of the learner (Kozulin, 2003). Hence the lecture-method of teaching can never be effective in facilitating learning. The Russian word *obuchenie* which translated into English means a unitary 'teaching-learning' process beautifully illustrates the indivisibility of what are usually considered two separate activities. The foundation of all human learning is thus a mediated learning experience during one's childhood. Conversely, in the absence of an effective MLE during childhood, the child's ability to learn from direct interaction with stimuli, its ability to be modified by new experiences, what Feuverstein calls the learner's autoplasticity, is affected, and this is likely to lead to learning failure at school (Feuverstein et al., 1980, pp.41-44). Thus all learning is inevitably situated in time and socio-cultural space. Human learning is always mediated, either interpersonally or intrapersonally, that is, through another human being or through one's own cognitive processes.

Thus all human beings learn by being socialized into a particular culture. To learn is, therefore, essentially to assimilate the culture one is born into. This is what constitutes our cultural schema. Individual cognition is thus in an important sense the internalization of the culture mediated through interaction with a more knowledgeable member of the community. More importantly language, in particular oral language is the tool with which cultural processes are mediated by the adult and internalized by the child–all of which show how culture, cognition and language are interrelated through social interaction.

Under normal circumstances, this process happens informally at home, in our familiar social interactions with other people and is the basis of all the knowledge we gather at home, and which we bring to school-our 'cultural capital' (Moll, 1988). But, once we enter the formal learning environment of the school, we start experiencing difficulties. This is because schools have a culture of their own, which is different from our home culture. This does not mean that schools become a problem just because they have a different culture; it only means they could become a problem when this culture is not effectively mediated.

Schooling involves assimilation into the culture of literacy, by which we mean a process of theoretical learning that becomes increasingly disembedded and abstract. It is, therefore, not surprising that all learners experience difficulties, at least initially. The situation becomes especially difficult for children from minority or marginalized cultures (Kozulin, 2003) as apart from the need to learn to become literate in their home language as well as in a second language, they also need to become academically literate; what makes the situation more complicated is that they do not have any one at home to help them with the literacy demands of school education. Unlike learners from literate families, who have access to guidance in acquiring such skills at home, these learners look up to and are hopelessly dependent on such help and guidance from teachers. But sadly enough, reality being what it is, teachers do not find the time or have the inclination, or as in most situations, lack the skills to play the pro active role needed to help these learners. In other words, these 'disadvantaged' learners lack (mediation of literacy practices) of instructional practices that could help learners relate theoretical learning processes demanded at school to their empirical learning processes at home (Kozulin).

This means that these children are at a double disadvantage – disadvantage at the level of literacy practices, and disadvantage at the level of acquiring these practices in a second language to which they have very little exposure. So, when teachers fail to mediate the language, that is, model it through concrete, strategically structured activities, or, what is better called a process of 'scaffolding', and focus only on form in a theoretical way, as is happening in India, language learning becomes a crippling burden, and, naturally, alienates these learners. Hence these learners are not deficient or uneducable as some may choose to think; the fact is they have not been provided the basic condition of learning—MEDIATION—of literacy practices. The solution, therefore, is to provide such mediation at school.

It is not as if mediation is required only during childhood and early schooling; given that schools, colleges and even workplaces are essentially social communities, each constituted by a unique body of assumptions, practices and processes, human life itself becomes in an important sense a process of ongoing socialization into different cultures at different levels, at different points of time; what is more to the point, successful socialization always involves mediation in some form. It is in this sense that people in trades, professions and businesses today speak of the need for 'cognitive and social apprenticeship' which is essentially a process of mediation. To put it differently, mediation, or being other-regulated, is an integral part of all learning processes. Whenever and wherever learning is not happening, be it at school or elsewhere, it is a signal that mediation is not happening and so the best way of responding would be to provide such mediation through scaffolding of learning activities.

Curricular and Pedagogical Implications

Need for Inclusive Practices

As is clear from our discussion of the socio-cultural theory of learning, culture is not a homogeneous, monolithic content to be obligatorily transmitted to all learners in schools. It is a child's unconscious process of assimilating the immediate human environment in which it grows up, the form and shape of all early learning experiences of children as they interact with the elders in the family and the community which means that culture is necessarily plural and specific to the social environment in which the child grows up. The implication is that curricular practices in schools have to be inclusive of the learning processes and social practices of all groups of students, particularly those from marginalized backgrounds, if education is to be meaningful to these learners

–this is the minimal requirement of education, if by education we mean a process of freedom, as Paulo Freire (1978) would put it. It also means that if the early life experiences of these children from poor and illiterate families are ignored or devalued in some subtle way, effective learning cannot happen (Genesee, 1994; Kozulin, 2003). It is a sad reflection on the ineffectiveness of ESL classroom practices in many parts of the world that students from these social groups are usually passive–what Freire referred to as 'the culture of silence' (1987) among these students. But, in actuality, the silence of these groups is not a reflection of stupidity but an expression of helplessness and sometimes, even resistance in the face of instructional practices that are designed to ignore the knowledge, experiences and learning processes these children bring to school. The schema theory of reading (Razi, 2002:1-18) also emphasizes the need for materials and tasks to build on the cultural schema of learners. Education, therefore, should not become a melting pot where learners have to shed their cultural identity; on the contrary, it should become to use the words of late Indira Gandhi, something like a sugar bowl where every ingredient maintains its uniqueness while contributing to the whole. In the TED context this would mean classroom processes where every learner could assert and draw on her cultural identity-what Cummins refers to as helping learners to find their voice (Genesee, 1994: 33-58).

Emergent Tasks/Activities

The power and ubiquity of home culture in children's lives and the examples cited so far have a twofold curricular implication for TED:

(a) the content of our curriculum and the construction of tasks and activities in class need to be 'emergent' and local – 'emergent' in the sense that these have to emerge from the learner's personal and cultural needs, to be negotiated through interaction between the teacher and the students– 'local' in the sense that the content should be built around the learner's life experiences, her knowledge and socio-cultural practices so that the content becomes meaningful and, hence, easily accessible to the learner. (Genesee. 1994: Freire, 1998;: Kozulin, 2003) This is why encouraging learners to use English to talk about themselves and their experiences becomes particularly important in the ESL class- this could be effectively done through activities focusing initially on self-disclosure, later on self-expression and much later on self-exploration, that is, through activities that become increasingly complex, cognitively and linguistically (Schmelzer, 2005; 200-215).

(b) as for content and learning processes that are unfamiliar and new to these learners, the academic content and tasks should be mediated by the teacher, by which I mean the abstract, theoretical learning processes on which academic success depends have to be made accessible to the learner. This can happen effectively only when these processes are related to the concrete life experiences of learners. In terms of activities to help learners understand, this would mean transposing theoretical content in empirical terms as well as transposing personal, empirical experience in academic, theoretical language (Moje, 2001; Cope, NCELTR; Schmelzer, 2005).

In other words, Mediated Learning in the TED setting would mean acknowledging the home background of learners whenever there is a possibility of doing so and, more importantly, situating abstract academic tasks within the framework of the knowledge and personal experiences of learners. Apart from bridging the gap between school and home, such practices also facilitate the process of interrelating identity, academic content and language use in a coherent framework. As Genesee says (1994: i-x), ESL teaching can be effective for these learners only to the extent it brings together the whole child, the whole curriculum and the whole community. In other words, teaching can become effective only when it successfully scaffolds the learning task as well as the learning process by building bridges between theoretical learning and every day empirical learning . The fact that some academicians have successfully used what they call 'ethno-maths' and 'ethno-science' (Schmelzer, 2005) to scaffold and teach school math and school science only emphasizes this point. There is a need, therefore, to relate, wherever possible in ESL classes, scientific and every day concepts through concrete, problem-posing activities that build on the knowledge and learning processes of these learners. TED could thus become a kind of ethno-ELT, something similar to what Canagarajah calls 'pedagogical safe houses' (2004), though the full implications of such a possibility have not been worked out yet. This way, the home background and cultural practices these children bring to school, which now constitute a source of disadvantage, could become a resource, a source of empowerment. This is the only way content of education can effectively engage and motivate the learners. For motivation does not happen before the learning task is set up as is made out by some academicians it arises from the task itself. As Shor & Freire (1987) point out, an effective learning task brings with it its own motivation. Allwright also talks about the need for negotiated interaction in the ESL class and others like Widdowson, Breen, Candlin and Prabhu (1987) speak of emergent, process and procedural syllabus-all of which argue in favour of a process as against a product approach to learning.

Language Teaching as Tool Mediation

A fundamental premise of socio-cultural theory is that language is an important tool which helps mediate our interaction with the world and later with our own selves-what Vygotsky calls tool mediation in our interpersonal and psychological processes. In this view, language is not only a medium of expressing our thoughts; it is the process of experiencing them. In fact, as already pointed out, language and, more particularly, the spoken word is the primary cultural tool which is internalized by the child in her early interpersonal processes and which later becomes modified as inner speech to regulate her own self. That is, language has to be modelled as a social tool before it can effectively become a psychological tool for the learner. Given this dual potential of language-to socialize as well as conceptualize-memorably captured in Cummins' distinction between BICS (Basic Interpersonal Communication Skills) and CALP (Cognitive Academic Language Proficiency) tool mediation would mean a process of interrelating cognitive and language learning tasks, a process of scaffolding language learning through a thinking skills programme, as has been attempted in many ESL programmes abroad. Mohan's Knowledge Frameworks (Early, 2005) is an example of a tool that could be used to analyse and bring together the cognitive as well as the linguistic needs of these learners.

But in a second language learning situation as in India, where English is learnt as part of the academic curriculum, teaching CALP poses special difficulties. While there are difficulties particularly for 'disadvantaged' learners in learning to use language cognitively before they have had the opportunity of using it for social purposes, what really makes the situation complicated is our continued focus on form and the theoretical, abstract way in which we teach the language. One way of making language learning meaningful and accessible to these learners even in the early stages is by helping them acquire simple comprehension and communication strategies, (Canagarajah, 2004) by focusing on what Canale calls 'Strategic Competence'.

As for CALP, the Hallidayan approach to language has shown how language is not just form but a systemic and functional resource for making meanings, a tool for critiquing traditional meanings and a powerful social semiotic. This socio-cultural approach to language has an immediate relevance for TED in that it emphasizes the need to stop focusing on isolated words, sentences and grammatical structures in the name of form and to start focusing on functions and corresponding discourse structures of language so as to help learners understand how language is used to construct academic genres and discourse, to create specific meanings.

In particular, Critical Discourse Analysis and Critical Language Awareness, two offshoots of the Hallidayan approach, have fruitful implications for the TED curriculum. They can be used effectively to show how language is used to construct and privilege certain forms of knowledge and discourse practices and, conversely, how it can be used by the learner to contest such practices. This means using CDA in the TED context for two important purposes: a) to select texts that focus on issues and discursive practices that are likely to impact on the lives of these learners; b) in a situation where the teacher has to work with a text prescribed by others, CDA and CLA can be used to create awareness among learners about language choices available to them for creating different genres and forms of discourse. This can be done through activities, focusing, for example, on how language is used differently to express a similar content across a personal narrative and a scientific report; this can then be used to mediate the underlying difference between the demands of empirical learning and those of theoretical learning. In fact, the rewriting of a personal account using the register of science, the critiquing of a text where language has been used to legitimate certain kinds of biases are some of the activities which have been effectively used in a few ESL programmes abroad to create metalinguistic awareness among learners (Schmelzer, 2005).

Critical Literacy as Content and Practice

Language is best learnt as part of a wider and more inclusive activity, which means that TED has to become part of a critical literacy programme. Why critical literacy and not cultural or functional literacy programmes? Given that these learners come from a background of illiteracy and discrimination, any learning activity that is not informed by critical thinking can only result in superficial learning. Many ELT professionals speak about the educational value of deep processing of texts. Empowerment can happen only when these learners acquire a capacity for systematically critiquing practices that are disempowering. In terms of curriculum this would mean the prioritizing of reading skills, the scaffolding of the ability to read the word critically, through problem-posing by the teacher (Freire, 1998). While reading the word meant within traditional literacy programmes an implicit acceptance and uncritical assimilation of fixed, immutable and authoritative meanings given by a hallowed tradition, in these post-lacanian, derridayan times, it necessarily means questioning and critiquing the word, to defer its meaning as Derrida (1982) would put it. That is, reading needs to be seen as a top-down, subjective process of semiosis, or meaning making, which by encouraging a process of questioning the text is likely to be 'liberating' for the reader; what is more important by being able to critique the word, the learner acquires the ability to critique the traditional, immutable world views underpinning the word. It is in this sense that reading becomes a transformative process. As Paulo Freire says (1998), by reading the word, we are reading the world and so by critiquing the word we are critiquing the world view and power structures implicit in the traditional interpretation of the word.

But there is likely to be an objection here. We know that these learners lack basic competence in English and so the question is likely to be posed-how is it that we expect these learners to critique words and world views when they find it very difficult to understand even simple texts? I would respond by pointing out that literacy programmes can be designed at different levels for different target groups, For example, it is possible for this purpose to use texts containing simple stories like the story of Casablanca. What I mean is that teachers can design tasks and activities that focus on issues implicit in the story and by making these accessible to the learner through a process of scaffolding, the learner can be helped to access the story and the narrative at deeper levels. In fact, in New Zealand and Australia, as part of delivering alternative ESL programmes to children from minority cultures, the narrating of anecdotes and personal experiences by children has been used as a spring-board for discussing deeper issues that are slowly brought into the open by teachers through a continual process of questioning and reframing of issues. Depending on the commitment and skill of the teacher, ordinary daily events and personal experiences of learners can be used to articulate deeper issues. More importantly the mediation of language by the teacher in such situations and the scaffolding of key words and discourse structures specific to the activity can help learners absorb language relevant to the task. The point I am making is that critical literacy is a skill that can be built up successfully in any situation, provided the teacher is professionally committed and believes in continually scaffolding tasks and learning processes until they become accessible to the learner. In short, language teaching has to be embedded in concrete, problem-posing activities and tasks that focus the attention of the learner on functions, words and structures specific to academic genres and discourse forms. Such practices have an educational value for these learners in particular, for as Foucalt (1971) says education is in an important sense the appropriation of powerful discursive practices.

Teaching as Scaffolding

The most important activity, unique to socio-cultural theory, and crucially needed to help these learners internalize the instructional processes, is what is called 'scaffolding', which is a process of continual structuring, or restructuring of the learning task so that it becomes accessible and available for internalizing by the learner. This demands exceptional commitment from the teacher. She cannot stand aside and watch, as is being done these days by teachers in some schools in the name of CLT; on the contrary, she has to actively intervene in the learning process; she has to scaffold not only the learning task to make it more accessible to the learner, but also the learning process, by which I mean being able to respond contingently to the changing levels of the learner. This would mean not only identifying the current level of performance of the learner but also identifying and making explicit her potential level, as revealed in her interaction with the teacher. Krashen (1985) also talks about the facilitatory role to be played by the teacher for effective learning to occur. He says input has to be made comprehensible for learning to occur and Long (1981) goes one step further and says input can be effective only when it elicits interaction and that it is only through interaction that the teacher's input is made comprehensible. But Vygotsky goes even further and shows how in order to make learning effective, the teacher has to continually scaffold the process of interaction. Unlike input modification, which is directed at the language and the learning task, scaffolding is focused on the learner and the learning process (Kozulin), and therefore is likely to be more effective. It is a process of being 'finely' tuned in to the learner, of being in continual touch with the changing levels of the learner and in that sense is uniquely contingent, unlike any other teacher-directed activity .

For example, in an ESL programme designed for learners with low proficiency in English, a teacher successfully used a few cognitive functions and their corresponding discourse structures within a kind of template to structure and scaffold the task of constructing personal narratives modelled on the structuring of stories in literary texts (Early, 2005). The key stages in a typical scaffolded activity are: (a) getting the learner interested, (b) simplifying the task, (c) inviting participation, (d) providing direction, (e) modelling the task response, (f) organizing guided performance, (g) eliciting independent performance. In many ESL programmes in Australia, scaffolding has been used as part of discourse, cognitive and academic literacy apprenticeship programmes (Cope, NCELTR). Unlike other teacher-assisted activities, scaffolding restructures not only the task but also the learning experience. It is in this sense that scaffolding is different from what is called 'teacher-assistance' and, other conventional techniques of supporting student activity.

ZPD/Potential Level

At any point in time, the learner is usually at two levels- the actual current level that becomes manifest in unaided performance and a potential level which is elicited only through interaction (Vygotsky, 1978; Kozulin, 2003). To be effective, teaching has to address the potential level, which shows the learner's propensity to learn. The current level, which refers to what the learner is able to perform on her own without any teacher assistance, shows only what the learner already knows, not what she is capable of learning. Unlike most theories of assessment which believe that intelligence is what one is born with and that it does not respond to educational intervention, Vygotsky's theory of scaffolding and what he calls the learner's Zone of Proximal Development (ZPD) are premised on a theory of intelligence as a continually evolving ability to modify one's behaviour in response to a change in the environment (Feuverstein, 1980; Kozulin, 2003). The point to be noted is that this intelligence is a dynamic process which responds to instruction. Applied to TED, this would mean that teaching should lead development instead of following it (Kozulin, 2003). This can happen only by scaffolding tasks at the potential level of the learner, not at her current level of performance. By scaffolding the task at the potential level, by which I mean gently pushing the learner to produce output ahead of her competence and by gently goading the learner on to make her output comprehensible, a situation is created which stretches the learner's capacity and results in development. It is only through such scaffolding of the learning process that the potential can be effectively actualized. As for the intrapersonal, conceptual processes of the learner, which at any point in the learning process tends to lag behind the interpersonal, communicative processes, the teacher has to continually and contingently scaffold them so that they unfold in interaction and finally catch up with the interpersonal, instructional processes.

Dynamic Assessment

As we all know, evaluation is in an important sense the process of acquiring comprehensive information about the learner. Unlike traditional assessment, which is premised on the fixed, immutable concept of intelligence as a static phenomenon which focuses primarily on the performance of the learner, vygotskian assessment takes on board the dynamic and dialectical processes of learning. Instead of focusing on what the learner already knows, which in a sense depends on the learner's social background and hence has an elitist bias. Dynamic assessment redefines it as a dialectical process that needs to look not only at what the learner can do by herself, but also at what the learner is capable of doing in the interpersonal context, that is, in response to instruction (Vygotsky, 1978; Kozulin, 2003). This is a more comprehensive assessment of the learner as it takes into account not only the current level but also the potential level, not only the intrapersonal processes but also the interpersonal processes of the learner. It is also a more open-ended, democratic approach to assessment as it emphasizes not only the past performance but also the present potential of the learner. It is premised on the zone of proximal development, the cognitive space in which new learning is constructed; by responding to what happens in this space and by focusing instructional processes on this ever-changing level of the learner through continual and contingent scaffolding, the potential of the learner is effectively coaxed into actualizing itself.

Thus Mediated Learning ensures not only learning but learning that is ahead of development –Krashen also talks about the need to teach at one step above the current level of the learner, what he calls i+1 ,but it is only Vygotsky who has made the concept operational through his ZPD. To put it more aptly, mediated learning illustrates the truth that the only way teaching can be effective is by leading development, not by tagging it.

A Professional Plea

Thus, in contrast to the present transmission style of teaching ELT, which necessarily alienates these learners, Mediated Learning, a socio-cultural perspective on TED, has the potential of being effective because it locates and effectively addresses learning within socio-cultural processes that are meaningful to learners. To reiterate the key implications for TED:

(a) motivation and engagement are processes that emerge from the materials and tasks, from the dialogic learning processes in the ESL classroom , which imply activities that build on the home background of learners and instructional processes that build bridges between the text and the socio-cultural context of the learner;

(b) content of the curriculum needs to become a process of helping learners become critically aware of themselves, their environment and issues likely to impact on their future lives;

(c) language is to be seen as a potential for meaning-making, by which we mean a tool to be used by learners to generate personal meanings and to critique meanings that have the potential to disempower them, which necessarily involves mediating language used in specific genres and discourse practices as part of teaching critical literacy skills;

(d) teaching is a process of continually scaffolding learning tasks and processes to identify and nurture learning potential of students so as to lead development;

(e) assessment is a process of gathering information about the potential level of the learner, as revealed in her responses to instruction, what Vygotsky calls the learner's zone of proximal development

In short, TED is a process of leading and nurturing developmental processes in the learner through problem-posing embedded in concrete activities and dialogic processes.

All said and done, the effectiveness of TED ultimately depends on the continual commitment and ongoing critical reflection on the part of teachers. How best teachers can be helped to become reflective practitioners is a story that has to be told at another place and time.

This is only an invitation on my part to fellow teachers to seek relevance and professional growth in activities nearer home, to help TED become a thrust area of Indian ELT through prioritizing it in action research and project work. There is a perception that TED as a socio-cultural perspective on ELT is not ELT proper, that it is ELT plus, that it lacks professional rigour. I would only respond by saying that relevance is not something that can be decided by whatever happens to be visible and fashionable today-relevance is not a given thing, (Shor & Freire, 1987) but a process of making whatever it is we are doing and believe in doing relevant to our learners and the profession. In the same way, rigour is not the readymade application of criteria and practices that have managed to gain acceptance in the west, it is a genuine process of making our own practices and theories rigorous enough-in other words, rigour is a process of making something rigorous (Shor & Freire, 1987).

I would like to conclude by quoting the late Charan Singh who in a particular context said that given the massive illiteracy and poverty of people in India, politics cannot afford to be driven by whatever happens to be popular at the moment, but by what is genuinely likely to transform people's lives in the long run. I would like to make a similar plea for education. Education, being the site where possibilities for the future are made and un made, and given the kind of problems poor people face for lack of quality education, we should do whatever is possible in our context to help education become more meaningful and relevant to the lives of these learners so that better career opportunities and better life chances become possible for them. TED is one small step in what could become a long journey.

In this context, I would like to acknowledge my debt to Robert Bellarmine, who gave a new purpose and relevance to my professional life by scaffolding the idea of TED as a genuine and productive way of building social relevance into our professional work.

Works Cited

Aggarwal Yash, 'Quality Concerns in Primary Education in India, Where is the Problem?', New Delhi: NIEPA, pp. 1-17.

Allan Michael, 'Cultural differences in Teaching and Learning', Paper presented at the AARE International Educational Research Conference, Parramatta, 2005.

Alexander Robin, *Culture and Pedagogy*, Blackwell Publishing, 2001.

Allwright D., 'Why Don't Learners Learn What Teachers Teach?- The Interaction Hypothesis', In Singleton and Little, ed. Language Learning in Formal and Informal Contexts, Dublin: BAAL/IRAAL, pp. 3-18.

Avermaet Piet Van, 'Socially Disadvantaged Learners and Languages of Education', Intergovernmental Conference, Languages of Schooling: Towards a Framework for Europe, Strasbourg, 16-18 Oct., 2006.

Blackledge Adrian, 'Language, Literacy and Social Justice: The Experiences of Bangladeshi Women in Birmingham, UK', *Journal of Multilingual and Multicultural Development*, Vol. 20, No. 3, 1999, pp. 179-193.

Breen M.P. and Candlin C.N., 'The Essentials of a Communicative Curriculum in Language Teaching', *Applied Linguistics I,* pp. 89-112.

Bruner J., *Actual Minds, Possible Worlds,* Cambridge, MA: Harvard University, 1986.

Canagarajah S., 'Subversive Identities, Pedagogical Safe Houses, and Critical Learning', *Critical Pedagogies and Language Learning*, ed. B. Norton and K. Toohey. Cambridge: CUP, 2004, pp. 116-137.

Canale M. and Swain M., 'Theoretical Bases of Communicative Approaches to Second Language Teaching and Testing', *Applied Linguistics I.* pp. 1-47.

Cloud, 'Special Education Needs of Second Language Students', Educating Second Language Children: The Whole Child, The Whole Curriculum, The Whole Community, ed. Fred Genesee, New York: Cambridge University Press, 1994.

Cope Nicholas, 'Apprenticeship Reinvented; Cognition, Discourse and Implications for Academic Literacy', NCELTR, Macquarie University.

Cummins Jim, 'Knowledge, Power, and Identity in Teaching English as a Second Language', Educating Second Language Children: The Whole Child, The Whole Curriculum, The Whole Community, ed., Fred Genesee, New York: Cambridge University Press, 1994, pp. 33-57.

Cummins J., *Language , Power and Pedagogy: Bilingual Children in the Crossfire*, Clevedon: Multilingual Matters, 2000.

Cullip Peter, 'Scaffolding Literacy Learning : Vygotsky in the Classroom Centre for Language & Communication Studies', University Malaysia Sarawak.

Derrida Jacques, 'Difference', *Margins of Philosophy*, Chicago & London: University of Chicago Press, 1982, p. 17.

Dighe Anita, 'Pedagogical Approaches to Literacy Acquisition and Effective Programme Design', 2003, pp. 1-26.

Early Margaret, et al., 'Teachers' Professional Knowledge in Scaffolding Academic Literacies for English Language Learners', *Prospect,* Vol. 20, No. 3, December, 2005, p. 63.

Egbo Benedicta, 'Critical Pedagogy as Transformative Micro-level Praxis', University of Windsor, Ontario.

Feuverstein R., et al., 'Instrumental Enrichment: An Intervention Programme for Cognitive Modifiability', Illinois: Scott, Foresman and Company, 1980.

Foucalt M., 'Orders of Discourse', Social Science Information, 10, 1971a, pp. 7-30.

Foucalt M., *The Archaeology of Knowledge*, London: Tavistok, 1971b.

Freire P., *Pedagogy of freedom: Ethics, democracy, and civic courage,* Lanham: Rowman & Littlefield Publishers, 1998.

Freire P., *Pedagogy of Hope*, New York: Continuum, 1994.

Freire P., *Pedagogy of the Oppressed, 20th Anniversary Edition*, New York: Continuum, 1997.

Hoai Huong Le Pham, 'The Mediational Role of Language Teachers in Socio-cultural Theory', New Zealand, (Bibliography details not available)

Kozulin Alex, et al., 'Vygotsky's Educational Theory in Cultural Context', Cambridge University Press, 2003. ISBN 0521528836.

Krashen S., *The Input Hypothesis: Issues and Implications,* Longman, 1985.

Literacy in the Context of the Constitution of India, Advisory panel, National Commission to Review the working of the Constitution, New Delhi:Vigyan Bhavan, 2001. pp. 1-15.

Long M.H., 'Input, Interaction and Second Language Acquisition', In Winitz H. ed., *Native Language and Foreign Language Acquisition, Annals of the New York Academy of Sciences,* 379, 1981, pp. 259-78.

Louis Prakash, Indian Education at the Crossroads, 2002.

Moje Elizabeth & O'Brien David, 'Constructions of Literacy; Studies of Teaching and Learning in and out of Secondary Schools', Lawrence Erlbaum Associates, 2001.

Moll L., 'Some Key Issues in Teaching Latino Students', *Language Arts, 65 (5),* 1988, pp. 465-472.

Moore Alex, *Pedagogy, Curriculum & Culture*, Routledge, 2000.

Morgan Brian, *The ESL Classroom: Teaching, Critical Practice, and Community Development*, University of Toronto Press, 1998.

Nieto S., *The Light in Their Eyes: Creating Multicultural Learning Communities.* New York: Teachers College Press, 1999.

Norton Bonny and Tooley Kelleen, Critical Pedagogies and Language Learning. Cambridge University Press, 2004.

Prabhu N.S., *Second Language Pedagogy*, New York, Toronto: Oxford University Press, 1987.

Rajabalasubramanian Aruna, 'Deliver us from this Darkness', Formal Education, and Lower Class Children in Tamil Nadu, India, Diss, The Graduate School, Syracuse University, 1997.

Razi S., 'The Effects of Cultural Schema and Reading Activities on Reading Comprehension', Canakkale Onsekiz Mart University, Turkey, 2002, pp. 1-18.

Schmelzer Michael Allen, 'Making a Difference, Transforming Lives: Mediating Practices in a Culture of Empowerment at Santa Cruz School', The Ohio State University, 2005.

Shor Ira and Freire Paul, *A Pedagogy for Liberation: Dialogues on Transforming Education*, Greenwood Publishing Group,1987, ISBN 0897891058, 9780897891059.

Soundararaj Francis, 'Education, Sustainable Development and Educational Management', Quality Higher Education and Sustainable Development, NAAC Decennial Lectures, Bangalore: NAAC, 2004, pp. 19-46.

Thomas Robert Murray, 'Overcoming Inertia in School Reform; How to Successfully Implement Change', Corwin Press, 2002.

Travieso-Parker, 'Lourdes, Policies, Pedagogy, and Practices: Educational Experiences of Latino English Language Learners in Virginia', Diss,Virginia Polytechnic Institute and State University, 2006.

'Universalization of Secondary Education', Report of the CABE Committee, New Delhi: 2005, pp. 1-56.

Vygotsky L.S., *Mind in Society: The Development of Higher Psychological Processes,* M.Cole, V. John-Steiner, S. Scribner, and E. Souberman, ed. Cambridge, MA: Harvard University Press, 1978.

Wertsch J.V., *Culture, communication and cognition*: Vygotskian perspectives. Cambridge: Cambridge University Press, 1985.

Wertsch J., *Vygotsky and the Social Formation of Mind*, Cambridge, MA: Harvard University Press, 1985.

Widdowson H.G. and Brumfit C.J., 'Issues in second language syllabus design', in Alattis et al., 1981, pp. 199-210.

Derrida J., 'On Love and Being' <http://in.youtube.com/watch?v=dj1BuNmhjAY&feature=PlayList&p=D49B3109A97ED3CE&playnext=1&index=39>.

Literacy and Numeracy Innovative Projects Initiative, <http://www.ag.gov.au/cca> Commonwealth of Australia, Department of Education, Science and Training, 2006.

Thanasoulas Dimitrios, 'Constructivist Learning', Greece, <http://www3.telus.net/linguisticsissues/constructivist.htm>.

<http://books.google.co.in/books?id=SssLoenALFkC&pg=PA110&lpg=PA110dq=perspectives+on+Teaching+ESL+students+from+marginalized+cultures&source=web&ots=q0eX76VqvD&sig=giU3NX_q8PQQVTkWR05Z9R0a6nc&hl=en&sa=X&oi=book_result&resnum=4&ct=result#PPR18,M1-constructions of literacy>.

Alistair Cumming, et al., <http://www.csse.ca/CJE/Articles/FullText/CJE19-4/CJE19-4-07Cumming.pdf>.

<http://etd.rau.ac.za/theses/available/etd-08222005-123305/restricted/Chapter5Part2.pdf>.

15

Empowering the At-Risk Learners

Dr. Francis Peter S.J.

Why Ted?

Access to English in Indian society has traditionally been inseparable from access to privilege. English has been serving an important gate keeping function– determining who gains access to the best jobs and to future cultural, economic and political power. Though seen as a colonial imposition, English even if least loved, there is no denying is much needed.

The fact of globalisation and its consequent burgeoning commercial, economic or technological contact with far flung nations has irrevocably boosted the position of English as a language of opportunity. It has catapulted us to the new, IT-enabled economy. India's development road-map will need more English speaking youngsters to move away from the traditional agrarian sector to the jobs in the organised sector. Even as the booming economy is throwing up new and attractive jobs, if India is not able to match the demands with competent, computer savvy English speaking young work force these industries would begin to source employees elsewhere.

Focus on English

It is striking that out of the 3,60,000 who passed out of engineering colleges in 2008-09, nearly 2,00,000 remained unemployed largely because they did not know English. THE BPO and outsourced jobs employ over 2 million English speaking Indians. This flattering scenario comes with a serious warning that the current supremacy and economic advancement would be stymied if adequate and efficient training in English is not provided.

The focus now shifts to understanding who are those for whom English is a nightmare, those who badly need English but find acquiring it hard? What are the principle reasons for their not being able to learn this language. Where does the problem lie – with these learners, teachers, material, methods of both instruction and evaluation or a combination of all these? Where should an effective agenda for change begin? Perhaps this problems needs to be tackled from all angles and simultaneously, concomitantly.

Who are the Disadvantaged?

Let us in these pages focus on this largest group of victims-the disadvantaged learners, try to study their problem and suggest a viable agenda that can send them rattling the rails of success. By the term 'disadvantaged' we refer to those who have repeatedly failed in English examinations or just managed to scrape through, even when their performance in other subjects is commendable. The entire 2 lakhs unemployable engineers referred to above would be embraced by this definition.

Yet such a definition would become a blanket and elastic term conveniently stretched to include any individual or group one likes to promote, because everyone in some way, at least for some time, in some form is disadvantaged. The definition lacks explanatory adequacy and is not scientific enough to include all who are really disadvantaged and only those who are disadvantaged.

Any attempt to seriously respond to the existing reality needs to begin with a greater conceptual clarity. There is no denying that some group of learners exhibit lower scholastic attainment than others. We need to identify rather than individuals with issues that are idiosyncratic, cluster or groups that are disadvantaged with debilitating experiences. We need to look for extraneous factors that give rise to poor performance. Our search then would lead to 'distal' causes that though are not self generated currently contribute to and work against their confident acquisition of the desired linguistic competency.

A comprehensive perception would see them as those with inherited multiple handicaps stemming from systemic denial of opportunities. These multiple disadvantages expose the population to social, economic, cultural, psychological, locational, educational contingencies and make coping with them difficult. The vulnerable are not the same as the poor. We are speaking of more than lack or want. In the words of Chambers (2006) vulnerability 'refers to defencelessness, insecurity and exposure to risk, shocks and stress' and the inability to cope with them. The heuristic matrix of vulnerability goes well beyond the money-matrix and includes the vagaries of nature, the whims of the dominant groups. In local terms these would largely apply to the scheduled caste and scheduled tribes. It is this group who because of the adverse repercussions of globalisation, the stranglehold of socio-political factors, inclement weather, etc. exhibit now a high probability of future loss.

These are the core of the disadvantaged group (termed the vulnerable) and these are the object of our current intervention. This would differentiate the target group from the others who exhibit temporary residual self imposed and accidental disadvantage and also the temporary poor. We isolate and pay attention to those who for generations have been subjugated by forces and systems that leave them deprived – those who are 'sinned against rather than sinning'.

The concept of disadvantage can be represented in the form of a three ringed circle.

1 The deficient
2 The deprived
3 The vulnerable

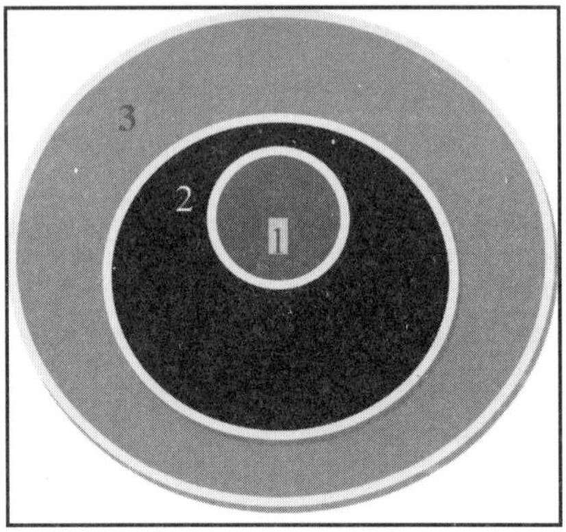

Circles representing the layers of disadvantage

All three circles include those 'disadvantaged' (with 'd' in the lower case) in one sense of the other. The outer ring specifies the pathologic and psychological deviation that prevents an individual from acquiring the TL – these we term the deficient; the inner ring includes those who to their portfolio of deprivations added vulnerability. These would be elbowed out of existence in the changing equations resulting from the forces of globalisation; these who badly need English are denied the emancipatory tool of English. Far more devastating than the so called digital divide is the language divide (those who can use English and those who can't). In an outsourced market driven economy those who can use English are rewarded while those who can't are reduce to live largely through manual and physical labour. These are the most vulnerable and these are therefore the core of the disadvantaged – the disadvantaged with a capital 'D'. In practical terms these are the marginalised, uninitiated, living in far flung hamlets, battling with the vagaries of nature to eke out their existence – those in danger of being eliminated.

What problems cripple their learning?

Having identified the target group our next job is to understand what affects their current learning efforts. Even though the root cause may be 'distal' factors in Feuerstein's sense the learning pathologies they result in 'proximally' are the question at issue. We begin by enumerating some of the factors that affect learning negatively teased out after prolonged observation and reflection; these listed below could broadly be grouped as belonging to the affective and cognitive domains.

- low self esteem
- diminishing desire to learn
- crippling fear of failure
- poor achievement motivation
- lack of sustained effort
- steep forgetting curve (of what has been learnt)
- passivity – let rather than make things happen
- poor scholastic skills

A Minimum Agenda Teaching/Learning Model

There arises a debate whether this group of disadvantaged learners need a customised learning/teaching procedure different from the one the rest of the learners are put through. If the two groups are as different as a wedding from a funeral, can the 'cakes baked for the funeral serve the marriage table'? Experts such as Bernstein and Labov have argued that there are differences in the ways meaning is perceived and expressed based on cultural factors. Bourdieu (1993) suggested the term 'cultural capital' to explain the advantage middle-class children have over their working class peers. The advantage is in terms of tastes, knowledge and ideas associated with a particular class. Because the teachers share the cultural capital of the middle-class learners from this category they are rewarded with greater educational success. Is it true that the mainstream cause them to remain poor achievers? If so should there be a different content and approach to learning for these different groups?

The issue is vexatious requiring deeper research and policy decision. However, if in the ultimate analysis all education needs to fall in line with employer requirements there is no purpose in labouring the point about creating a curriculum designed exclusively for the disadvantaged. We'd rather look for an enriched programme and a separate route more suited to the needs of the target group to achieve the same language competency acceptable to the job market.

Moving along these lines of working out a strategy to enable these learners acquire a comparable level of proficiency in the TL we need to evolve approaches to overcome their A pedagogy that must include procedures that would help the disadvantaged.

An Enriched Teaching Paradigm

In order to make good the wants suffered by the disadvantaged learners, providing larger doses of the same medicine served at the mainstream teaching programme, in the form of compensatory education, remedial programmes imposed outside school timings can be of little help. We need an Enrichment Programme that focuses on the 3'H's i.e. the head, heart and the hand. It must restore the higher mental processes and make it an active part of the learners' repertoire. A combination of an affective, cognitive and strategic process as detailed below can possibly help the learning processes by making the slow learners,

- make the learners feel wanted, appreciated and progressing
- change their self concept from that of a passive recipient to an active participant and generator of information.
- develop intrinsic motivation to work on a task because of the personal significance of the task for the future and in the present proper approach to an issue and work habits learnt in the process
- identify successful learning strategies, techniques and processes and accompany them in their progress through scaffolded learning
- provide occasions that reinforce their learning till they become spontaneous and automatic.
- enable introspection and insight and understanding of one's own thought processes and strategies used, and the underlying reasons for their success and failure.
- acquire proper thinking skills, discursive reasoning and develop their cognitive functions.
- learn concepts, vocabulary and strategies necessary for problem solving situations.
- Support for coping with failures and frustration
- tapping their preferred routes to learning
- focus on syntax and connected language.

Principles Underlying the Pedagogy

Rather than a specific teaching method it is classroom procedures that need to define the approach to the at-risk learners. Based on the insights gleaned, we identify the principles of the classroom procedure as those providing affective (value the learning), cognitive (strategies to learn) and behavioural (strategies to deal with failures, frustrations) support to the learners under consideration. In the following paragraphs we shall attempt to expand these three areas.

The Affective

The most fundamental requirement arguably, is to attend to the affective aspect of these battered learners. For the easiest way to change the learners' behaviour is to help them first value themselves. This huge barrier that obstructs learning for the at-risk learners is an injected and cultivated low self esteem. It is not the failure to achieve which produces low self-esteem. Not all disadvantaged learners who fail will have a low self-esteem. It is important to know what value language learning presents to them. It is rather the reaction of significant people that cripple one's self-concept. Self-esteem is, therefore, a product of social interaction. Self-esteem in language learning is part of global self-esteem as shown graphically (adapted from Lawrence 1996: 10)

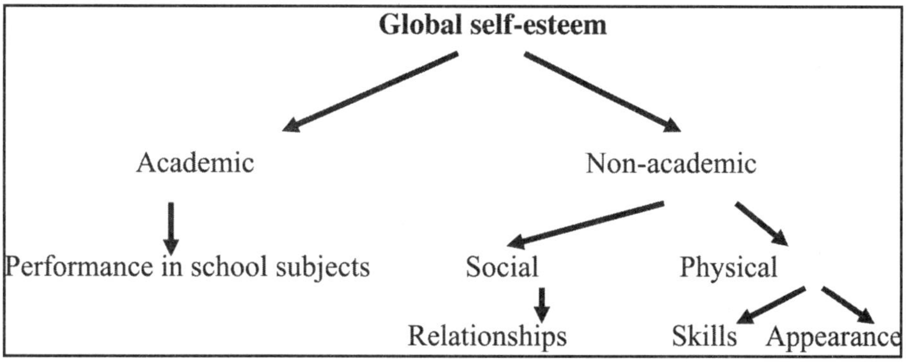

Teachers can play a major role in shaping learner self-esteem through acceptance, genuineness and empathy in their relations with learners. A very important factor is expectancy effect because students tend to behave according to the teacher's belief in their worth. Learners tend to fulfil teachers' expectations even if the latter downgrade their abilities. This illustrates the importance of teacher's behaviour that can have a powerful impact on learner self-esteem and learning outcomes.

(a) Pathos-ethos-logos

Reinterpreting the triads Aristotle spoke of (although in the context of rhetoric) i.e. pathos, ethos and logos, makes a practical approach to teaching these at-risk learners. Refurbishing self image (pathos) and ensuring a collaborative, nurturing, non-threatening classroom atmosphere (ethos) needs to come before actual language teaching (logos). Any attempt to force the head to learn before the heart is ready, would be like putting the cart before the horse! Only when these learners feel accepted would they drop their defences in the classroom and find their own voices. The pedagogy must do enough to make the learner feel confident and motivated before being exposed to the target language. It should unleash motivation, involvement and participation of the learners in question. As Pit Corder (1981) points out, given motivation, learners cannot but acquire a new language if they are exposed to it. If then learner confidence and motivation are sine qua non for language learning these must be ensured for the group in question whatever be the approach adopted.

In fact, the Pathos intertwines with Ethos, a non threatening and cooperative learning atmosphere and both ethos and pathos progress simultaneously rather than successively. So rather than like decorative icing sitting just on the top of a cake, pathos and ethos like nuts and raisins adding flavour and richness to a cake need to encompass the entire learning process. Acceptance, genuineness and empathy throughout the teaching/learning experience distinguish the teacher's relations with the target learners. The teaching/learning envisaged is an ongoing process where the teacher/facilitator shapes learners' self-esteem by being caring enough to know when his/her selected program is not meeting the needs of his/her students, then perceiving the need for course correction, he is flexible enough to make the necessary changes to make these accommodations and is practical enough to equip them ultimately with 'learning to learn' skills. While overtly focussing on the content, the whole exercise covertly works on expanding the learner's self concept from being one of a dependent personality toward being a self-directed human being. The lesson, or content signified by Logos, comes after these stages are ensured.

The bedrock of the learning process for the disadvantaged remains the self perception. We shall try to understand how to make these learners open up and let go. All human beings seem to be endowed with two apparently contradictory principles; one is the creative and the explorative and the other is the critical and cautionary. The first encourages the individual to explore, expand and think out of box while the second prescribes caution and restraint. This second is the face saving principle that ensures the ego does not get shattered by adventurous and often dangerous endeavours. These two principles often go hand in hand for nothing great or new can be achieved unless one dares and takes risks and the principle of caution or preservation makes sure nothing extreme or foolhardy is attempted that might damage the person; this is nature's gift to ensure one does not gets carried away by the onslaught of emotion. In the case of disadvantaged learners however, due to cumulative negative experiences it is possible an individual or an entire lot may have a sharpened sense of the critical that cripples trialling and experimenting with language. Therefore, it is important for these learners to temporarily muzzle the critical and give free rein to the creative spirit. And that must be the line on which the pedagogy for the disadvantaged needs to be shaped. Errors need to be underplayed and encouragement focussed on. Accuracy is consciously overlooked in order to encourage fluency. There would be multiple presentation of the learning matter permitting different routes and rates of learning that Ellis speaks of.

The Cognitive

The affective factor, all said and done is but a prologue to the more substantive cognitive modifications to follow. And this next stage focuses on learner preparedness which is realised by helping learners appreciate why to learn, what to learn and how to learn. Also, in order to overcome the acquired deficiencies, the scheme must help them

(a) unleash discursive thinking,

(b) become efficient at learning by using effective learning strategies and

(c) cultivate the ability for the mind to impose a pattern in the disparate linguistic data presented to it.

Coming to the first, it must be noted that our schools while training their students in the LSRW skills and possibly their sub skills, neglect a very vital skill intrinsic to success in language learning i.e. thinking skills. As Edward de Bono (1994) observes, 'On the whole, education does a poor job at equipping people to think.' There are occasions when it seems that the better 'educated' a person is, the less he/she is able to think'. Specialized knowledge, facts, and the ability to quote opinions, even in interesting combinations, are not at all the same as skill in thinking. If our pedagogy as Rose and Nicholl (1997) point out needs to shift to how students produce knowledge rather than how they merely reproduce it; for learning is not about just storing information, in which case a book shelf or a computer would be considered most learned. The use of thinking skills such as analytical, lateral, problem solving, critical, creative, and reflective need to be woven into the learning process. In the earlier stages of language learning the ability to identify, define, analyse, scan for pattern, work out rules, etc. are some of the skills Woodword T (2008) considers important in promoting language learning.

(a) The Strategic

Another feature that deserves attention is learning strategies which account for how learners acquire new L2 rules and how they automatize existing ones following conscious or subconscious processes. We are referring to a repertoire of ideas, plans, steps, techniques and behaviours that the learner finds helpful in collecting, storing, retrieving and using the information learnt.

These can be further broken down as cognitive strategies which concern what learners do to learn (e.g. mental or physical manipulation of the material); metacognitive strategies which is about what learners do to regulate their learning and its efficacy as also monitoring their own comprehension and production. Then there are memory strategies which are about ways to remember and store information using mnemonics, analogy, similarity, humour, repetition, etc. Compensation strategies help learners cope with carrying on a conversation overcoming gaps. In the process of learning they need to be made aware of and in command of their own process of learning. In the process of learning the disadvantaged learners would profit by the knowledge of the strategy they use, its significance, how to employ, monitor and evaluate that strategy as well as to which activities these strategies can be transferred. These strategies says Oxford R.L. (1994) pertain to 'control, goal directedness, autonomy and self efficacy'.

(b) Syntactisation Process

Another important cognitive factor pertains to the need for the learners to process the input, either consciously or unconsciously, if what is learnt has to become available to them as output. The raw language data unless reflected upon does not become part of the learners' repertoire. The progression from itemized learning, from lexis to syntax is the highway to language competence. We have repeated reminders from stalwarts such as Widdowson (1989) who makes an insightful distinction between 'analysability and accessibility'. In the process of SL acquisition learners reveal two types of language: the pragmatic mode or as Givon (1995) calls it 'pre-grammatical mode' where the structures are loose and paratactic – e.g. non-prepositional utterance, vertical construction, etc. and the second is the 'syntactic mode' ('Givon's 'grammatic mode') which reveals tight 'grammaticalised' structures akin to the formal discourse. There appears to be a twin knowledge system that needs to be perceived and accounted for, if the acquired system can be made useable for the learners. The learners must be assisted to transit from the first to the second stage.

This concern is reflected by many theoreticians in the profession who posit a dyadic process in language learning a learner has to sail through. Chomsky to begin with, agreeing with de Saussure before him distinguishes between 'competence and performance'; Krashen (1981) who speaks of 'the acquired language vs. monitored language' and Tarone's 'Capability Continuum' refers to the need for transition from the lexical to the syntactical mode.

The notion of 'Declarative and Procedural knowledge' also implies a shift from controlled processes (dealt with in the short term or working memory and under attentional control) to automatised processes stored in the long term memory (retrieved quickly and effortlessly). Through this process, what starts as declarative knowledge (knowing 'that') becomes procedural knowledge (knowing 'how') which becomes automatic (declarative) through reflected use. Again, Car and Curren (1994) making a distinction between 'Rule based and exemplar based learning' suggest that input unless reflected upon remains superficial, enabling most basic comprehension but offering little help in the production skills with any accuracy. Skehan P. (1993) is of the opinion that language learning goes through three stages: lexicalisation-syntacticisation and relexicalisation. In the first stage (lexicalisation) learners eager to express meaning mainly rely on lexical elements and ignore and overlook the form of their utterance. In the second stage, (syntacticisation) the learner's UG operating on the language material at hand develops a rule governed system. In the third stage, (relexicalisation) under real time pressure due to the inadequacy of composing rule referred utterances the learner indulges in stringing lexical chunks together.

Our target group then need to focus on and be adept at combining analysis with access. Therefore, one important way is to help them turn raw data into reflected data in order to make the passage from pre-grammatical to the grammatical utterance possible. The process of stretching their relatively fluid, simple, unstructured and inefficient interlanguage is to provide for a recurrence of the target structure and get them to reflect on the data, hypothesize and test rules and integrate them through deployment.

The Social

A child as we know learns a language through meaningful and repeated interactions where adult caregivers who interpose themselves between the child and the environment. But for the group under study, the crippling and constrictive imperatives of their existential realities restrict their interactions with persons outside their stratified community. The absence of mediation where the elders interpret and organise the stimuli around the learners is a serious drawback.

Thus, their impairment results from denial of opportunities for a wide range and types of real time interaction and interpretation of realities and experiences around them. Then, what the disadvantaged learner needs is exposure to quality and prolonged verbal interactions. Simply stated, with the restricted opportunities for interactions in English in the classroom and their near absence outside, finding alternative routes to learning becomes imperative. Someone needs to caringly mediate meaning for them.

Feuerstein consciously chooses the term mediator rather than instructor or teacher because the role of the mediator is much larger than those of the others. In Mediated Learning Experience (MLE), a mediator – an intentioned and experienced individual – interposes himself/herself between the stimuli and the organism receiving it, in our case the disadvantaged learner. He/she mediates the world to the learner by 'selecting stimuli, scheduling them, framing and locating them in time and space, grouping certain stimuli or segregating others, providing certain stimuli with specific meaning as compared with others, providing opportunities for recurrent appearances; bringing together objects and events that are separate and discrete in terms of temporal and spatial dimensions; rejecting or deferring the appearance of others; and through this providing the organism with modalities of selecting, focusing and grouping objects and events' (Feuerstein 1979:365-66)

Interestingly, De Bono (1994:53) also identifies the need for MLE when he says 'when children continually ask "why", they are not seeking in an adult sense any causal explanation. For them the need is to fill in the gaps in their perception of reality (and their ability to communicate what they experience). In the absence of an adequate connecting experience they create their own myths to explain/understand the reality perceived.' The comforting thought is that if the Disadvantaged learners did not get adequate MLE in their early childhood leaving mental gaps and perception difficulties, this damage can be corrected. It is affirmed that 'the more an organism was subjected to Mediated Learning Experience, the greater the amount and quality of this mediation, the higher the capacity of the organism to use direct exposure to stimuli for learning and change' (Feuerstein & Rand 1975:18).

Classroom Methodology

A classroom methodology specific to the target group integrating the affective, cognitive and the social features elaborated above could possibly follow the following steps not very different from the procedures of Task Based Learning:

A. **ICE Breaking** – A feel good group game or activity related to the theme of the day aimed at relaxing and lowering affective barriers and helps the learners 'find their voices'.

B. **Introduction** – where the problem to be tackled in the given exercise is explained and perhaps illustrated in a pretask; the concepts, vocabulary, rules and relationships needed for the task are introduced and appropriate strategies for solving the problem are discussed.

C. **Teacher initiated Interaction** – It is obvious that the at-risk learners would be reticent in a mainstream classroom. It is the teacher who is vested with power to control, direct and permit student participation. When the teacher does not provide adequate opportunities and even encouragement, these learners would remain reticent. When the teachers avoid what Tsui (1996) points out as deterrents of 'willingness to communicate' i.e. intolerance of silence, uneven allocation of turns, incomprehensible input, and lack of or short wait time, these learners would blossom.

D. **Independent Work** – where students work on the task which provide for

   (a) *Identification Thinking*: promotes noticing and recognising issues from the text

   (b) *Interpretative Thinking*: is a process of adding semantic and psychological meaning from their existing knowledge,

   (c) *Affective interpretation:* processing and adding meaning by feeling

   (d) *Analytical thinking*: helps reflect on what is noticed and endeavour to understand its significance.

   As part of the group discussion process every member in every group needs independently to write the findings and be prepared to present it before the whole group. Throughout, the teacher acts as a 'guide by the side' supervising, ensuring use of target language and providing constructive feedback to prevent frustration.

E. **Group Discussion** – is usually problem solving in nature involving exploring, suggesting, defending and refuting

F. **Grammar Focussed Reflection** – where learners' attention is drawn covertly where possible, to the salient features of some specified grammar, spelling, context, declensions or conjugations, collocations, etc.

G. **Summary**- is where an evaluation of the work is done and its significance to life and other learning situations are suggested. A reflection on the different strategies employed by the learners and a comparison of their appropriacy and efficacy is attempted. The learners are also asked to anchor their learning by spend time reflecting on a) learning points i.e vocabulary, expressions, pronunciation, etc. learnt and b) action point i.e the learner initiated action to proceduralise the knowledge gained.

The process of group-discussion and summation, pay special attention to the learners understanding what strategy they are employing, why and with what success; they are also given an opportunity to compare the relative merits of the strategies other students have employed and judge what is most suitable for them. The summation concentrates on the relevance of each strategy and to what classroom and real life situation they can be best transferred to.

Conclusion

It is obvious, that with the opportunities that the knowledge era offers improving education is a key ingredient in human and economic development, allowing millions to escape from poverty; our new development road-map needs more people in the organised sectors which require English.

Though, achieving such goals requires a huge investment in education at all levels, and a shortage of resources is a common problem in development contexts. In India, however, this is not now the main problem. Several interviewees complained that although they regarded funding and budgets sufficient, they were unable to ensure these resources reached the schools and classrooms.

With even a small number of trained and dedicated project managers, of people who can monitor and supervise projects, and of trainers at all levels even this humongous project (in terms of the numbers of children and teachers affected) is possible to deliver effectively and quickly.

The pool of educated adults is small in comparison to the large numbers of children who need to be taught. English teachers tend to be in especially short supply. Anyone who can speak English can usually find a much better-paid job elsewhere in the economy, making both recruitment and retention of English teachers difficult, particularly in rural areas.

Work Cited

Aristotle, 'On Rhetoric' tr. George A. Kennedy, New York : Oxford University Press, 1991.

Bernstein Basil, 'Social Class, Language and Socialization', In Power and Ideology in Education. ed. Jerome Karabel and A.H. Halsey, New York: OUP, 1977.

Bruer John, T., 'Schools for Thought: A Science of Learning in the Classroom', Massachusetts Institute of Technology Press, 1993.

Chambers Robert, 'Vulnerability, Coping and Policy', IDS Bulletin Vol. 37, No. 4, Sept. 2006.

Corder S., Pit., 'Error Analysis and Interlanguage' Oxford: OUP, 1981.

de Bono Edward, *Water Logic,* Penguin, 1994.

Feuerstein R. and Rand Y., 'Mediated Learning Experience: An Outline of the Proximal Etilogy for Differential Development of Cognitive Functions, New York', (Reprint) 1975.

Feuerstein R., et al., 'Learning to Learn: Mediated Learning Experiences and Instrumental Enrichment' in Special Services in the Schools. Vol. 3, Nos. 1 & 2, 1986.

Green, *The Pursuit of Inequality,* New York: Pantheon House, P. 1981.

Krashen Stephen, 'Second Language Acquisition and Second Language Learning', Oxford Pergamon, 1981.

Oxford Rebecca L., 'Second Language Teaching and Curriculum', University of Hawaii at Manoa, 1986.

Skehan Peter, *A Cognitive Approach to Language Learning:* Oxford: OUP, 1998.

Topping K.J., *Parents as Educators,* Cambridge: Brookline Books, 1986.

Tsui A., 'Reticence and Anxiety in Second Language Learning' in K. Bailey and D. Nunan ed. Voices from Language Classroom, Cambridge, CUP, 1996.

Widdowson H.G., *Linguistics* Oxford University Press, 1996.

Woodword Tessa, 'I think therefore I learn' English Teaching Professional, 58 Sept. 2008, p. 35.

16

Moving Forward in Tertiary-level ELT: Hard Curricular Choices

Makhan L. Tickoo

Lead in: Speaking at the annual day function of the Delhi Public School (DPS) at Noida – an upcoming city close to Delhi, on December 27, 2007 the Central Board of Secondary Education (CBSE) Chairman expressed his concern over the fact that the dominance of the '3 Cs' in the lives of today's youth was being allowed to hamper their growth towards the '3 As'. The 3 Cs he singled out are computers, cricket and cinema and the 3 As aptitude, attitude and altitude. As he saw it 'overindulgence in the 3 Cs not only costs students their valuable time but could also be of such an influence to hamper their growth and stunt them in achieving 3 As – aptitude, attitude and altitude in their personal life and professional career' (*The Times of India* 2007). The Chairman received a warm applause from his audience of parents and teachers for his 'straight talk'.

As students of the English language some of us may find it difficult to understand how 'indulgences' like the ones named above, could influence a teenager's or any human being's 'altitude' which the dictionary defines as 'the level above the sea of an object or place' or, for that matter, their 'aptitude' which we understand to be one's natural ability or skill in learning. But if one takes the Chairman's concern at its face value, one can try to understand the obvious reason for his timely warning and advice to the gathering of teachers and anxious parents.

What apparently won the CBSE Chairman applause was his candidness in reminding his audience of the need to make sure that the '3 Cs' do not mar the students' chances at the end of school examinations which currently are the system's only gateway to institutions of higher learning, more particularly to the coveted IITs and IIMs which every ambitious middle class parent today wants their son or daughter to gain admission to.

The statement above took me back to an event that I had, not long before it became known, witnessed as a grandparent. Our granddaughter, who was a Class 6 student of another DPS, had come home with a weekend home assignment set by her class teacher. It was to list as many as possible of the great novelist, Charles Dickens' books of fiction. She naturally approached me, a teacher of English, for help and, given my built-in habit of seeking support in books, I borrowed a couple from the university library which listed the main publications of the great novelist in their references. The number came to around 40 and I was more than satisfied with the outcome. I also made myself believe that she was equally happy with the outcome.

However, being a child of the early 21st century, she decided not to give up on another source known to her. Without breathing a word about it, she was at work looking up the relevant pages on Charles Dickens in the website of her personal computer. A surprise awaited me when we greeted each other early next morning. It was that she had added at least a dozen titles to the ones I had helped her put together. As a grandfather I felt proud and hoped she would keep relying on that rich resource (one of the 3 Cs above) as a better alternative to what I could even at my best do for her.

As for the other 2 Cs above I am once again only half convinced about the wisdom of their being viewed as mere indulgences. Cricket may be a passion more true of India than of many other – perhaps more developed – countries. But like other sports, cricket too, I believe, is capable of doing more good than harm. Nor can one dismiss the rich potential of good cinema as a source of both entertainment and education. What is important, however, is for parents and teachers to equip and enable their wards to become capable of making good choices in a world where the number of offerings keeps multiplying.

Setting the Task: That leads me to the main point of this paper. One's preferences, whether one likes it or not, are governed by one's priorities. For the CBSE Chairman above, they seemed to have been on the school-final examinations and the results thereof. For me as a grandparent, it was the desirability of a growing child very dear to me gaining autonomy as a learner. In making any choice one inevitably pays a price. And this is as true of schools/colleges or a whole system of education as it is of one or more individuals who are responsible for making the choices.

English teaching professionals at the tertiary-level need to make choices and the more thinkfully they make them, the better ought normally to be the returns. But what are some of those choices and what makes them difficult in this day and time?

Understanding Some Curricular Choices

The first appears to be the most obvious one in 2008. English teaching has become a large and fast growing enterprise of our world and India happens to be among its largest single settings as far as both the size and scope of the enterprise are concerned.

To understand where we stand today let me seek support in a recent research-driven source on ELT in the world. It is a book entitled *English Next* by David Graddol published in 2006 which looks at English in the world of the early 21st century, its present and predictable future.

On the basis of what he was able to gather in his research all over the world during the last few years, Graddol comes to two conclusions which, in my judgment, need to be heeded by decision-makers in colleges and universities of India. The first can be said to foreground the more pleasing aspect of the scenario inside our vast and great country. Here is a part of what he found.

In his description Graddol refers to how policy-makers in the West view India's growing strengths in English language, its teaching, acquisition and use. He quotes the Worldwatch Institute, a United States based think-tank, and what it says in viewing the state of the world in the early years of the 21st century. Here is part of the warning it gives its readers: 'India and China are planetary powers that are shaping the global biosphere who, if they were to consume as much per capita as Japan, would require a full planet earth to meet their needs.' It goes on, 'many are fearful of the political consequences of such a shift of economic power.' (33)

An elementary student of Economics should, it seems to me, find it easy to dispel the fears of the above think-tank at least for now by pointing out that a majority of India's more than a billion people are still unable to afford two square meals a day. A nation which in 2008 has been accorded the dubious distinction of having the largest number of men, women and children who require better nutrition than they can currently afford, is unlikely to make such giant demands even on the limited resources that exist in today's world. That, however, is not part of our present concern. What is obvious in the above warning is that the world is waking up to the reality of India's fast growing English-literate population.

But there is also the reverse side of the coin among Graddol's findings. Here is a relevant part of that: 'universities play a key role in developing knowledge economies; international surveys of the attractiveness of a country as an outsourcing destination routinely assess the quality and number of local graduates. For example, a report by the international consultancy McKinsey, in December 2005, indicated that although India produces 2.5 million university graduates each year, only a quarter are "suitable" for employment by multinationals or their Indian outsourcing partners. Within five years, India may find itself short of 150,000 IT engineers and 350,000 BPO workers – such as the kind needed for Call-Centres.' It goes on, 'the chief handicaps are weak spoken English skills, especially among graduates of non-elite schools and the uneven quality of college curricula and faculty.' Graddol concludes his quoted text by warning that 'such shortages lead to high staff turnover, and escalating wage costs, which erode India's competitive advantage.' (75)

These latter set of findings in Graddol's research appear to have found valuable support in an inside-the-country study done in working with some representative English-using workplaces in India. The study was done by two ELT practitioners who had worked for the corporate sector in South India and had over a few years closely observed the market trends and demands in that sector in the principal cities in that region. Based on their study they highlighted several remediable failures of the existing system of English teaching in colleges/universities. In particular they emphasized the urgent need to make provision for the following:

'(i) being aware of individual areas of lacunae, (ii) using English extensively for transactional communication, (iii) interacting fluently with people who belong to predominantly 'English' culture, (iv) socializing with counterparts/clients outside business discussions, (v) comprehending various regional accents and flavours of expression.' (Shobhaneswari and Dass, December 2005: 51).

As an essential first step every curriculum planner or practitioner working in or for tertiary-level English will need to take the above well-attested findings into account and explore appropriate means to readily respond to them. They must put to work every available avenue to meet the pressing requirements of this section of the society. On a modest scale this has already begun to happen in a small but steadily growing number of colleges and universities. Over the last few years the State-run system of higher education in Andhra Pradesh has, for example, been investing its resources to provide short-term training to equip and enable every undergraduate teacher to teach oral-aural communication. Autonomous colleges in more than one South Indian state have been doing so with much greater though varying success over a much-longer period. What then are the choices and how can the policy-maker/and curriculum designer decide between them?

An obvious long-term answer should be to look at the feasibility of each such response at work. Let me refer to an actual example to make the point. The example shows at work some of the variables that may be found at work and therefore require attention in implementing a workable curriculum renewal plan.

Some five years ago at an international seminar held in Chennai two senior teachers of English working inside the same university, viz. the University of Pune, presented individual case-studies based on their personal observations as curriculum implementers while providing their students communicative abilities in English for use in the new type of workplaces. The presentations were made at the open discussion session of the seminar. Here is part of what I noted down in listening to the two presentations, the first of which was about a college in Pune that stood out for its relatively rich resources, both human and material, the second about a district-level college somewhat away from the main city centres. What should interest the reader is what each presentation highlighted.

The former gave an account of how much a professionally trained lecturer was able to achieve with support in the college's computer lab and through her planned use of the college's rich stock of audio and visual cassettes and by encouraging her students' regular home listening to good TV and radio programmes in English; the latter mainly brought out the failures caused by, among other things, the limited and poorly maintained aids, large and crowded classes, non-provision of tutorial hours, unreliable power supply and above all, the majority of learners' failure to find opportunities to use their learnt knowledge and usable skills outside their characteristically acquisition-poor classrooms.

What an analysis of the two presentations showed was that to make a success of a new communicative programme the ready availability of relevant resources—men and materials—plays an important part, but even more so does a well-motivated class and a well-equipped teacher. More crucial than both towards making a lasting impact may turn out to be the presence or absence of opportunities to put to regular use the learnt communicative skills and abilities outside the one-hour-a-day teaching-learning. Offering a course that guarantees credible results must significantly depend on the system's preparedness to make it work. Such a system must also, among other things, raise and meaningfully respond to the currently ignored basic need for putting in place trial-tested and reliable means for the end of the session assessment and evaluation, which in the case of spoken English – both listening and speaking – is as yet rarely found in most of our institutions, be they secondary and tertiary.

A second important criterion may, in my judgment, be even more crucial. It is a question of priorities which I briefly referred to above. For ELT professionals it becomes a question of deciding where to place their bets. In a situation where the language is assigned, no more than four or five class hours a week and the class is overly large, an obvious question to ask may, for example, be 'Which of the four language skills —reading, writing, listening and speaking—should receive greater attention and more time and why?' In making that decision some of the following questions must receive attention.

What is/are the primary aim(s) and objectives of English teaching in the institution?

What proficiency levels are the students likely to have when they enter the course?

What level of relevant language proficiency can be assumed as given in planning the course? How much time is allowed and with what frequency – how often will the language be taught/learnt in the classroom; and what opportunities for use exist outside the language classroom? Does the college attract a larger/smaller than average number and percentage of non-English medium students or, equally importantly, rural as opposed to urban students? Not unimportant but difficult to possess at the curriculum planning stage would be an informed understanding of the socio-economic background of the majority of the students in the class/ course?

Finally, what resources – human and material – are or will be placed at the course-planners' and practitioners' disposal to make a success of the programme?

The answers to the above questions will vary and most may demand careful studies of the societal variables as essential preliminaries. What may, however, offer a few clues to the kind of workable answers that are and must be made in such circumstances should be actual examples of comparable curriculum renewal projects. For this I shall seek support in two examples of graduate-level innovative courses offered a quarter century ago. The facts I refer to in both cases are based on materials that were available then and should normally be available to anyone today who seeks to know about what happened in the implementation of the two innovative projects. However, the conclusions I have drawn are, I must admit, subjective. They are based on an admittedly partial understanding of factors and facts. There is therefore a lot of scope for interested scholars in future to draw their own conclusions-based on a different, perhaps better informed, approach to them.

Curriculum Renewal in Undergraduate ELT: Two Illustrative Examples

The two courses were offered roughly at the same time in the city of Bombay (now Mumbai) in the 1980s. They were offered by two neighbouring university departments or Boards of Studies, viz. Bombay and SNDT. In what follows I briefly refer to them in that order.

a. The reform in Bombay—a larger and more established university—was informed by the at that time just emerging 'Communicational Approach'. Accordingly, it mainly aimed at putting to work real-life communicative skills and abilities towards giving the graduating student the communicative competence that would be required for use at places of work and also in pursuing higher studies. To realize those well-defined objectives the following were some of the aims and beliefs that went into the design of the undergraduate English curriculum.

In their forcefully expressed suspicion of the prescribed textbook as an 'aid' that acted more as a restriction than as a facilitator for or support to both teachers and students, the curriculum planners accorded it no place in the reformed syllabus. They also found the existing system of examinations incapable of judging the real linguistic proficiency achieved by the student and therefore argued for the need to design and develop an alternative system of examinations capable of judging the abilities required for using English in real-life contexts.

The alternative came in the form of a detailed syllabus which incorporated the aims, detailed the preferred methodology and the accompanying materials to go with that and offered guidelines for a well-defined alternative system of exams. No textbooks or source books were prescribed. In their place there was guidance on the type of materials that would help equip and enable the teacher and students to work towards success in achieving the defined curricular goals. A small number of books whose authors had –in part or in full – attempted materials capable of helping students realize those aims, were alluded too.

b. The reform at the SNDT, a much smaller and younger university for women, was based on a study of both what the students needed and wanted and also their specific needs in terms of the four language skills and what was known of the sub-skills inside each. The university decided to and set about preparing its own materials which focused on the chosen skills and sub-skills giving weighting as found necessary. It also gave internal tests a defined role in the overall assessment and made provision for skills/sub-skills to be evaluated by that mode. Perhaps most importantly, it made the compulsory reading of a minimum number of supplementary readers part of the essential core of the curriculum and made well-defined provision for judging that reading and also the essential skills of spoken English through the year-long internal assessment. Marks that counted towards final end-of-the-year grades were assigned to that assessment.

What were the main similarities and differences between the two?

Only a partial answer can form part of what is found below.

Both reforms stood out for highlighting the need for a different set of materials from the ones that had been used for several generations. Rather than carry on with the usual literary texts, both therefore saw the need for texts capable of foregrounding current English and its essential genres. Both placed much value on a more reliable and relevant system of evaluation and assessment. Both but more pronouncedly Bombay, relied on learner efforts to realize the specific aims that were well-defined.

But the two reforms measurably differed on several essentials as also the emphases within each. Whereas the Bombay reform removed the need for a Board of Studies prescribed textbook and gave the teacher the choice of materials to choose for reaching the communicational goals, the SNDT reform made reading—both intensive but especially extensive—obligatory in the understanding that a major cause of failure was that most students did not read enough and the majority failed often to read what they did, for meaning. It also used internal evaluation to make sure that additional reading of several books became a valued part of the examinable syllabus. Both taught spoken English but only the SNDT was able to make its assessment a part of internal in-college tests. However, the SNDT reform also ended up by giving teachers working in most colleges much less freedom by assigning the task of producing the full package of materials for use to syllabus makers and materials writers most of whom worked for the university.

I have discussed the two reforms critically in a few earlier papers. So have others. However, people interested in tertiary-level English teaching reform should find a lot of value in their study of both reforms using primary sources of information. As an outside-the-system observer with my bias and beliefs I noticed the following:

(i) Most Bombay teachers wanted textbooks, and most of them ended up relying mainly on one of the recommended books.

(ii) With the textbook becoming optional, the better-equipped student—often someone who was a product of a better school—confidently depended on his/her own proficiency to attempt the 'communicative' test items. In most such cases it worked although it also may have meant no additional reading on their part. The average student found the recommended book(s) too demanding and in a majority of cases worked for and mainly relied on grammar and word-stress related questions at the final examination to gain the minimum passing mark.

(iii) Bombay's reform was radical—well-defined and defended but very new. It markedly suited the small percentage of better-placed colleges or a few where the teacher was measurably more proficient, fully prepared for and committed to making the reform work.

(iv) The obligatory reading of books at the appropriate levels of challenge helped provide a lot more exposure to most students at SNDT. The year-long internal assessment helped make it real by obliging the student to read the prescribed texts.

(v) A majority of SNDT teachers liked their control in classrooms; students welcomed that too. Making the learner a participant in active learning remains a challenge.

(vi) Major curricular changes threaten the teacher; they need careful—often long-term planning to make them acceptable to the majority. In general there seems to be much truth in the understanding that especially in large mainstream systems of education a successful curriculum in action—one that seeks the teacher's appropriation of it in his/her everyday teaching—has to be 'a patient pursuit of the possible'. (Bruner)

Conclusion

Unlike Robert Bellarmine and a small few other ELT practitioners in today's profession who have attempted to carve new paths to progress, I have, much like the majority, failed to adopt new ways into reform. This brief exercise in understanding a few choices in tertiary-level ELT may show that too. However, I would like to conclude by suggesting that we have reached a stage in our profession where choices are not all that easy. One of the main reasons is that the factors that enter any worthwhile decision-making process are complex and also much larger in number than ever before. Tertiary-level ELT is being forced to respond to the fast globalizing market place. In doing so, I believe, that it can ill-afford to ignore its other equally pressing obligations. These include:

(a) the growing need to respond to students from weaker sections and first generation learners whose numbers are fortunately on the increase;

(b) the real aim of higher education and especially education through English being not just the development of skills for the fast expanding job markets but also contributing to a knowledge society, adequate attention also needs to be paid to the larger aims. English today is India's most important language of knowledge —one that empowers graduates to be not just consumers of knowledge which techniques alone and by themselves make possible but, more importantly, participants in the production of knowledge. India of tomorrow cannot afford to remain a recipient of products produced elsewhere. It has to become the equal of the best with a workforce comparable to the very best in the world. To do this tertiary-level ELT must not allow technique to displace content but bring in technique alongside content i.e. the language in its fullness with the riches of literatures of all types.

The ELT profession, as Henry Widdowson pointed out in 2004, has 'lost its innocence'. It now knows that there are no final answers, only good (or not so good) questions. A good curriculum must be not just workable in general, it must be practicable in the circumstances where it has to operate. Above all it must be an answer to the carefully studied special needs of the particular institution. The widespread belief that imported approaches with their support in other experiences especially in the West can meet all our requirements may no longer be helpful. Nor may the accompanying belief that characteristically local factors in our multilingual classrooms are constraints to be confronted rather than essential conditions to be accepted and worked with, be found true any longer. Although it is true that certain facts about teaching and learning are universal and certain qualities set apart good from not so good and definitely bad teaching, what is also true is that for many aspects of the curriculum the nature of the institution and its resources must be kept in mind in making the inevitably hard choices. A good curriculum must be designed in full view of the factors that operate in a particular institution. The need to accept the shift to localization must be taken seriously.

Our choices are thus hard and our answers must be based on a studied view of not just the pressures that operate in the fast changing world of today but also in the growing recognition that education and inside it usable English has to be made a reality for every graduating student. And it must now be done without marginalizing the learner's own language, however minor that may be. English in India must grow inside India's multicultural and multilingual ethos; it must both accept help from and offer help to the learners' own literate languages.

Works Cited

Graddol D., *English Next,* British Council, London, 2006.

Shobhaneswari T.J., and Mridula Dass, 'Observations on Market Trends and Teaching in India', *The English Classroom* Vol. 7, December 2007, Bangalore: RIESI, 2005.

The Times of India, December 28, 2007, p. 12.

Widdowson H.G. and A.P.R. Howatt, 'A Perspective on Recent Trends', *A History of English Language Teaching,* 2nd edn, Oxford University Press, 2004, pp. 353-372.

17

Lexical Phrases and Their Role in Language Acquisition

Manjula Duraiswamy

In a communicative approach which accepts that learners learn best when they participate actively in the learning process. Opportunity should be provided for meaningful engagement with the rules behind language forms. This engagement can be brought about through a methodology based on 'chunks' or' lexical phrases' by which learners perceive and assimilate information about the underlying patterns of language. The key principle of this approach is that 'language consists of grammaticalized lexis, not lexicalized grammar' Michael Lewis (1993.)

Background

Willis (1990) provides a design for language teaching-based on a lexical syllabus and emphasizes that instructional methodology should focus on words use in different language environments. While this lexical syllabus subsumes a structural syllabus, it also describes how the structures are used in a natural environment. However, Sinclairs (1987) and Willis (1990) lexical syllabuses are word-based while Lewis lexical syllabus 'explicitly recognizes word patterns for de-lexicalized words, collocational power for relatively semantically powerful words, and longer multiword items, particularly institutionalized sentences, as requiring different and parallel pedagogical treatment' (Lewis 1993). This teaching model recognizes 'observation – hypothesis – experimentation', in direct contrast to the more orthodox 'presentation—practice – production' model which relies on a rule governed process instead of the retrieval of 'chunks' of language structures from memory. Sinclair, Nattinger, De Carico and Lewis are representative of an important pedagogical shift from the past as they challenge a traditional view of word boundaries, emphasizing, on the other hand, the need to 'notice' patterns of lexis and collocation.

Classroom Methodology

The classroom methodology that this approach incorporates can be described further as:

1. Observation

In this stage attention is focused towards features of language incorporated in the 'chunk' through activities involving 'noticing' and real-life language experiences. The learner has direct experience of language in use.

2. Hypothesis

This stage helps the learner navigate through language finding explanations for linguistic phenomena involved in a piece of text. In short, the learning of grammar rules is facilitated through an understanding of patterns of language use; the learner forms an impression of the way language items work in different contexts.

3. Experimentation

The learner now confirms understanding of language learnt through exploratory language use in carefully scaffolded contexts.

Consolidation

The learner reformulates and trials structures in different contexts and relates language use to appropriate grammar terminology.

The Curriculum

Brindley (1984) and Nunan (1988) have described curriculum design as a negotiative process between teachers and learners, where learners are involved in decisions on context selection, methodology and evaluation.

Teaching language is a complex social and cultural activity and 'chunks' methodology incorporates sensitivity towards learners, dealing effectively with psychological challenges and diverse capabilities.

In this learner–centered approach involving the use of 'chunks' in the language classroom goal-setting is undertaken collaboratively and methodology and study mode are tuned to student requirements. Students feel involved in their programme as they try to uncover unifying networks supporting 'chunks'. A significant component of this curriculum design is fashioning teaching around learner interests and resources, and helping learner participation in a pedagogically reliable process.

The actual teaching programme revolves around choices based on an initial assessment of learners and their needs. A selection of texts-based on interests and appropriacy is finalized and each unit is exploited for meaningful sentence fragments. These 'remembered fragments' form the basis of language learning as the recycling of language is inherent with understanding how grammar systematically coordinates and manages language output.

The direct teaching of grammar is the conclusion, not the starting point of a teaching unit; learners have already used the language forms in different meaningful contexts before being asked to study the underlying grammar. By providing a holistic learning experience similar to a child's first experiences with language learning, this approach encourages language acquisition by engaging the learner in conative, metalingual and poetic functions, aiding long-term memory, and activating language fluency and confidence in the learner.

The Process

The classroom activities described here employ techniques which can be modified and adapted according to context. I have used these activities in my classes for about 15 years and have observed tangible results with both adult learners and children. With an informed approach the lexical approach can be adapted to suit the requirements of different syllabuses and programmes.

Activity 1: The Oracle

Activity type: Role play, group activity
Description: This is a Reading/Speaking activity based on Oracular pronouncements using expressions from a text that is just beyond the learner's reach.
Aims: Noticing, language enhancement through internalizing of 'chunks', awareness raising about higher levels of language use and grammar as an inbuilt component of lexis.
Level: High school and above
Time: 40 mins
Materials: Any suitable prose text

Procedure:

1. Pick out seven expressions from a prescribed text and ask the class to underline them in the text. (5 mins)
2. Make groups and appoint an Oracle for each group. (3 mins)
3. Each group discusses the expressions and their meanings. (10 mins)
4. Each Oracle now steps away from the group and hides behind a book to create the atmosphere for Oracular pronouncements. (5 mins)
5. The group asks questions. Each one in the group is allowed one question and he/she has to explain the Oracle's reply so that the others understand the response as it applies to their context.

e.g.

1. **Student:** Will I pass my math test?
   Oracle (reading from a strip): 'when conditions are favourable'
   Student: Favourable conditions would mean preparation and practice before a test. I should work hard at my math problems!
2. **Student:** Will my friend talk to me again?
   Oracle: 'Strike a balance'
   Student: Both of us should make an effort to understand each other.
3. **Student:** Will India win the series?
   Oracle: 'A possible way of saving the situation'
   Student: If our batsmen score high runs we might be able to win after all.

   (idea from Drama Techniques in Language Learning, Alan Maley and Alan Duff (1981)

Activity 2: Found Poems

Activity type: Pair work
Description: Writing activity
Aims: Noticing, enhancing facility with expressions, awareness raising about 'chunking'
Level: Middle school and above
Time: 40 mins
Materials: Any suitable prose text

Procedure:

1. Tell the class that a child has eaten a dish kept in the fridge for guests and has penned an explanation for his mother. Write the message on the board, adding some background information for interest.

   'This is just to say I have eaten the plums that were in the icebox and which you were probably saving for breakfast. They were so delicious, so sweet and so cold'. (5 mins)
2. Now present the text as it was originally written. How does it suddenly change from being 'not a poem' to being a poem? Discuss reasons. (10 mins)

This is just to say
William Carlos Williams

I have eaten
the plums
that were in
the icebox
and which
you were probably
saving
for breakfast

Forgive me
they were delicious
so sweet
and so cold.

3. Now mark out a suitable passage in the prescribed text and ask the class to work in pairs to rearrange the lines to create poetry. (15 mins)
4. The poems can be written and displayed on the walls. (10 mins)

Activity 3: Activity Type: Pair Work

Description: Listening activity
Aims: Noticing, enhancing facility with expressions through awareness of collocations.
Level: Middle school and above
Time: 40 mins
Materials: Radio, TV news broadcasts, etc.

Procedure:

1. Ask the class to listen to a broadcast everyday at the same time for a week and write down any word combinations that they think are interesting or useful.
2. They should also note how many times a word appears in different combinations. Eg. pleasant scenario, changing scenario, present scenario (3), etc.
3. The class can create word webs for the collocations.
4. They can then try to create a news bulletin using their favourite collocations.
5. In pairs they can read and listen to the bulletins.

18

Key Issues in Developing a Parallel Course in Writing for Under-privileged Students

Aysha Vishwamohan

This article describes a parallel/remedial intervention programme in ESL writing carried out at IIT Madras to enhance the writing skills of disadvantaged learners. This is a corpus-based writing research that first teases out the needs and lacks of these learners and then attempts to address them systematically. It also shows how such a parallel training can make a real difference for tertiary-level learners who lag behind their classmates primarily due to problems stemming from their socio-economic background.

The Context

In 1990, a nation-wide research was conducted by Damyanti Singh from the Curriculum Development Cell at IIT Kanpur. The programme, NEST or Need-based English for Science and Technology was based on the special needs of various learner groups. The survey noted that while speaking is the top priority of the students, writing occupies the second place. It was concluded that:

> written discourse is the very essence of traditional NEST at a higher academic level, but the training in the art of technical and scientific writing must be given to the students during the college years. Our students are keen to be taught the style of scientific and technical writing as they are quick to recognize the writing

> areas most needed for their careers (Nest Folder 1990:27).

Clearly, for the IITians, effective writing skills are of paramount importance. Possibly very little is done to help the group in question in this area. It was decided that the students of this Preparatory Course (PC) would form the experimental group. The official website of the IITM describes the objective and the participants of the PC thus:

> one year preparatory course for SC/ST candidates is offered to improve their intake in the B.Tech programme. Generally 30 to 40 candidates from the non-qualified candidates list in the ranking order of JEE are taken. In this programme they have to undergo courses in Mathematics, Physics, Chemistry and English for the two semesters and successfully complete the courses. On their successful completion, available discipline/branch in the B.Tech programme will be allotted from the vacancies of that year's quota for SC/ST candidates. The course is residential. The students are eligible for all concessions during the period of coaching on par with the regular students in the matter of admission to the B.Tech programme. The Joint Admission Committee finally decides the admission of these students.

Learner Profile

The learners at the preparatory course that formed the experimental group for this research were first-generation learners from regional medium schools coming from socially and economically underprivileged segment of the society. Needless to say, despite learning English for the past fifteen years or so most of them before joining the IIT have had a very uneven exposure to English language. However, this is not a reflection on their cognitive abilities, which are quite well-developed. Another perceptible feature of this group was that there was no common mother tongue, as the learners come from diverse linguistic backgrounds. These learners are found lacking, particularly, in productive skills, viz. speaking and writing.

Research Objective

It was observed by the subject as well as the English language teachers that in spite of some practise in writing during the first semester, the PC learners were still unable to write reasonably error-free English; and this caused problems in communication, and consequently, stress for the reader. It was evident from the samples that the writers had difficulties with every aspect of written communication. Some of the major problems were: faulty arrangement of words and sentences, difficulties in forming structures, errors in spellings and punctuations, and inability to choose the appropriate word for the context. Another observation was that although the participants were successful in grammar-based activities, like error correction in isolated sentences, 'fill in the blanks' exercises, etc. they faced serious difficulties when it came to writing a full-length piece of prose, logically connecting sentences, and developing outlines. For this particular study, at least hundred pieces of writing were collected before arriving at the above conclusion (Allwright & Bailey 1991: 38-40).

Research Questions

The research focused on three relevant questions:

- Is there a need for the learners of the Preparatory Course (PC) at the IIT Madras to improve their ESL writing skills?
- Can there be a marked improvement in the writing skills of the participants of the PC at the IITM if a parallel course in writing is administered?
- Which approach works better—process or product—while teaching the ESL writing skills to this group?

The Expected Outcome of the Research

The research was grounded in the belief that given a parallel course in writing the participants of the Preparatory Course can cope with the complex academic demands at the IITM. The parallel or experimental course can co-exist with the already existing syllabus. The expected outcome is that at the end of this course, there would be a discernible improvement in the quality of writing of the students, especially in the domain of cohesion and coherence as well as selection of appropriate vocabulary.

The Hypothesis

The research was based on the hypothesis that if a short-term parallel course in writing is administered to the learners of the PC, there would be considerable improvement in the writing skills of the students.

Analysis of the Questions

The questionnaire was used to elicit responses on the following areas:

1. ***The mother tongue of the participants:*** This was necessary to draw attention to the fact that there was no common MT in the class. The use of L1, therefore, could not have been employed in the set-up.

2. ***The skills needed by the participants:*** This question gave the learners a chance to reflect in their own skills, their individual strengths and weaknesses, and the skill which, in their opinion, they needed most.
3. ***Most useful activity:*** This part of the questionnaire was framed in order to elicit feedback on the classroom activities.
4. ***Preferred mode of doing activities in the English classroom:*** This part was devised to understand the mode of writing preferred by the learners.

The Process of Developing the Parallel Course

Rationale

It was realized that the students can show an overall improvement in their ESL writing skills if given a three hours a week parallel course. The concept is in correspondence with the recommendations of a University Grants Workshop in 1977, conducted at the Indian centre's of Lucknow, Shillong, Mysore, Bombay, and Kurukshetra. It stated:

> Short and highly intensive 'bridge' courses should be organized at the commencement of the academic year for students who are found to be deficient in their command of the English language, to help them come up to the standards expected of students at the degree level. The duration of the course may vary from two to four weeks, but there should be 4 to 5 hours of instruction in English everyday (UGC National Workshop 1977: 152).

However, going by the writings of the students, it was clear that a parallel course with limited duration may not meet every writing-related problem of the students. As Griffin observes, 'the major question confronting any theory of responding to student writing is where we should focus our attention' (Fathman & Whalley 1990:178).

It was decided to concentrate on the content rather than the form (although the debate between the effectiveness of the two is never ending) for two reasons. Firstly, once the learners become confident with the content-related area, they would decidedly communicate better through their writings. Secondly, form based instruction and assessment become rather mechanical, and students tend to lose interest with excessive stress on grammar, particularly so in a parallel course.

Despite the learnings towards the content-based writing, it was felt necessary that attention of the participants should also be drawn towards the form of their writing. To address this issue, a list containing the common inaccuracies in grammar was drafted, and was made accessible to the learners.

As part of the parallel course, the learners were made aware of the following:

- Organization of a paragraph/essay—choosing the appropriate topic sentence, developing the 'body', and the concluding paragraph/sentence.

- Mechanics (spellings/punctuation, with greater emphasis on former).
- Signposting/Use of logical connectors.

Students' errors in spelling were also classified, based on the data collected. It is obvious from the samples that some of these errors are so acute that they cause a severe strain for the readers. This problem was addressed in the following ways:

(a) a list was compiled consisting of the relevant correct spellings, and was distributed among the students.

(b) occasionally the learners were given dictation in order to reinforce their spellings.

Key Aspects of Organizing Text

Students were made aware that a successful paragraph exhibit three important qualities: it is complete, it is unified and it is ordered. A complete paragraph provides as much information as the reader requires. A unified paragraph is structured around the central idea and has a consistent tone and a point of view. An ordered paragraph is marked by its coherence.

Students were also told that the conventions of a paragraph in English may differ from those of other Indian languages. A paragraph is something which one can see. It starts away from the margin, which is called indentation. Alternatively, the paragraph can start at the margin with the rest of the text, and be separated from the paragraph before by a blank line. A paragraph usually is made up of several sentences. While it is possible to have a one-sentence paragraph, these are quite rare. In general, each paragraph is about one main idea, when moving on to a new point; one should start a new paragraph (Sherman 1994: pp. 72-74).

Structuring Texts

Students were made aware of the fact that writing a text follows a specific structured order. Most texts follow a certain pattern, such as statement or definition, classification, comparison/contrast, examples, conclusion. As writers (and readers) learners should be sensitive to those subtle markers which signify a shift from one sentence to another.

Rearranging jumbled sentences of a paragraph is an exercise which can be used successfully.

Writer-reader Relationship

Learners were made aware of the principles of clarity, reality, relevance, and honesty.

Coherence and the Schema Theory

Consider a paragraph as the following:

Make your friends go green with envy, literally. If you are the kind that feels more in tune with the natural world, Sri Lanka can prove to be a treasure trove. While even happy employees whine on Sunday evenings, you know you really hate your job when the frequency and intensity of your complaints take on gigantic proportions. When your child starts feeling better, you tend to stop giving her medicines. The last shipment of goods has not yet showed up.

Learners were told that although the above paragraph looks like a paragraph, it lacks logic and coherence. This is because the text lacks a schema. An important aspect of the organization of schemas is that simpler schemas can be 'embedded' within more complex schemas. Or, to put it another way, schemas can be hierarchically structured. The writing schema contains within it a number of sub-schemas; the schema for writing implement, a writing surface, a language, and an entity that is trying to communicate. It must be realized that readers do not read in a mental vacuum. They are influenced by personal mental constructs. These can include their experiences, expectations, emotions, and attitudes towards the topic and the writer. Personal constructs differ from reader to reader. So, for successful writing, a writer needs to find those constructs that he has in common with his readers. The common ground a writer and his readers share comprises the wide context of culture, the context of restricted culture, and the brief context of specific situation. As part of the process approach to the teaching of writing, students were introduced to the techniques of free writing, writing one-minute papers, fish-bowl method, and mini-lessons. They were encouraged to write in pairs as well as groups. They were also given continuous assignments on writing an effective beginning, middle and conclusion of an essay. To enhance their vocabulary, the PC learners were given a basic list of words, helpful in their writing. This list included common words which students at their level must be aware of. Additionally, they were also given a list of word-formations and antonyms of the commonly used words.

The Use of Model

The model approach to teaching and learning of writing has its share of takers and detractors. Most teachers of writing believe in providing models to the readers with all that is 'appropriate' and 'correct', was the belief I fervently subscribed too. However, an intense reading of the theories of ESL writing has made me question some of the classroom practises. In her paper *The Use and Abuse of Models in the ESL Writing Class*, Cynthia Watson reflects that though models provide an effective input, 'model-based composition teaching is product-based composition teaching' (Watson 1982: 6). The writer cites two strong reasons against the use of models: 1) Models engender a tightly controlled composition, and 2) Models foster an unduly sheltered environment which offers false reassurance. While Watson makes a good case for not using a model for ESL writing, it has been noticed that models can be effectively used to generate ideas and take a stand. Learners however, should be cautioned against blindly imitating the model as well as against 'lifting' expressions, vocabulary, and various linguistic structures.

Feedback

When teachers give feedback, the focus should be on form or content or both. Researchers have also looked at the quality of comments of the teachers. The L2 research on composition has focused both on how teachers correct form and how they respond to content. A three-pronged approach as the following was adopted to elicit feedback: Feedback by the instructor, peer-editing/review and self-evaluation.

Findings

During the parallel course, learners were asked to compose several pieces of work. It was found that writing can be better facilitated in a classroom situation if the instructor narrows down the focus to one/two micro skills rather than engage in 'improving' all the skills (grammar, vocabulary, organization, sociolinguistics features, discourse strategies, etc.). Despite the presence of errors in writing, it was observed that continuous writing and expressing themselves lowered the inbuilt inhibitions of the learners. The osmosis effect of writing was reflected in the other productive skill, which is, speaking. As a result, formerly reticent and withdrawn participants gradually started expressing their opinions, probably encouraged by their improved abilities of constructing (relatively) error-free sentences in English. This reiterates the notion that 'linguistic and communicative competence manifests itself in language behaviour receptively and productively' (Stern 1983: 344). The occasional use of L1 vocabulary in the writings of the learners varies, and instructors should encourage the learners to express themselves in the best way available to them. This further leads to democratization of teaching where students' conditions are reflected in the teaching/learning context. However, because of the limited time-frame, it is important that English remains the prominent language of discourse in classroom. It was observed that the participants of the 'parallel course' respond better when there is sufficient instrumental motivation and when their sociolinguistic (learning with peers vs learning with the teacher) preferences are taken into account.

Scope for Further Research

English empowers and breaks the caste/class boundaries, thus facilitating the upward mobility of the underprivileged students. This fact should be taken as a positive reason enough to launch further studies.

Future researchers can work at exploring the *process approach* wholly or in part, to teach writing. Research scholars/teachers can attempt developing *short/long-term collaborative writing projects*, where writing is considered 'a literacy event' (Nunan 1992: 104). Collaborative writing can lead to projects that are more challenging and complex than those produced by individual learners.

Collaborative groups draw upon the strengths of the individual members in a group. For instance, one member may excel in critical thinking and may generate ideas, while other may be strong in vocabulary and/or syntax. Further research can therefore focus on the impact of collaborative writings on the overall performance of the students. To ensure the successful functioning of collaborative group, the teacher/researcher should ensure that all group members understand the assignment, decide on the major features of the project, and agree on the goals of the writing project. Next, the tasks should be divided among the members of the group. Nevertheless each member shares responsibility for the whole product. The writing project should be duly revised and drafted according to schedules, and procedures can be established for reviewing each other's components as they are written. Collaborative writing can also draw from built-in peer review. Cooperative learning promotes effective instruction of thinking skills and creativity.

Some of the web resources for fostering collaborative writing projects, such as *MoonEdit, Reduce, WikiWiki Web* and *Writerly* can be used as an effective tool for empowering the learners. Collaborative writing is especially useful for students from science/management background, where a significant portion of technical writing is done not by individuals but by different groups. Analysing verbal interaction among the members of a collaborative writing group during the writing process can also yield vital information about the cognitive/affective factors at play while writing. Future researchers can also look at the chapter on Interpretation of data and concentrate on developing any of the three areas of thrust: grammar, vocabulary and organization.

Understanding individual frustrations of the ESL writing students is another area which can be investigated into. The teacher/researcher can attempt to understand the phenomenon of negative attitude towards writing in English, its causes, and suggest solutions, if possible. The internet can be intensively exploited to explore the area of web-based teaching, through which students are taught how to write different writing genres.

Conclusion

Writing is an essential skill and its position cannot be undermined. For the students of the PC at the IITM it is their lifeline, which can enable them to get integrated in the mainstream courses, therefore, preparing these learners to write in English, is a responsibility which no teacher of the PC can afford to ignore. Continuous research of this nature, therefore, should be encouraged.

Works Cited

Allwright Dick and Bailey, Katherine M., *Focus on the Language Classroom*, Cambridge: Cambridge University Press, 1991.

Fathman Ann K. and Whalley Elizabeth, 'Teacher Response to Student Writing: Focus on form Versus Content', Second Language Writing, Barbara Kroll ed., Cambridge: CUP, 1990.

Nunan David, *Collaborative Language Learning and Teaching*, Cambridge: CUP, 1992.

Sherman Jane, *Feedback*, Oxford: Oxford University Press, 1994.

Singh Damyanti, NEST—*A Programme on Need-based English for Science and Technology*, Language Studies Unit, Curriculum Development Cell, Kanpur: Indian Institute of Technology, 1990.

Stern H.H., *Fundamental Concepts of Language Teaching*, Oxford: Oxford University Press, 1983.

'Syllabus Reforms in India, Recommendations of the UGC National Workshop 1976-77', New Delhi: University Grants Commission.

Tudor Ian, *The Dynamics of the Language Classroom*, Cambridge: Cambridge University Press, 2001.

Tyson Rodney, 'Peer Review and Sense of Community in Academic Writing', IATEFL *Brighton Conference Selections*, 2003.

Watson Cynthia, 'Models in Writing Class', *TESOL Quarterly*, No. 1, Vol. 16, 1982.

19

Error Correction Strategies for ESL Student Writing

Anam Govardhan

Introduction

Writing is the most important language skill used for effective communication in the literate world. Yet, it is also one of the last language skills a student learns in a formal classroom. In spite of its importance, teaching writing skills receives the least attention both at school and college levels. A cursory look at the funding and scheduling of classes at every level of education shows that neither the policy-makers nor the administrators treat teaching writing on par with teaching other subjects like biology, chemistry, mathematics, sociology, psychology, etc. Due to the low priority accorded to teaching writing at the college and university levels in the United States, it is not uncommon to find the least experienced in the English departments or part-time instructors, or graduate assistants being assigned to teach writing. The priority assigned to teaching writing does not appear to be different in other countries like India, Nigeria, Malaysia, etc.

Several studies have shown that while listening and speaking skills can be acquired by both native speakers and second language learners through exposure and interaction with speakers of a language, writing and reading require specific training because neither of them is entirely linguistic (Taylor 1976). To be able to write on a paper or slate, a student must have muscular coordination; likewise, to compose on a computer, he or she must have keyboard experience. In addition, he or she should know the invention techniques, process of selection, organization of ideas, and rhetorical rules applicable in a specific language to reflect his or her experience adequately (Arapoff 1967). In other words, to know how to write successfully even in a first language, a student has to learn separate sets of rules applicable to the rhetoric of the language, grammar, and organizational structure of the text. In the case of a student learning English as a second language (ESL), he or she has to acquire 'what amounts to a new language at least the language of standard edited English and perhaps even formal academic English' (Raimes 2). Even assuming that an ESL student is subjected to rigorous training to master writing skills, we cannot be sure whether what he or she produces in writing is effective because the effectiveness of writing does not depend on how much rigorous the training one has undergone, or how much time one has spent on a piece of writing, but on how relevant and well-organized the facts are, and how well the writer has used the various rhetorical strategies to persuade a reader.

While both native speakers of English and English as second language learners have almost equal level of difficulty in acquiring writing skills, writing instructors do not make the acquisition of writing skills easier for either of them. The difficulty, according to Blair (1983), often arises out of instructors focusing on form or structure to the exclusion of content and rhetorical principles under the assumption that the student writers begin as architects and therefore, should be forced to inhabit pre-fabricated houses to learn how houses are built (4-5). Unfortunately, the focus on form leads to emphasizing the final product to the exclusion of the several stages in the composing process. The over-emphasis on the final product also leads to the intolerance of 'errors' and 'mistakes' in student writing as reflected in the 'bloodied' student papers. Therefore, I would like to focus in this paper on assumptions about errors, on strategies used to correct errors, and their implications for teaching writing.

Assumptions about Errors

In 1950s and 60s, the structural linguists popularized audio lingual method of teaching English as a second language. Under its influence, the language teacher assumed that the relationship of 'error' to 'learning' resembled that of 'sin' to 'virtue'. According to this method, ESL students are required to avoid errors in their writing by all means (Brooks 58). Unfortunately, in order to produce error free sentences, a learner has to observe and practice the right model many times. At the same time, the writing instructor is expected to prevent mistakes from occurring in the first place by drilling the correct structures in the class, and if a mistake is committed by a student, the instructor is required to correct it at once, and then repeat the correct pattern several times for the benefit of the whole class.

The structural linguists also introduced the concept 'contrastive analysis', according to which, a teacher can predict that the students are likely to commit mistakes in the second language if it differs vastly from the structure of the target language. In addition, the contrastive analysis helps to identify the difficulties of the second language learner in speaking and writing to 'interference' from specific aspects of his or her first language. The interference, according to Richards (1971), refers to learner's use of strategies of assimilation and strategies of communication (212).

In the late 1960s, studies in transformational generative grammar and cognitive psychology paved the way for the emergence of 'error analysis'. The error analysis deals with the differences between the way people learning a language 'speak' and the way adult native speakers of the language 'use' the language. From an initial stage of cautious enquiry, 'error analysis' has now become a well-developed technique useful in determining the sequence of development in second language acquisition (Dulay and Burt 130). As a result, there is a perceptible change in the attitude of the language teacher, who is no longer 'a revenge thirsty monster wielding pen and red ink to bloody a stunned freshman's paper' (Kroll and Schafer 243). Instead, teachers view errors as offering exceptionally interesting clues to the linguistic and cognitive processes. Corder (1967) has rightly observed that one cannot learn without goofing. Today, teachers recognize the fact that ESL students are bound to commit errors like children learning their first language, and therefore, the errors they (ESL students) commit should not cause undue concern. This attitude among language teachers has led to a shift in the pedagogical focus from preventing errors to learning from errors.

Types and Sources of Errors

Selinker (1967) traces errors in a second language student writer to the developing 'interlanguage' of that student, and therefore the errors should be viewed as proof of that student's developing proficiency in a second language. According to this theory, a learner views the second language through the prism of his or her first language, and slowly moves toward the second language. In the process, he or she has to go through a stage (interlanguage) when both the linguistic systems are at work. The mistake a learner commits at this stage should be viewed as evidence of progress towards the second/target language. This view shows the progress that has been made from the 'contrastive analysis', which identifies mother tongue interference as the source of many errors in second language learning. By using the 'contrastive analysis', the errors in the usage of articles by the Japanese and Koreans are traced to the absence of articles in those languages (Duffin 1977). Similarly, the frequent dropping of definite article in the writing of Indian students is traced to the lack of rigid distinction between definite and indefinite articles in several Indian languages. Likewise, the errors in word order and sentence construction in ESL writing of Czech students are traced to their mother tongue (Duskova 27). Dulay and Burt (1974) also refer to the interference of Spanish in the learning of English by Spanish speaking children (132). However, these findings are inconclusive as some researches contend that a writer's writing skills in the first language, instead of being a hindrance, forms the basis of new hypothesis in a second language (Edelsky 1982).

We also have ample evidence to suggest that errors in ESL student writing are viewed differently by teachers depending on whether they are native or non-native speakers of English. Some researches (Corder, 1967; Selinker, 1967; Kroll and Schafer, 1977; Raimes, 1978; and Zamel, 1985) suggest that writing instructors should look at 'errors' and 'mistakes' in ESL students' writing problems differently. The 'errors' are those that interfere with the understanding of the message while 'mistakes' are those that are attributed to a learner's failure to use his or her linguistic proficiency of the second language. Non-native teachers of English, who may not know the expectations of native English teachers, tend to focus on sentence level problems and accommodate their students' rhetorical differences. The way one looks at 'errors' and 'mistakes' also differs depending on who is looking at the writing samples and the purpose of the writing task. For example, Kantor, and Powers (2002) report that raters, who participated in their survey, used the following criteria while grading ESL student writing: (a) rhetorical organization, including introductory statements, development, cohesion, and fulfilment of writing task, (b) expression of ideas, logic, argumentation, clarity, uniqueness and supporting points, (c) accuracy and fluency of English grammar, and vocabulary (d) amount of text. Therefore, an ESL student is required to focus not only on the sentence level grammar and development of ideas, but also on the rhetorical conventions in the second language, which are not widely taught in the classroom.

Error Correction Strategies

Structural linguists' contribution to language pedagogy is very significant. In spite of the negative aspects of 'contrastive analysis', we need to acknowledge its importance in compiling an inventory of the areas of difficulty which a student faces in learning a second language and to which a teacher may direct his/her attention. Similarly, 'error analysis' has helped ESL teachers to broaden their understanding of 'errors' and their significance in acquiring a second language. As a result, an ESL teacher may expect his or her students to commit them whey they write in English as the 'mistakes' and 'errors' help the teacher to gauge the progress a student makes towards acquiring the second language.

A review of literature on 'error correction' also suggests that a systematic analysis of 'mistakes' and 'errors' provides useful insights into the process of language acquisition, and therefore, a teacher's correction strategies should be such as not to embarrass or frustrate students. Experienced teachers are also aware that students receive positive feedback favorably and mostly ignore the negative feedback. Since learning a second language in a classroom environment depends on a student's needs to learn it, his or her attitude towards the target language, and his or her experience in learning a language in the past, research in error correction suggests that ESL teachers need to take into account the attitudes, motivation, personality and past language learning history of ESL students before providing feedback to them (Cardelle and Corno 1981).

The field of 'error correction' is still a developing one. In the absence of findings of empirical research to determine how different error correction strategies affect a student's developing proficiency in the second language, ESL teachers are unsure whether 'all second language errors be assigned an equal status within any given learner's grammar, and which of the student's errors be corrected and how to correct them' (Hendrickson 1976:1). Harris and Silva (1993) answer ESL teachers' dilemma when they suggest that the errors should be categorized as linguistic deficiency, rhetorical differences, and performance related, and each one of them should be addressed depending on its effect on successful communication.

In the past, a traditional language teacher (corrective analyst) would have circled an error in red, explained its seriousness, and warned the students against repeating it. On the other hand, a 'contrastive analyst' would have attributed the same error to the interference of the learner's first language. Today, an 'error analyst' will accept the interference factor but recognizes that a learner is not passive and a slave to his first language. Also, the 'error analyst' will attribute the error to the application of wrong strategy and try to help the learner to overcome the confusion arising out of over-generalization. The error analyst is also confident that the errors are likely to disappear only if teachers guide students to see all the different routes that led them to the error in the first place (Kroll and Schafer 244-245).

Under the influence of 'error analysis', there is a perceptible change in the psychology of language pedagogy among ESL teachers. The emphasis has shifted from the 'product approach' of the contrastive analysts to the 'process approach' of error analysts. Errors are no longer studied to produce taxonomy of what errors learners make. Instead, errors are studied in order to find out a psycho-linguistic explanation of why a learner commits an error. Also, instead of attacking individual errors and try to eliminate them through drill, error analysts try to find out the source of the non-standard forms in ESL student writing. Furthermore, errors are not viewed as a result of the failure to learn the correct form. Instead, they are attributed to learner's ignorance of rule restriction, incomplete rule application, excessive use of over-generalization, and inappropriate use of hypothesis to arrive at false concepts. Finally, writing instructors perspective has also shifted from teaching to eliminate the errors to learning from them with the aim of supporting a student's active learning strategies.

In spite of the importance given to error correction in second language teaching, no current standards exist on whether, when, which, or how student errors should be corrected or who should correct them. There are a few widely accepted linguistic criteria to correct grammatical and lexical errors, and much of what has been published is yet to be empirically investigated. Hendrickson (1978) tries to answer the five fundamental questions confronting the second language teachers. He contends that just like parents who correct the errors of their children in a gentle manner, teachers need to correct the errors of the students in a friendly manner, for such an approach to correction helps the learner to discover the functions and limitations of the syntactical and lexical forms of the target language. Secondly, Hendrickson warns that drawing the attention of students to every error they make will not guarantee that they will not repeat them and hence, the teachers should consider which ones are to be corrected and which ones are to be overlooked. Thirdly, according to him, only the 'global errors' that affect the intelligibility of the message needs to be corrected. Fourthly, the teacher should avoid using correction strategies that might embarrass or frustrate a learner. Lastly, Hendrickson advocates peer correction as it might help the learners to recognize errors in a friendlier atmosphere (389-391).

Wingfield (1975) also suggests five less intimidating techniques to correct errors in the writing of ESL students. According to him, the teacher should provide clues to enable the learner to make self-correction. He follows it by correcting the script, and providing marginal comments and footnotes. When needed, the teacher orally explains the errors to individual students, and finally, he uses the error as an illustration for a class explanation (312).

According to Duke (1975), personalized instruction to correct errors in student writing will work successfully. Unfortunately, such a strategy has very limited application in large composition classes. On the other hand, Blair (1983) suggests that writing instructors should engage ESL students in a meaningful and often personalized writing before requiring them to write on academic topics. Such a strategy may work in remedial writing classes, which are normally restricted to 15-20 students in a class but not in a large class with students of varying abilities. Self-correction and peer review are also advocated as means to bring awareness in ESL students about their problems in writing. As per this view, such awareness will lead students to develop their own strategies to overcome them. The problem with this strategy is highlighted by Wingfield (1975), who observes that though self-correction is the best way to extinguish an error, it may also lead to confusion if the students are not provided with the clues. Therefore, he suggests that a teacher may talk to students individually about the errors they commit, and if there is an error sufficiently common for the whole class, the class may be given a quick drill exercise to consolidate the explanation (311-313). Even this strategy has limited application as several studies have shown that 'rote learning' and 'drill exercises' do not eliminate errors in ESL student writing completely.

Till now, we have seen only the error-correction strategies. However, we also have a few researchers suggesting error-avoiding strategies. For example, we notice that most errors in the writing of ESL students refer to 'form' and an excessive emphasis on 'form' is bound to make a student to look at writing as a 'mechanical act of transcribing one's ideas, when the language itself rather than the purposes for which the language is used becomes the focus' (Zamel 198). Therefore, if the emphasis on 'form' is lessened, the students will have an opportunity to explore the invention techniques and use writing to discover meaning, which is what writing is all about. In other words, the teacher in the ESL writing class should respond 'not so much to student writing but to student writers' (Zamel 97). This strategy requires ESL writing teachers to spend as much time on 'invention' techniques as they currently do on 'language'. In order to teach both of the above, ESL teachers engaged in teaching writing need to have more freedom, resources, smaller classes, and support of the administration.

Conclusion

Writing in English is a complex and difficult task for both native and non-native speakers of English. Also, there is no foolproof method which prevents errors from occurring in ESL writing. However, over the years the ESL teacher's attitude towards a learner's errors has changed and teachers do not frown upon errors any longer. Instead, they consider the errors significant as they throw light on the strategies used by the learner to acquire writing skills.

Though the literature on error correction in ESL writing is quite speculative and relatively scant, some implications for error correction with regard to whether, when, which, how, and by whom can be drawn from the observations made by Wingfield (1975) and Hendrickson (1978). Also, since the aim in the ESL writing class is to facilitate the acquisition of writing skills, the following error correction strategies, in my opinion, will be found useful:

(a) Creating a supportive classroom environment in which the teacher plays the roles of facilitator, consultant, or motivator can make students feel confident to express their ideas and feelings without worrying about errors (Wess 5).

(b) The correction of errors that have stigmatizing effects upon the listener or reader and frequently occurring errors will help the learner to write more acceptable English (Hendrickson 396).

(c) Peer correction or self-correction with teacher's guidance will be very useful too (Wess 5).

(d) Needs analysis of ESL students' expectations and clear understanding of curriculum objectives. It may also be helpful to write instructions in planning lessons and activities facilitating the successful teaching of writing.

Works Cited

Arapoff Nancy, 'Writing: A Thinking Process', *TESOL Quarterly,* 11.1. 1967, pp. 59-67.

Blair Linda, 'ESL Students and Writing Acquisition Theory', *Education Resources Information Center Document,* <http://www.eric.ed.gov.search> (ED242196), 1983.

Brookes Nelson H., *Language and Language Learning,* New York: Harcourt Brace Jovanovich, 1960.

Cardelle Maria and Lyn Corno, 'Effects on Second Language Learning of Variations in Written Feedback on Homework Assignments', *TESOL Quarterly,* 15.3. 1981, pp. 251-261.

Corder S.P., 'The Significance of Learners' Errors', *International Review of Applied Linguistics,* Vol. 5, 1967, pp. 161-9.

Cummings Alister Robert Kantor and Donald E. Powers, 'Decision-Making While Rating ESL/EFL Writing Tasks: A Descriptive Framework', *The Modern Language Journal* 86.1. 2002, pp. 67-96.

Duffin Beryl, 'A Study of Writing Problems in a Remedial Program for EOP Students', *Education Resources Information Center* (1977). <http://www.eric.ed.gov.search> (ED 153 473).

Duke Charles R., 1975:9, 'The Student-Centered Conference and the Writing Process', *The English Journal,* 64.9, December, 1975, pp. 44-47.

Dulay Heidi C. and Marina K. Burt, 'Errors and Strategies in Child Second Language Acquisition', *TESOL Quarterly,* 8.2. 1974, pp. 129-136.

Dulay Heidi C. and Marina K. Burt, 'Error Analysis in the Adult EFL Classroom', *TESOL Quarterly,* 9.1. 1975, pp. 53-63.

Duskova Libuse, 'On Sources of Errors in Foreign Language Learning', IRAL, Vol. 7. 1969, pp. 11-36.

Edelsky Carole, 'Writing in a Bilingual Programme: The Relation of L1 and L2 Texts', *TESOL Quarterly,* 16.2. 1982, pp. 211-228.

Harris Muriel and Tony Silva, 'Tutoring ESL Students: Issues and Options', *College Composition and Communication,* 44.4. December, 1993, pp. 525-537.

Hendrickson James, 'Error Analysis and Selective Correction in the Adult ESL Classroom: An Experiment', *Education Resources Information Center* (1976), <http://www.eric.ed.gov.search> (ED 135 260).

Hendrickson James, 'Error Correction in Foreign Language: Recent Theory, Research, and Practice', *Modern Langauge Journal*, 62.8, 1978, pp. 387-398.

Kroll Barry M. and John C. Schafer, 1977:2, 'Error-Analysis and the Teaching of Composition', *College Composition and Communication,* 29.3, 1978, pp. 242-248.

Raimes Ann, 'Problems and Teaching Strategies in ESL Composition', *Education Resources Information Center,* (1978):2. <http://www.eric.ed.gov.search> (ED 145 482).

Richards Jack C., 'A Non-Contrastive Approach to Error Analysis', *English Language Teaching,* 25. 1971, pp. 204-219.

Selinker Larry, 'Language Transfer', *General Linguistics,* Vol. 9. 1969, pp. 67-92.

Taylor Robert. C., 'Errors and Explanations', *Applied Linguistics* 7.2, 1986, pp. 144-166.

Wess Robert C., 'Publishing Student Writing: An In-class Model', *Education Resources Information Center,* (1979): 5, <http://www.eric.ed.gov.search> (ED 185564).

Wingfield R.J., 'Five Ways of Dealing with Errors', *English Language Teaching Journal,* Vol. 29, 1975, pp. 311-313.

Zamel Vivian, 'Writing: The Process of Discovering Meaning', *TESOL Quarterly*, 16.2, 1982, pp. 195-209.

Zamel Vivian, 'Responding to Student Writing', *TESOL Quarterly*, 19.1, 1985, pp. 79-101.

20

Involving Learners in the Assessment Process: A Case Study of Disadvantaged Learners

V. Saraswathi

Let us travel down memory lane and go back to our student days. Each one of us remembers cherished moments of ecstasy as well as nightmares of agony. The anxious, tension-ridden waiting for the results, the frustration and disappointment at getting a score much below our expectations or the pleasant surprise of performing much better than we had anticipated—these form an inevitable part of our student lives. Examinations constituted the necessary evil, a part of the process of growing up and we had learnt to live with them—at least those of us who were brave enough. The shy, diffident, quieter ones amongst us have often contemplated suicide on getting the results, and some have unfortunately succeeded in it as well.

Assessment in yesteryears had the finality of death. Its purpose was to distinguish the sheep from the goats, nothing more, nothing less. If you scored the first marks, you became the instant hero. If you failed you were branded as dumb and imbecile and became the butt of everyone's ridicule. With the advent of humanistic psychology, however, the practice of assessment has undergone a sea-change. The instructional value of testing has gained significance. According to Brennan 'the process of evaluation is wasted if the information is merely recorded and no further action is taken. The whole purpose is that of refinement of the curricular process, of education: consequently the outcomes, of evaluation must feedback as action in relation to the process, the pupil, or both' (19:93).

This change in attitude to assessment is supplemented by a change in attitude to errors as well. One need no longer be ashamed of making mistakes. Errors form an inevitable part of language acquisition. In fact, it may be argued 'No errors – no learning'. A lot of things that we call mistakes can also be seen as learning steps. Students should be encouraged to experiment with language so that they can take more learning steps. When my student comes out with his own coinage and says 'braveness' instead of bravery, I am no longer upset or angry but try to understand the way the grammar construction process works in his idiosyncratic dialect. If Shakespeare could 'But me no buts' why can't my learner also be creative?

These attitudinal changes, however, have not yet percolated to the classroom, where the real action takes place. Most of our Indian classrooms continue to be quite traditional in their approach to testing. Teachers are strict and distant and learners are scared. Examination fever still remains very much of a reality, more so for the disadvantaged learner. For the purposes of this study we would accept Gulliford's definition of a slow learner as 'of average or good intelligence' but with a 'marked discrepancy between their educational achievements and their ability as judged by intelligence tests or their general performance in everyday affairs or non-academic aspects of schooling'. According to Brennan 'slow learners are defined as pupils who do not have above average intellectual ability or severe intellectual retardation or any other primary handicap but who are unable to cope with school work considered normal for their age group ... they may exhibit some insecurity arising from their exercises of failure' (1974:16). He also suggests that further improvements depends upon the development of a more rational and continually planned approach to the provision of facilities for slow learners, mainly within the ordinary schools.

We have used the case study approach to explore an alternative approach to assessment that would promote language acquisition in slow learners by involving them in the process of assessment. Three slow learners from I year B.A. Economics class of a City College constitute the sample. We have attempted to involve them in the process of evaluation through the adoption of various technical strategies discussed below. We strongly believe that such enlistment of learner participation in the assessment will,

(a) increase learners' confidence in themselves,
(b) involve them in the process of 'learning to learn' and ultimately,
(c) promote L2 acquisition.

Earlier we had pointed out that examinations are a 'necessary evil'. They are necessary because they serve as an indicator of progress and offer feedback to the curriculum framers. And they are evil because of their side effects that cripple learning. Examiners are accused, often rightly, of being prejudiced and impressionistic. Unfortunately, first impressions are not always the best impressions, but teachers are trapped by them.

Research studies reveal that teachers' ratings are coloured by their attitudes towards learners. These attitudes and general impressions may be based on just a few key criteria such as frequency of hand raising, frequency of correct answers or frequency of time –wasting. This prejudice is further aggravated when the learner knows what the teacher thinks of him. It sets in motion the 'self-fulfilling prophecy' (Insel and Jacobson 1975). When the teacher constantly tells the slow learners that they are lazy and stupid, they often gradually adjust their behaviour so as to conform to the teacher's image of them. Their self-esteem, receptiveness and level of aspiration are all adversely affected, and they cease to take efforts to learn. One of the magnificent obsessions of student life is to get good grades in order to get the approval of others. The disadvantaged learner has to get used to the disapproval on the other hand; this demotivates him and destroys any enthusiasm he might have had. The ethos of competitive assessment gradually turns a failure in academics into a failure as a person. Dr Samuel Johnson pointed out: 'by exciting emulation and comparisons of superiority, you lay the foundation of lasting mischief; you make brothers and sisters hate each other.' Marks and grades are often impersonal and 'hopelessly inadequate to convey the load of meaning that we sometimes believe we are putting into them and which other people desperately try to get out from them again' (Rowntree, 1979: 70).

If marks and grades have such pernicious effects, perhaps it is time we explored other ways of assessment. Chater suggests that teachers could share responsibility for assessment with learners. Pupils may be encouraged to read, mark and discuss each other's work. Ultimately from peer evaluation, they can graduate to self-assessment. This weans them away from a total dependence on the teacher's judgment and develops in them a sense of confidence about the use of language.

The focus of assessment could shift from measurement to description. Marks emphasize the ranking of children in the order of merit, and establish how different one learner is from another. Descriptive assessment, on the other hand looks at the individual in his/her own right, rather than in comparison with others. Here is a sample assessment of a fifth form student: 'I see, Jane that you have taken much more care this time with presentation. Addresses, date, etc. are exactly right. You have also provided plenty of information about your qualifications and reasons for applying for the job —this is well-expressed and arranged. If you received this letter, would the applicant get the job? Read it aloud, then we can discuss what improvements you might make' (Chater 1984: 21).

In the light of the discussion above, we conducted a few case studies. Three weak learners from I year B.A. Economics 1996-97 class of Ethiraj College, Chennai were selected. They had studied through the medium of Tamil at school; in the college, they had chosen to write their examinations in Tamil even though the teaching was mainly done in English. They were asked to write a set of free compositions. As a first step towards self-assessment they were asked to engage in peer evaluation. Later the teacher sat with each one of them and gave them an oral descriptive evaluation.

Here are a few sample corrections: Essay on 'Violence in Films'

* Why are birth in violence, why are end in violence in see the film.
This is modified by their peers as 'How the violence started and ends...

* 'Because they lose their on our education. All people start following the violence method. So the violence scene spoiling our future life.' This was modified by their companion as 'Moreover, they are not interested in education. All people start following the violence. Violent scenes spoil their future life.'

These corrections, of course, do not indicate a significant improvement to the original version. At best it marginally clarifies the writer's intent. But that is beside the point. For the main purpose of the exercise was not language acquisition, but rather awareness raising and confidence building. The students were able to identify at least some errors, in their peer's work. And they had developed enough self-confidence to say boldly that these were errors. Later when the researcher accepted their versions, there was a sea change in their attitude; their self-image rose high. Their dignity as human beings were restored. No longer they were the downtrodden, at whom fingers pointed; now they too could point out others' mistakes. This revelation has done tremendous good to their ego. Now, in classes they no longer remain the silent spectators. They have the courage to stand up and ask for clarifications when they don't understand what the teacher says. We have not as yet asked them to do any self-assessment; it is evident that they are moving in that direction. They are willing to revise their work before submission and make corrections, where they think necessary. In the ten tasks they have written, there has been a definite improvement between the first and the last tasks. This suggests the development of the ability for self-assessment.

This small research project as well as the researcher's experience of teaching disadvantaged learners for nearly three decades has enabled her to arrive at certain strategies for assessment, when promoting learning.

1. Encourage the Learners – Don't Frustrate Them

This could be done by pointing out their strengths before moving on to their shortcomings. Each learner has some skill he is proud of: good vocabulary, neat handwriting or mastery over spelling. Consider remarks like the following. 'Ram, your spelling is excellent. Why don't you improve your handwriting next time?' Such comments are sure to touch a chord in the learner's heart. He feels happy that at last he is being recognized as an individual. This makes him feel good. Now he attains a frame of mind which can accept criticisms. 'If you recognize what's good in me, I can accept what you think is bad about me.'

2. Give Detailed Comments in Addition to Marks

Descriptive assessment appeals to a learner's intellect as well as emotions. It could help him in the process of self-actualization. Consider for instance, a learner who receives his/her answer script with a mark 2 out of 10, and a remark 'This simply won't do'. Unwilling to digest this, the learner jumps to conclusions. He is sure that the teacher is biased and doesn't like him. Or worse still he thinks that the teacher has not bothered to look through his script carefully. A detailed comment as outlined above is sure to prevent such a possibility.

3. Involve Learners in Evaluation

As tried out in the experiment reported above, learners could get slowly interested in peer evaluation and self-assessment. This is sure to raise their self-confidence and also restore their faith in the teacher's sense of justice and fair play. In fact, it may be worthwhile beginning learner training at the evaluation end, as the wash back effect of evaluation on the curriculum is significant.

4. Let your Evaluation Instruct, not Punish

It would be better if the teacher–assessor dons the role of the defence counsel rather than the judge. His/her duty is not to sentence errant learners but rather understand them and protect them. The feedback should be educative rather than retributive. A learner should be given opportunities to learn from his mistakes, not reel under them.

A proper approach to assessment, on the lines of participative pedagogy is bound to prove a source of empowerment for the disadvantaged learner. Let us struggle with some humanism in evaluating our disadvantaged learner. Then language acquisition is sure to take care of itself. As the old Chinese verse goes 'Tell me and I'll remember; teach me, I'll understand; involve me and I'll learn; share my concern and I'll change'.

Work Cited

Chater Pantine, *Marking and Assessment in English,* London: Methwin, 1984.

Brennan W.K., *Shaping the Education of Slow Learners,* London: Routledge & Kegan Paul, 1974.

Rowntree Derek, *Assessing Students: How Shall we know them?* London: Harper & Row Ltd., 1979.

Saraswathi V., 'Learner Evaluation: A Humanistic Approach', *The Journal of English Language Teaching,* Vol. 31, 6 November–December 1996.

21

Assessment and Motivation in English Language Teaching

S. Devaki Reddy

The success of a teaching programme depends not only on the content and methodology of a course but also on assessment. Besides the design of a course, learners' abilities as well as their attitude, referred to as the cognitive and affective dimensions of learning, influence the outcome of the course (Gardner and Macintyre 1992, 1993). Stating that learning can be said to have taken place when language *input* results in language *intake*, Lewis (1993: 25) underlines the importance of several factors including affective factors such as students' attitude and motivation. Several other studies have emphasized the role of motivation for success in language learning (Gardner & Lambert 1972; Niederhauser 1997; Dornyei 1998 cited in Rubdy 2002). Learners' motivation, in turn, may be influenced by assessment (Stern and Solomon 2006). This article describes how assessment was used with a view to promote learner motivation in a course in English offered to university students.

Assessment and its Testing

The terms 'assessment' and 'testing' have been defined differently, with some language practitioners making a clear distinction, and others using them interchangeably (Clapham 2000). In this paper, *assessment* is used as an umbrella term for observing student performance whereas a test means an instrument used to assess students. Further, a distinction is made between formal and informal tests. A formal test is administered on specified dates and is usually standardized, such as a mid-semester or annual examination, whereas an informal test is administered by a teacher in the classroom and is often unannounced. An informal test may or may not be scored, but the marks are not included for the award of the final grade. Formal tests are scored, and the marks included for the final grade.

Tests can be Helpful

Tests are rarely perceived as pleasant tasks. In fact, in several countries, tests such as the public examinations at the end of school are considered so significant that they drive teaching and learning, a phenomenon referred to as *washback* (Bachman 1991; Taylor 2005). In some schools, the entire final term is devoted to helping students 'revise' the portions on which students may be tested in the exam.

Tests, however, can be very useful. As Welsh and Metcalf (2003) observe, assessment may evoke negative reactions, but the right kind of assessment 'is much more palatable and easier to swallow when one knows that real results and important information are brought to light as a result of this activity' (cited in Stern and Solomon 2006:23). Describing the advantages of taking tests, Barrett (2004:5) states that 'tests do not prove that you cannot do something. They can only suggest that you could do something'.

Tests can be used to assess students' strengths and weaknesses so that the course of instruction can effectively address the needs of the learners. The information can also be used to measure students' progress after a phase of instruction. Called diagnostic tests, such tests are usually given at the beginning of a course. When designing a diagnostic test, attention is usually paid to known or predicted areas of particular difficulty for the learner. (Davies et al., 1999).

Informal tests in the formative stage of a learning programme are believed to be reliable indicators of a learner's proficiency. Describing the importance of informal tests, Tomlinson (2005: 43) observes that 'it is much fairer to test typical performance than to treat stressed performance as real'.

Tests may also be administered periodically to determine whether a learner has learnt what has been taught. Such tests are called *achievement tests*. To ensure effective learning, therefore, it is recommended that 'courses are best designed to include a variety of assessment techniques' (Heywod 2000:149).

Motivation

Tests may also be used to motivate learners. Motivation relates to a person's willingness to do something. A person's interest in an activity in anticipation of external rewards such as verbal praise, prizes or good grades in an examination is termed extrinsic motivation. When an individual is driven to do something because of a desire for self-fulfilment or to achieve feelings of self-worth, he/she is said to be intrinsically motivated (Rubdy 2002).

Several factors can affect a learner's motivation. Studies have asserted that motivation and success are positively correlated although it is not clear whether motivation leads to success or success enhances motivation (Lightbown and Spada 2003). Assessment practices do play a role in motivating learners (Norris 2000). Positive assessment experiences can motivate people to learn further and build on their strengths while negative assessment experiences can discourage people from future efforts. Negative experiences may range from a failed driving test to getting lower grades than expected (Haines 2004: 10).

Motivation is said to increase when tests challenge a learner, highlight the gaps in the learner's knowledge and indicate what he/she has to know at a particular stage in the learning process. When learners become keen on improving their performance, learning may become an end in itself. In other words, learners may be intrinsically motivated. Second language learning is a cyclical process. According to Gan et al. (2004) strong motivation, positive attitudes, and effective learning effort may result in 'increased language attainment and the feeling of progress, which may in turn enhance motivation and facilitate further effort' (cited in Inozu et al., 2007).

The Teaching Context

This part of the paper describes how testing was used in a course titled 'English for communication' offered to students in an undergraduate programme, where the medium of instruction was English. The objective of the course was to help students improve their written and spoken communication skills. The paper, however, focuses on the efforts to help improve students' grammatical knowledge, and the tests used for this purpose.

The students in the course are high achievers in school, as admission to the institute is based on a national competitive exam. Some students who score good marks in English in their school-final exams feel that they do not need further instruction in English. The course also has some students with low levels of motivation for various other reasons. Diagnostic tests have helped us understand that there is often no correlation between high scores in English and students' performance in the test. The tests have also helped to overcome the challenge of teaching such students and provided insights for the designing of the course.

Methodology

In the first week of the course, after the course objectives were explained, the students were asked to write essays on specified topics. This was the first informal test. In the following class, students were given another test. Handouts containing correct and incorrect sentences were distributed in class. The sentences were illustrative of the errors commonly made by students. Students were asked to distinguish between correct and incorrect sentences. At this stage, the students were not required to correct the sentences or identify the errors. The answers were then supplied and the students were asked to put down their scores on their sheets. Students were very happy when they got good scores. However, when they realized that they had been unable to identify an incorrect sentence, they were eager for an explanation.

The next stage involved correcting the sentences. Students were often able to correct the sentences, without being able to describe the error. When asked if they were aware of the reason for correcting a sentence, some of them stated that the sentence did not 'sound' correct. From my experience of teaching the course over several semesters, I have observed that students very rarely get all the answers right, establishing the relevance of instruction in this area. In the following classes, the nature of the errors in different sentences was discussed and illustrated with more examples. For example, texts were used to show how the use of different tenses, voice or pronouns affect the meaning in communication. Students began to realize that there were aspects of language that they needed to learn about. As the test was informal, students were not anxious about their performance. Many of them began to participate in classroom discussions. The exercise also provided an opportunity to draw students' attention to the importance of grammatical accuracy. The teaching of grammar continued through the semester, sometimes through explicit instruction and sometimes by contextualizing it. During the course, students were taught to write effective paragraphs, essays, reports and reviews and made to understand the significance of different aspects of writing skills, including grammatical knowledge.

By around the third week of the programme, the essays written by the students were corrected and returned. The scores, however, were not written on the students' scripts. Separate scores were given for the content of the essays and grammatical accuracy. Students were called individually and shown the scores for each of the parameters (Appendix 3, column 2, indicates the marks for grammar). Further, sentences that contained different types of errors were picked from the students' essays. Students were given a generalized feedback, without specific reference to any individual. The students were then asked to edit their own writing. This provided an opportunity for students to apply what they had learnt. After students had acquired a little familiarity with various concepts, they were given written texts that had errors in them to correct and improve. Students were also asked to assess the writing of their peers. I have observed that their ability to identify and correct errors gave them a sense of mastery and the confidence that they could progress in their learning.

Tests were thus used not only for assessing students' achievement but also to enable them to discover the gaps in their grammatical knowledge. A lack of awareness, for example, may explain why students used expressions such as 'listened the news'. Students' attention was drawn to aspects of English grammar such as the use of transitive and intransitive verbs. When they were made to understand, for example, that an intransitive verb is not followed by an object and were taught how to find the information about the verb in a dictionary, they were able to appreciate the significance of the knowledge.

Students were also told about other sources of information about language such as websites and books. Using tests to teach concepts and directing them to websites also helped to utilize class time effectively and promote independent learning (See appendix 1b). As the class had students with various levels of proficiency in English, they had problems with different aspects of the language. Each of them was directed to the appropriate sources. It was when they began to understand concepts and realize that their learning could help them improve their proficiency that they began to take an interest in what was being taught.

The informal classroom tests were followed by a formal achievement test and the papers were graded. (Appendix 2 contains questions from the formal test; Appendix 3, columns 3 and 4 show their performance in grammar and paragraph writing). Explicit instruction in grammar was found to be useful because when students write paragraphs and essays, they tend to avoid expressions that seem incorrect. An analysis of students' performance in tests has shown that students who score well in essays or open-ended questions do not always score well in discrete point tests that examine their grammatical knowledge (Appendix 3, e.g., students 3, 6, 9). On the other hand, some students who score well in objective type questions get fewer marks in tasks such as paragraph writing (e.g. students 1, 11, 16). The advantages of form-focused instruction in language learning have been well attested (Freeman 1995; Lightbown 2000).

After every test, generalized as well as individual feedback was given to the students. The objective of the test and the possible answers to the questions were discussed in class. Students were encouraged to go through their answer scripts and seek clarifications when necessary.

At the end of the course, students are required to give their feedback on various aspects of the course, including testing and feedback given by the teacher. The course on English communication has usually been evaluated positively. Although several factors such as the teacher, the content of the course, the methodology, the classroom atmosphere and the testing determine the success of a course, my experience suggests that the methods of testing have had an impact on students' motivation to learn.

Discussion

Testing was viewed as an important dimension of the language programme. The scores of the students in grammar in the first informal test and the first formal test were compared. When the results were reported in class, a few students came forward to ask how they could improve their performance. It should be pointed out, however, that in the informal test, the marks for grammar were based on students' essays. In the formal test, the scores for grammar were based on a discrete point test. The results of the test show that the performance of fifty per cent of the class had improved since their first informal test, while that of the other half had not improved. On the whole, the scores reflect an improvement by about three percent (Appendix 3, column 5). More importantly, the comparison of scores at an early stage in the programme helped to emphasize the fact that efforts could lead to better performance.

Feedback was an important part of the programme. Through the semester, care was taken to give detailed feedback to students after every test. Further, sources of information were provided in order to promote independent learning (Appendix 1b). Informal tests also helped to highlight the fact that the objective of tests is not merely to judge students' levels of proficiency or intellectual abilities but also to help them learn.

Conclusion

The paper has described how testing was used to promote learner motivation. The fact that a few students showed an interest in improving their performance, indicates their motivation to learn although it is difficult to determine whether the motivation is intrinsic or extrinsic. In a teaching programme, informal tests can be used to help students understand what they need to learn and how they can improve their proficiency. Moreover, informal tests make testing appear less dreadful. Formal tests may be used to determine whether instructional goals have been met and to assess students' progress. Evidence of progress made by students, even if marginal, can help demonstrate how effort can lead to success. If the tests are followed by constructive feedback, it may foster intrinsic motivation. As testing can influence learners' attitudes towards learning, due attention should be paid to this aspect of a programme.

Appendix 1 a

(Sample Sentences from Informal Test 2)

Correct the following sentences if necessary.

1. There was so much noise at home that I couldn't listen the news.
2. She is knowing the truth.
3. We have heard so much about him that we are all looking forward to meet him.
4. People who worry often get ulcers.
5. After the death of his father, the prince was overthrowed.

Appendix 1 b

Answers for test 2 and explanation. For each sentence, the key word/s that can be used to get more information from the Internet, as well as useful links are provided (accessed on 23rd April 2008).

1. There was so much noise at home that I couldn't listen to/hear the news.

The verb listen is an **intransitive verb** and is not followed directly by an **object** (noun, noun phrase, etc.); it needs a preposition before its object (Swan, 1996: 579). Some verbs may be used transitively or intransitively. For example, the verb hear is used transitively in 'hear the news' and intransitively in 'hear with the ears'.

Key word/s for reference on the internet: transitive verb

Link: http://www.arts.uottawa.ca/writcent/hypergrammar/trnsintr.html

2. She knows the truth.

The verb *know* is not usually used in the progressive **tense** (verb + -ing). Verbs in English that describe a state, do not take the **progressive form**, whereas verbs that describe an event do take the progressive form.

Key word/s: verbs not used in progressive

Link: http://www.englisch-hilfen.de/en/grammar/state_dynamic_verbs.htm

3. We have heard so much about him that we are all looking forward to meeting him.

The phrase 'looking forward to' should be followed by a noun or a word **functioning** like a noun, such as *meeting* (gerund) in the above sentence.
More examples:
'I am looking forward to the party.'
'I am looking forward to going there.'

Key word/s: gerunds after prepositions

Link: http://www.englishclub.com/grammar/verbs-gerunds_2.htm

4. People who worry ofter get ulcers.

In the sentence, the word *often* may modify either the word worry or get. A modifier says something more about or adds to the meaning of another word, and should be placed close to the word it modifies. As the word *often* appears to modify the word preceding it as well as the word following it, it is called a **squinting modifier**. When a word modifies two words, two possible interpretations of the sentence may arise, giving rise to ambiguity. Here are some of the ways in which the sentence may be rephrased:

- Often, people who worry get ulcers.
- If people worry often, they get ulcers.

Key word/s: Squinting modifiers

Link: http://www.oregonstate.edu/dept/eli/buswrite/squinting_modifiers.html

5. After the death of his father, the prince was overthrown.

The past tense and participles of regular verbs are formed by adding –d or –ed to the base verb. Examples are phone-phoned, enter-entered and dread-dreaded. **Irregular verbs**, however, do not follow this rule (Quirk and Greenbaum, 1973), as the word overthrown in the given sentence shows. Most dictionaries list the participle forms of irregular verbs.

Key word/s: Participles of irregular verbs

Link: http://www.usingenglish.com/forum/ask-teacher/25535-tenses.html

Appendix 2

Sample questions from the formal achievement test used in class

A. Correct the following sentences if necessary.

1. Each of the boys was asked to give an explanation.
2. He having started early in the morning and reached well before sunset.
3. Trying to get a glimpse of the singer, the lights went off.
4. I thought the illness would effect my chances of passing the exam.
5. We are supposed to meet tomorrow, isn't it?

B. For each of the questions in this section, follow the given instructions.

6. Complete the sentence using the appropriate form of the verb in brackets.

   If people did not like such clothes they ______________ (not buy) them.

7. Write the following sentence in reported speech.

   Sita: 'I can lend you my dictionary.'

8. Use suitable articles where needed.

   Only liquid which can dissolve gold is mixture of hydrochloric acid and nitric acid.

9. Change the voice in the following sentence.

   Radiation from nuclear fuels can alter the genes in body cells.

10. Combine the sentences to form a simple sentence.

    Mohandas Karamchand Gandhi was born at Porbandar on October 2, 1869. He was the fourth and last child of his father's fourth and last marriage.

Appendix 3

Students' performance in Test 1 and Test 2 – Scores in percentage

Student No.	*Grammar 1*	*Grammar 2*	*Paragraph 2*	*Difference in grammar scores between Test 1 & test 2*
1	**60**	**80**	65	+ 20
2	**75**	**87**	80	+ 12
3	**65**	**40**	75	– 25
4	**75**	**93**	80	+ 18
5	**55**	**63**	60	+ 8
6	**50**	**40**	55	– 10
7	**75**	**73**	70	– 2
8	**60**	**67**	60	+ 7
9	**65**	**60**	80	– 5
10	**70**	**47**	65	– 23
11	**60**	**87**	50	+ 27
12	**60**	**47**	60	– 13
13	**60**	**40**	60	– 20
14	**70**	**53**	70	– 17
15	**50**	**53**	50	+ 3
16	**65**	**87**	70	+ 22
17	**45**	**35**	50	– 10
18	**65**	**50**	50	– 15

19	**65**	**87**	70	+ 22
20	**70**	**87**	75	+ 17
21	**75**	**87**	80	+ 12
22	**50**	**67**	60	+ 17
23	**55**	**43**	60	− 12
24	**50**	**73**	50	+ 23
25	**60**	**57**	65	− 3
26	**80**	**93**	75	+ 13
27	**45**	**57**	50	+ 12
28	**75**	**60**	70	− 15
29	**55**	**97**	65	+ 42
30	**50**	**47**	60	− 3
				102
				+ 3.4

REFERENCES

Bachman L., 'What does Language Testing have to Offer?' *TESOL Quarterly*, 25, (4), 1991, pp. 671-704.

Barrett J., *Aptitude, Personality and Motivation tests- Assess your Potential and Plan your Career*, 2nd edn, New Delhi: Kogan Page India Private Limited, 2004.

Clapham C., 'Assessment and testing', *Annual Review of Applied Linguistics*, 20, 2000, pp. 147-161.

Davies A., et al., *Studies in Language Testing*. Cambridge: Cambridge University Press, 1999.

Freeman D., 'On the Teaching and Learning of Grammar: Challenging the Myths', *Second Language Acquisition Theory and Pedagogy*, ed. F. Eckman et al., NJ: Lawrence Erlbaum, 1995.

Gardner R. and Lambert, W., *Attitudes and Motivation in Second Language Learning*, Rowley, Mass.: Newbury House, 1972.

Gardner R. and Macintyre P., 'A Student's Contributions to Second Language Learning', Part I: Cognitive Variables, *Language Teaching*, 25, 1992, pp. 211-220.

Gardner R. and Macintyre P., 'A Student's Contributions to Second Language Learning', Part II: Affective Variables, *Language Teaching*, 26, 1993, pp. 1-11.

Haines C., *Assessing Students' Written Work – Marking Essays and Reports*, Oxford: RoutledgeFalmer, 2004.

Heywood J., *Assessment in Higher Education*. London: Jessica Kingsley Publishers Ltd, 2000.

Inozu J., S. Tuyan and S. Cakir S., 'Overcoming Affective Barriers for Continuous Learning', *Asian EFL Journal*, Vol. 9, 4. <http://www.asian-efl-journal.com/Dec_2007_ji&st&cs.php> (accessed on 5th March 2008), 2007.

Lewis M., *The Lexical Approach: The State of ELT and the way Forward*, Hove, England: Language Teaching Publications, 1993.

Lightbown P., 'Classroom SLA Research and Second Language Teaching', *Applied Linguistics*, 21, 2000, pp. 431-462.

Lightbown Patsy M. & N. Spida, 'Factors Affecting Second Language Learning', *English Language Teaching in its Social Context*, ed. C. Candlin & Neil Mercer, Second Reprint. London: Routledge, 2003, pp. 28-43.

Niederhauser J., 'Motivating Learners at South Korean Universities', *English Teaching Forum*, Vol. 35, (1), <http://exchanges.state.gov/forum/vols/vol35/index.htm> (accessed on 13th March, 2008), 1997.

Norris J., 'Purposeful Language Assessment: Selecting the Right Alternative Test', *English Teaching Forum*, Vol. 38, (1), <http://exchanges.state.gov/forum/vols/vol38/no1/p18.htm> (accessed on 23rd April, 2008), 2000.

Quirk R. and Greenbaum S., *A university grammar of English*, England: Pearson Education, 1973.

Rubdy R., *What Insights can Motivational Theories offer Second Language Teacher Education? Teaching English in Non-Native Contexts*, ed. S.C. Chaudhary, Chennai: Professor V. Saraswati Felicitation Committee, 2002, pp. 23-41.

Stern L. and A. Solomon, 'Effective Faculty Feedback: The Road Less Travelled', *Assessing Writing*, 11, 2006, pp. 22-41.

Swan M., *Practical English Usage*, Oxford: Oxford University Press, 1996.

Taylor L., 'Washback and Impact', *ELT Journal*, Vol. 59, (2), 2005, pp. 154-155.

Tomlinson B., 'Testing to Learn: A Personal View of Language Testing', *ELT Journal*, Vol. 59, (1), 2005, pp. 39-46.

22

Positive Washback: The Power to Empower L2 Learners

J. John Love Joy

The Subjugated Students

The disadvantaged students of the present generation are victims of tremendous pressure from all quarters viz. parents, teachers, peers, siblings, relatives, neighbours and employers. The pressure to perform and in this competitive world, perform exceptionally well, seizes them the very day they step into an educational institution. This pressure mounts to unimaginable proportions as they inch their way up the educational ladder. Thus they easily become a commodity of saleable dreams, unwillingly shouldering the expectations of their many stakeholders and caretakers.

In this process, their freedom is clipped, creative skills are seldom exercised, critical faculty is left untouched, self-esteem is damaged beyond repair, and social usefulness is seriously jeopardized. Simultaneously, fear grips them, insecurity stares at their face, hatred and self-pity ensue, and disappointment and despair become their constant companions. Consequently, as the course is completed these shattered students crawl out of the institution almost unemployable to be battered by the harsh realities and demands of the real world.

Probing the Problem

Recent years have witnessed some genuine although isolated attempts, like a flash in the pan at improving second language education in India. The outcome of these attempts has not been encouraging though, and certainly there was nothing that made a wide and lasting impact. Why have these experiments not been so effective? Why have experts stopped searching for an answer and rather turn to the luring and lucrative training sessions for international examinations? Has ELT become a bag of tricks and a mundane collection of jargons? Are the teachers to be blamed for their outdated methodology? Or is it because of the ambitious amendments effected in the curriculum? Or is it rather the much hyped heterogeneous large classrooms with traditional screwed down furniture the problem? Could it be the different governments' ambivalent educational policies with hidden agenda the real hindrance?

Arguably, all these factors do influence the teaching-learning process. However, a close critical look at the situation would reveal a crucial but grievous, hitherto ignored layer of the educational set-up—the negative washback effect of the exams. In fact, the impact of testing on teaching has been shockingly negative and nothing concrete has been done to modify or transform testing and evaluation into a positive learning experience.

In the Indian context, the criminal neglect of testing has played havoc in the lives of learners yearning to learn, classroom exams have become a mere dry runs and rehearsals for the decision-making final tests. As Krishnaswamy & Sriraman (1995) comment,

> It is well known that students are not being taught in classrooms today, they are being coached today for examinations ... (p. 48).

One not too infrequently stumbles upon arguments suggesting that test-oriented teaching definitely mutilates the process of student empowerment. Others with equal vehemence may argue, 'How come test-oriented teaching is a hindrance to development?' In fact, testing in itself is not so appalling as long as it promotes genuine effort and learning inside the classroom. However, what actually cripples learning is the testing system which encourages rote-learning, that is, spoon-fed, undigested information, memorised, recollected and regurgitated on the exam day. As a result, testing remains unproductive or rather counterproductive. Testing if it has to be meaningful must follow the process approach of experiencing, understanding, applying and producing.

Term Defined

Washback has been discussed in language testing literature as the direct and indirect influence of testing on teaching-learning processes. Hughes (1989) defines washback as 'the effect of testing on teaching and learning' (p. 1). Prodromou (1995) refers to it as 'backwash' and defines it as 'the direct or indirect effect of examinations on teaching methods' (p. 13). McNamara (1996) refers to the term as 'the impact of tests on teaching programme ...' (p. 23). For Davies et al., (1999) washback is 'the effect of testing on instruction'.

Washback is said to have both positive and negative effects. Positive washback is a result of genuine testing procedures which encourage and inspire meaningful and useful teaching practices. Whereas, negative washback occurs when irrelevant, misguided or unproductive testing procedures are employed which try to constrict the teaching-learning process to fit their narrow and skewed views.

Classroom Practice in India

If we analyse the existing classroom practices, we would be bemused to see the teachers dominantly lecturing their day out, letting the students do nothing but listen to their learned input, (in fact, very little intake occurs). This attitude resembles the 'banking theory' which was criticized by Freire (1972) three decades ago. He compared education to the banking system,

> ... in which the students are the depositories and the teacher is the depositor. Instead of communicating, the teacher issues communiqués and 'makes deposits' which the students patiently receive, memorise, and repeat. (pp. 45-46).

In the light of the concept mentioned above, what transpires is that the teachers consider themselves as 'know-alls' and therefore underestimate the cognitive faculty, exposure and experience of the students by pouring whatever they know into the 'empty' vessels, i.e. the students. This attitude would, for sure, demoralize the students because,

> The more students work at storing the deposits entrusted to them, the less they develop the critical consciousness.... The more completely they accept the passive role imposed on them, the more they tend simply to adapt to the world as it is and to the fragmented view of reality deposited in them. (Ibid: p. 47).

Hence the role of teachers becomes crucial for successful implementation of any curriculum. Unfortunately, the teachers believe that teaching and learning are the same. They expect instant, total and absolute intake of the input presented under whatever conditions. Thus, antiquated methods that are not informed by the recent insights from cognition, psychology, linguistics, etc. are imposed; controlled practice and choral repetition are common sight, error is not tolerated, production skills are ignored for there is no interaction between teacher and student. Minimal and small group work among students is absolutely nil. Poor infrastructure further mutes the possibility of cooperative learning. In short, to quote Gupta (2004) irrespective of the approach adopted,

> Classroom methodology remained the same teacher-centred, lecture-based, and examinocentric dull procedure. (p. 266).

Despite the minimal teaching aid and abysmal infrastructure, teachers can do justice to their profession, provided they give more importance to the language skills and make the students practise in the classroom. In reality, all efforts of the teachers end up in preparing students for the examination which promotes parroting and reproducing.

What Needs to be Done?

We need to understand that genuine attempts made, in recent years, to improve the quality of teaching have turned futile. These attempts have failed largely due to ignoring testing. Teaching and testing should form the two legs education stands on. Unfortunately, relatively more energy has been spent on materials production, teaching techniques and teacher training. Testing procedures on contrary, have received scant attention, forgetting the fact that testing is part and parcel of the curriculum and equal importance is imperative. As Puhl (1997) has rightly asserted,

> We cannot change the instructional process unless we change the assessment process. It has been widely accepted that testing greatly influences instruction; and narrow testing has meant narrow instruction, teaching done 'to the test'. (p. 2).

Therefore, changes effected just in areas other than testing cannot yield the desired result if testing is not given due importance. In India, testing is not considered a vital aspect of teaching. It is by and large seen only as a judgmental and not an instructional tool. The first step towards changing the idea that testing is meant for judgment alone, is to make testing part of classroom learning process. Judging the students through standardized achievement test demoralises them.

Ideally, any test in an instructional setting should concentrate more on developing student's proficiency (Puhl, 1997) because education basically is meant to develop and not to judge or discriminate. As Skehan (1988) cautions, '... tests would not always be done *to* people, but *with* them' (p. 221; emphasis original), thus, calling for delegation of authority. Thereby, learning orientation should be given the upper hand, so that, the focus is on 'mastery and improvement rather than out performing others' (Baker & Wigfield, 1999: 455).

On the one hand, the primary aim of any testing practice in an educational set up should be made developmental. On the other, the testing pattern should give little room for reproduction or memory, so as to encourage the applicatory skills, learning by doing. Once application gains the upper hand, the three-hour end term paper-and-pencil examination would give way to classroom based continuous assessment. This change would result in a positive washback on teaching, hence creating enough room for the teachers and students to play an active role in the empowerment process.

The Right Time Indeed

The 'virtual' world has made knowledge available to everyone and it is just a click away from the sought. Feed in the website and in a few minutes the users will have more than they could chew. As a result, students today are challengingly informed and alarmingly secluded. Therefore, pouring in information is not what they need. What they are in need of is a place to prepare them to face and contribute to the real world; a place where they can enjoy the freedom of thought, practise skills, claim a sense of ownership, feel confident and serve to lead for the empowerment of the self and the society at large.

Bibliography

Baker L. and Wigfield A., 'Dimensions of Children's Motivation for Reading and Their Relation to Reading Activity and Reading Achievement', *Reading Research Quarterly*, 34/4, 1999, pp. 452-477.

Davies A., et al., *Dictionary of Language Testing*, Cambridge: Cambridge University Press, 1999.

Freire P., 4th edn, *Pedagogy of the Oppressed*, tr. M.B. Ramos, London: Penguin Books, 1972/1990.

Gupta D., 'CLT in India: Context and Methodology Come Together', *ELT Journal*, 58/3, 2004, pp. 266-269.

Hughes A., *Testing for Language Teachers*. Cambridge: Cambridge University Press, 1989.

Krishnaswamy N. and Sriraman T., 'English Language Teaching in India: Past, Present and Future', In Agnihotri, R.K. and Khanna, A.L., ed., *English Language Teaching in India: Issues and Innovations*, New Delhi: Sage Publications, 1995, pp. 31-57.

McNamara T.F., *Measuring Second Language Performance*, London: Longman, 1996.

Prodromou L., 'The Backwash Effect: From Testing to Teaching', *ELT Journal*, 49/1, 1995, pp. 13-19.

Puhl C.A., 'Develop not Judge: Continuous Assessment in the ESL Classroom', *English Teaching Forum*, 35/2, 1997, pp. 2-9.

Skehan P., 'State of the Art Article: Language Testing, Part I', *Language Teaching*, 21/4, 1988, pp. 211-221.

23

'Simply English': Spoken English Demystified

Lavanya Mavillapalli and Francis Peter

Introduction

It can reasonably be assumed that there are over 350 million English users and about 100 million English speakers in India. The distinction between the users and speakers is (Wikipedia's India) that users only know how to read English words while speakers know how to read English, understand spoken English as well as form their own sentences to converse in English. It is this new demographic advantage that makes India the favoured place for global business. According to a study, 'Roadmap 2012 – Capitalizing on the expanding BPO landscape', (Nasscom and Everest Group) the sector employs 7 lakh English conversant people, and has an annual turnover of about $ 11 billion. Over the next 5 years the BPO industry will give employment opportunities to about 2 million people. (www.bpowatchindia.com).

Along with this all flattering information comes also a note of warning that the current supremacy and economic rise would be stymied if India does not pay attention to training its generation next in English. (Graddol 2006).

Probably a relic of the Raj, even today in India, English skills determine social hierarchy. In fact, English is a tool to fight poverty, a language of opportunity, a pre-requisite for upward mobility. The importance of English for higher learning, job placement and promotion is obvious. Without English our students will not be able to enter the highly competitive job market. They remain excluded from the better paying jobs. The booming economy today is throwing up new jobs but we are not able to match the demand with enough skilled and qualified school drop-outs.

The Problem

If then English is what can help this nation connect to the global economy and emerge triumphant, how is the education system meeting this challenge of creating proficiency and competence in that language? 'Not having the English related soft skills is proving to be a serious handicap to these students, which is all the more regrettable insofar as it is system-induced. With the opportunities that come with globalization comes also the systematic exclusion of the underprivileged sections of the society. That is only because majorly they lack scholastic skills and specifically because of their parsimonious English skills.' (Peter 2008). And as Ashok Kamat, the Managing Trustee of Akshara Foundation observes this is a situation that 'should both numb us and excite us that we have nearly 190 million children in the 6-14 years age group. What is exciting about this number is the tremendous human resources we have access to if we are able to train and tap this huge pool of young citizens; on the other hand what is numbing is that any statistic beyond this tells you that our problems are in the many millions. What do I mean? ASER says that 51.9% of children cannot read Standard 2 level material—this means 98 million children need remedial help in language.' (HT 03 Feb 2006)

The question is, why cannot our massive system of education bring about the desired change? The ELT experts would point their fingers at the poor quality of teachers, unmotivated learners, uninspiring material and inefficacious methods. All of the above and more could be the reasons. But where does one begin the change process—introduce effective methodology, prepare alluring teaching material, work on the students or train the teachers? Strong arguments have been adduced in support of one or the other of these factors. There is a common feeling that the teachers are the weakest link today in the educational chain. Untrained, undertrained teachers with parsimonious language are the bane of the system. So teacher development seems to be the best bet, the ripple effects they can trigger and the generations that can benefit from such training puts teacher training above the rest of the available options.

However, the ground reality is truly staggering. In Tamil Nadu alone there are 37,000 primary schools (The Hindu, Wednesday, 16 Mar. 2005). It would take years to systematically train these numbers and there are other questions like who would handle classes while these are being trained and when would the next lot who by then would have been inducted, be trained. The cycle is vicious. A change in text or method would again imply a dependence on the teacher to efficaciously implement it and thereby requiring more training. Working on batch after batch of students motivating them and compensating for their limited competence out of class would be self-defeating. Obviously the many atomized approaches hitherto attempted have not been able to fracture the cyclic structure of this problem.

This is the reasoning that prompted *Susiksha* believe the answer lies in an integrated approach. Motivating and meaning making material supported by affordable technology involving an empowering methodology, the group believed can empower the teachers at the same time while enlightening the learners.

This would supplement the existing teacher without supplanting them.

Sarva Shiksha Abhiyan (SSA), the flagship programme of the government addresses a mammoth 131.69 million children in Primary (I- V) section. The scheme involves 23, 10,000 primary teachers and 14,39,000 upper primary teachers in 7,67,520 Primary and 2, 74,731 Upper Primary schools all over the country.

SSA's objectives include:

(i) All 6-14 age children in schools.
(ii) Bridge all gender & social category gaps at primary stage.
(iii) Universal retention by 2010.
(iv) Focus on elementary education of satisfactory quality.

The Tamil Nadu Unit of SSA, in making this vision concrete had assessed the requirement of the state accurately and set its priorities. One of the major objectives was evolving an effective model to enable children from the government schools speak confidently in English. Lavanya Mavillapalli and her team at *Susiksha*, an organization dedicated to 'enhanced learning' were happy to be entrusted with this arduous job. Guided and led by Revd Dr Francis Peter, S.J. Director, Research Academy for Communicative Excellence (RACE), Loyola College, Chennai, the team began to give shape to the dream that came to be called 'Simply English' Teaching (SET).

The Rationale

What was needed, we sized up was an affordable technology with an easy and wide reach that contacts and excites the learner even in remote corners of the state directly. Then followed a critical review of some of the earlier attempts made by EMRC (Educational Multimedia Research Centre), AMRC (Audio Media Research Centre) and ventures like BBC's 'The Tiger's Eye' to teach English through audio and visual media. It was concluded that these were structured well and executed well but met with only partial success possibly because (a) they were serialized, thereby preventing lateral entry, (b) they were not integrated into the curriculum, and thus became an additional and unwanted burden (c) the density of the target language soon caused ardent devotees to drop-out, (d) they were non-interactive, denying any role to the class teachers and (e) the content was not necessarily attuned to the socio-cultural milieu of the learners. The new approach would need to overcome the identified limitations while including the many positive qualities of these programmes.

The Methodology

The variety and range of the clientele, their varied level of language proficiency and motivation, the quality of teachers and infrastructure were issues that had to be tackled. The decision was to develop audio lessons to impart English speaking skills to absolute beginner level learners, which would be bilingual to begin with. In order to achieve this, affordable, reliable and target-specific English education was to be presented in a non-threatening and engaging manner. The roadmap was made and execution began in stages.

Step One: Identification and Assessment of the Target Group

SET had in mind the absolute beginner level learners present in the 37,000 state board schools in Tamil Nadu. The task began with a needs analysis of the target group (TG) and their levels of proficiency in English, using a bilingual questionnaire.

The characteristics of the target group (TG) could be stated as:

- no communicative knowledge of English
- minimal exposure to the language
- no scope for the use of English outside class
- low self-worth

On the perception that emerged from the analysis it was decided to group the learners from the government schools, proficiency-wise rather than according to the class they were in. The TG was designated as crawlers, walkers and flyers based on their current level of competence in English irrespective of biological age or the classes they are in.

Step Two: Formation of Syllabus

An integrated syllabus was framed keeping in mind the specific needs of the TG. Frequency, salience and immediacy of application have been the guiding principles in the selection of vocabulary and structures. SET has turned to Communicative Language Teaching Approach, Humanistic Approach, NLP for Language Learning, Multiple Intelligence and Community Language Learning for Inspiration. This holistic learning made sure of the integration of all skills in an interest engaging, learner centred, and learning by interacting approach. While the focus has been on functionality, care has been taken to knit relevant grammatical structures into the comprehensive course outline. The attempt is to give the learners not just specific vocabulary but to also enable them to become confident, independent users of the language. The requirement of the examination was not left out while focusing on the communicative nature of the language. The methodology adopted believed 'learning is a celebration' and believed learning is a result of construction not just instruction.

Step Three: Creation of Sample Lessons and Field-testing

Inspired by these principles sample lessons had been created and extensively field tested across a section of the TG. These trials and field visits supplemented by informal chats with practising teachers and BRTEs threw light on the stark ground realities. Rubrics in English were just beyond the reach of many of the teachers especially in the rural areas. For the learners, the density of English words in the lessons caused a severe strain. Rather than struggle through these lessons they tended to give up learning the TL. They had decided that they were not upto the task and just slumped back.

This meant thinking of ways of luring and exciting the learners and getting them glued to the lesson. There was a reluctant decision to introduce bilingual approach in SET. The content, it was decided must be contextualized and customized to interest and engage the learners. Once the lessons and the activities grab the interest and excite the learners, the density of English could progressively and imperceptibly increase culminating in near total English in content, rubrics and classroom management. The radio lessons would include songs, jokes, activities and games and anything which would make them focus on the use of the language.

The greater challenge related to the teaching community. Some had been frank enough to admit that they would be at a loss if they did not have a printed text they could read out to the children, often with meanings in MT penciled in. They also confessed inability to string a sentence of their own in English. With such restricted competence it was thought fit that SET should still supplement the existing teachers without supplanting them. They would have a Teacher's Manual printed in English and with an MT version as well. The teachers would be an integral part of the radio lessons though the Radio teacher would take care of complicated instructions and the actual teaching. The teacher in the classroom could manage with assisting the radio teacher, using predictable language. Nothing would be asked of the teacher that might embarrass them. A 'learning by doing' methodology would ensure that the learners acquire the target language if not because of the teacher, at least in spite of the teacher. It was hoped that the process would covertly help the teachers themselves get empowered maximizing exposure and extending their own interlanguage.

Step Four: The Final Version

The beginner level programme, the one launched on the 7th of November 2008, has sixty lessons. These sixty audio CDs come with a Children's Workbook, a Teacher's Manual and other supplementary material such as flash cards and posters. The bilingual audio lessons of SET use the radio as the medium of transmission. The broadcast is worked into the curriculum within the school hours. This affordable technology with a wide reach is used to support and enhance the teacher's competence or the perceived lack of it. The class begins with a pre-lesson where participants prepare for the audio lesson to be broadcast on that day. The digital version of the lesson is available for the class to play as often as required. In fact, it can serve the needs of adult education and other interested groups as well. The radio teacher in conjunction with the class teacher conducts the lesson and the accompanying activities. The post-lesson or follow-up is spread across four days – when with the help of the workbook and digitally recorded activities, the learners reinforce the teaching. The learning points of the previous classes are built into the progressive lessons to ensure reinforced learning.

Further Stages

The next mammoth task is to take the project forward, and work on the next two phases meant for the walkers and the flyers. However, a prolonged follow up and feedback of the project that is initiated need to be conducted. Insights gleaned from such close analysis would also feed into the planning and execution of the next phase.

Conclusion

We owe it to our nation to do something to uplift the children from the neglected sections – this is not an option but an obligation on our part. Much has been done in this state and much more remains to be done. It is time we critically looked at what is happening and particularly, what is not but should be happening in our schools with respect to equipping our students with adequate English Language skills. We need to immediately introduce sufficient and efficient changes to the teaching/learning approach in our institutions. More than looking for conclusive, comprehensive and dramatic results confirming the efficacy of the approach all we look at is to commit ourselves to the task ahead of us. If a significant number of limited proficiency learners exhibit greater propensity to speak English, this group would rest content. Our aim is capacity building and we are confident the headstart this programme provides would make them race on and compete with the rest of India's proud children.

WORKS CITED

Garddol David, *English Next,* British Council, The Hindu, Wednesday, March 16, 2005.

Peter Francis, 'Project Future Secure', *Jivan,* May-June, 2008, p. 17.

Kamath Ashok, 'Hindustan Times', 3rd February, 2006, www.bpo.watchindia.com

24

Reading to Respond: Activating Readers' Responses through Drama Praxis

Annie Kuriachan

We value a work of art either because of the reputation of its creator or because of the intrinsic merits of the work itself, and not because of the audience or the reader who brings meaning to it. If such a perception of reading is painfully narrow because it has ignored and sidelined the reader, the process of reading also must share the same blame as it ignores the new meanings and insights the perspectives of multiple readers bring to it. Thus, reading skill that has immense potential for stretching learners' interlanguage and language use is wasted by reducing it merely to a comprehension exercise. The need to recognize reading as a higher order skill for language enhancement that equips the readers to read in order to reflect, respond and perform is the need of the hour, especially, for most tertiary-level learners in the Indian context as they prepare to become globally employable.

This study highlights the role of the reader or the performer and the act of reading in making meanings as texts are read and reflected upon for performance. For this reason, the first part of the study deals with the theoretical underpinning of the transactional aspect of the Reader-Response Theory, and, the second part experiments with adapting and applying the theory in a classroom/play rehearsal setting using the concept of drama praxis.

While proponents of the New Criticism argued in favour of the text's autonomy, stating that the meaning of the text is contained within the text itself, the Geneva

School of critics, also known as the Critics of Consciousness, spoke of the human mind as capable of receiving impressions and also of questioning these impressions in the process of making sense of the world. This indeed marked the beginning of a shift of focus from the venerability of the literary text as the repository of the ultimate meaning to the acceptance of the existence of the reader's intelligence as capable of formulating and creating new meanings.

Likewise, the Reader-Response theorists asserted that any claims to the objectivity of a work of art is merely an illusion and that the reader's response to a work of art is all that matters. The theory was interested in what the text does to the reader than what the text is. Therefore the axiom on which the theory rests is that readers are not passive consumers of texts but are actively involved in constructing a meaning out of it, thus enriching the text and helping it to grow beyond it's immediate age and concern. In fact if the term 'reader' were to mean any person capable of evaluating the process of aesthetic experiences, then it could be understood from the words of Umberto Eco as summarized by the German Reception-Aesthetic theorist Hans Robert Jauss that, 'any work of art, seen as an open structure, requires the active co-production of the recipient and brings about a historical variety of concretizations without in the process ceasing to be one work' (1990:53-69). The Reader-Response theorists specified the role of the reader as one who discerns using his/her own faculty of reason, judgment and learning in order to arrive at the meaning of the text. They testified that the reader was one who was the actual, informed reader or competent reader with real aspirations, hopes, dreams and frustrations and for whom reading was neither a simple nor an innocent activity bereft of cultural, social, historical, educational and ideological positioning. For such a reader, the act of reading would become suffused by a complex pattern of discourse, avoiding passive consumption and active imposition of any particular meaning to texts. The process of reading could be understood as an ongoing communication between the writer and the reader that ensures the reader's active participation in the fulfilment/ realization of the text.

The Reader-Response theorists belonged to three different schools of thought based on their own special interests; but what is noteworthy is that they were concerned about the same issues regarding the reading of texts. The Transactional Reader-Response Theory affirmed in the words of their leading thinker, Wolfgang Iser, that reading is a transaction that happens between the writer and the reader. For him the incompleteness, the inconsistencies and the contradictions found in the illusions created by the writer of a literary work actually served as gaps or blanks that the reader had to fill in order to arrive at various interpretations. These gaps and unformulated meanings in a work of art were referred to as indeterminates that empowered the reader to an awareness of '... the possibility that we may formulate ourselves and so discover what had previously seemed to elude our consciousness' (2000:204). Wolfgang Iser in *The Act of Reading* (1978) also spoke of the reader's communication with the text as a dynamic process of self-correction whenever the reader's interpretation through the use of his/her imagination was incorrect. On the other hand the American Reader-Response theorist Stanley Fish, who worked on Affective Stylistics Reader-Response, spoke of the text as an action or an event done on the reader. Fish explained this by saying, 'meanings are actualized in texts in the process of reading through the interaction between the text and the reader's expectations, projections, conclusions, judgments and assumptions' (1980:2). Stanley Fish defended his case by stating that reading is an analysis of the word-by-word response of the reader that is corrected or ratified in the interpretive communities to which a competent reader automatically belonged. The third category of Reader-Response Theory, known as the Psychological Reader-Response Theory headed by Norman Holland, spoke of the reader as creating texts through a projection of fantasies and through a fulfilment of psychological needs by a transformation of unconscious wishes through a literary text. Holland asserted that 'identity themes' and 'stock responses to texts' came into being as a result of such psychological projections.

All these categories of the Reader-Response Theory have convinced us that the literary text does not exist unless the reader brings a materializing of meaning to it. In other words, the text lives as a result of the life that the reader breathes into it by reading the meanings within a text with the help of his/her own aspirations or even frustrations. Different readers read different meanings into a single text and perhaps this is the reason why the greatest works of art are enigmatic and fresh in their appeal. Indeed the mark of any great art is its ability to inspire the highest of thoughts in men and women anywhere. The reader synthesizes the meanings of his/her life with that of the text and concretizes the ideas. Thus reading is the process whereby the work of art is positioned between the effort of the author and the concretization of the reader. The reader is responsive, able and accountable with the result that reading takes on the nature of a discourse between the author, art and audience. The Reader-Response Theory has ensured that reading is a dialectic/dialogic process absolutely democratized and demystified for the reader and the work of art strengthened and enriched because of the plurality of meanings arrived at.

The Reader-Response Theory is to be validated especially in the classroom enterprise because of its inbuilt mechanism that focuses on the response of readers or learners. A majority of learners of literary texts today in the Indian classrooms are reluctant and uninterested in the production of meanings as they feel disempowered in a system that is based on a teacher-centric pedagogy. In applying the Reader-Response Theory to texts in class, this gross injustice can be rectified and learners can be attributed with innate and collective wisdom to formulate meanings. The theory also helps the teacher to go ahead with the business of motivating learners and facilitating language acquisition and stretching of interlanguage through a process of reflection and transformation. Thus the reflective practice of teaching and learning with the help of deliberating on experiences gains wider usage with its own attendant benefits. According to Pennington, reflective teaching and learning are, 'a means for (1) improving classroom processes and outcomes, and (2) developing confident, self-motivated teachers and learners' (1992:51). Paulo Freire, the well-known Brazilian educator, advocates a working pedagogy in which teacher and students, 'become jointly responsible for a process in which all grow' (1996:53).

Taking into account these views, the Reader-Response Theory strengthens the student-centric pedagogy of literature wherein active learning is pursued and by which the focus of literary studies shifts from content/aesthetics to process and practice. The active participation of the reader/learner in the process and analysis of reading that is stressed by the Reader-Response theorists involves an active engagement of the learner where the learner is enthused to fill in the gaps and indeterminacies in texts using the consciousness of their cultural, social, ideological leanings.

An illustration of active learning and reflective teaching can be noted in the process of a play-text being read in the classroom by many readers who will lose no time in structuring a life on it. The Theatre in Education (TIE) programmes that gained public reckoning in the 1950s in the western world capitalized on the twin effect of action and reflection in theatrical procedures and these programmes were also responsible for bridging the gap between the play on the page and the play on the stage. A major triumph for the TIE practitioners was the attention given to performance studies that by the 1990s came to be an important component of pedagogy. This has been so, because drama as a sound learning medium has always been a process of exploration as readers are expected to get under the skin of the characters of the play and live the situations that are in the play. In doing so, the reader improvises and adapts the world of the play according to the sum total of his/her experience and of the perception of the world he/she lives in. Theatrical practices involve for its practitioners a more than fair amount of spontaneous recreation and reshaping of the experience of the play-text world. Such improvizations or adaptations aid the reader/actor in engaging with the inner (sub textual) life of the drama, that is, its thematic coherence. In the words of Dorothy Heathcote, 'dramatic improvization is concerned with what we discover for ourselves and the group when we place ourselves in a human situation containing some element of desperation. Very simply it means putting yourself into other people's shoes and by using personal experience to help you understand their point of view, you may discover more than you knew when you started' (1967:44-48).

What one means by dramatic improvization is the manner in which readers/actors find current equivalences to situations in play-texts or scripts and thereby infuse the texts with an enriched dramatic life that is rooted in the reader's reality and experience. For example, Bertolt Brecht's *The Caucasian Chalk Circle* that speaks of social values about motherhood as nurturing, irrespective of biological considerations about ownership of land can be deconstructed into a series of readings that are Feminist, Marxist and Post-Colonial in spirit. Using the gaps, blanks and indeterminacies in the text, the reader can put together brief narratives from his/her own life in the form of short dramatic acts to define the interpretations made. It should be remembered that performance pedagogy will work if the aim is to establish or realize multiple readings and interpretations of the text rather than to descend to a mere presentation or mimicking of the situations found in the text. In this way, the reader/actor is empowered to grapple with difficult texts on her own terms without having to be anxious about producing politically correct readings. The reader's self-generated response liberates him/her from the restrictions imposed by dominant critical views and perceptions. The flexibility and range of ideas brought forth realizes the freshness of appeal for the text. Therefore, the most significant aim in teaching drama through performance is to integrate the creative and interpretative skills of learners as they discover the text.

Apart from improvization and adaptation as facets of performance pedagogy, we can also examine the principle of 'drama praxis' as being significant in guiding the reader/actor through a process of action, reflection and transformation. Praxis is a translation of ideas into action, making it, therefore, an important tool in the hands of practitioners who are not content with only a generation of ideas and thoughts but who also aim at acting on these ideas, and later, at reflecting on the action. Praxis was a word developed by the Brazilian educator Paulo Freire in 1970 to denote thought, action and reflection which together achieved the result of transformation in any situation. Praxis evokes the process that is involved in any action rather than in its end result because in the course of the process, transformation of the individual, the context, the theme and the perception of the situation can take place. The close similarity between Reader-Response Theory and Praxis operates on the agenda that new insights have to be gained not at the end of the situation but in the process of the unraveling of the situation. Thus for both these approaches, it is the journey towards self-discovery that matters, and not the destination at all.

In dramaturgy, praxis is significant because it brings together the thought that is developed theoretically and the action that is designed by experiences. Therefore, through praxis, a play becomes a live experience where each day's inquiry and spirit of adventure explore newer frontiers. Drama is enriched through praxis as meanings from individual responses are made by shattering established norms and conventional thoughts. Human experience that is at the heart of drama, praxis is studied by the teacher and the students to reflect upon issues pertaining to their own lives or to those in the societies they live in. The reflections gleaned by the group are then transmitted to the larger group, namely, society.

The complete picture of art conspiring to generate meaning through drama praxis can become clear through a study of the ten key principles of drama praxis underlined by Philip Taylor (2000:18-19) that make drama a lived and dynamic event which demands the ongoing and immediate interaction of teachers, students and their communities. The principles are:

1. Driven by inquiry
2. Teacher as co-artist (facilitator, director, interrogator, manipulator)
3. Promotes yearning for understanding
4. Well researched
5. Generates rather than transmits knowledge
6. Tightly balanced yet flexible structure
7. Pursues engagement and detachment
8. Powered by risk taking
9. Logically sequenced
10. Rich in artistry

The above principles have been adapted here to validate the claim of drama praxis to provide meaning through exploration. The issue that I wish to examine through these principles is that of women's empowerment, an issue that is of great concern among social thinkers, scientists and activists. Women have all along been silenced into fantasies, images and symbols by a society that fosters a gender-biased social construct. Therefore it has always been difficult for women to fight society's pervasive and subtle ways of blanking out women from its historical, social and cultural consciousness. The only panacea for this malady is through a process of redressal to restore the balance and position of women in society. The process can be through a recording of experiences that explore the past and present so that women can be positioned as active negotiators and producers of cultures in society, rather than as simply its consumers.

Why are women silenced and what needs to be done for them to be heard? I propose to use this example of the theme of the annual college play of Women's Christian College, Chennai, 600 006, South India, produced in the year 1999 by the collaborative efforts of thirty women students in the age-group 17-21, three women faculty members aged 36-45 and the director of the play, Gnani Sankaran, a theatre activist, and incidentally, the only man in the process. The director and the group evolved the play through a workshop method running to about ninety days of discourse, enquiry and execution.

The manner in which the play came into existence was based on the three elements of drama praxis, namely, action, reflection and transformation. Experiences of the members of the group formed the foundation of the play that enquired into the theme of repression of the great women who fought for the freedom of the Indian nation. The nature of the play was a documentary-drama of those parts of history forgotten in archives; yet what seemed to amaze the participants was the shared experiences of women of the past and the present. The participants underwent a process of transformation through a realization that they have to be in charge of their destinies and of their faculty of reasoning. The impact of the transformation was in the empowerment of all the participants as they took stock of their positioning in society, and involved themselves in a wholehearted participation of bringing to consciousness the contribution of women to society, and as they became leaders in charge of their lives through the process of the play and after it.

I would like to examine the evolution of the play by adapting it to a slightly changed set of principles from that of Taylor's, to prove that drama praxis is an important tool for practitioners to transform people and situations.

Principle 1: The Question Within

An image in popular Indian advertisements that invade Indian homes through the aegis of mass media about the selling proposition of the marriage of daughters and the education of sons was presented to the group.

This was done deliberately by the director to help the participants measure their sensitivity to gender-bias. How aware were the students to subtle messages of socialization? How amenable were they to accept these messages without question? If they raised objections to such prejudices in society, what prompted them to speak up?

The questions within the mind of the director were externalized to spark off a process of reflection within the minds of the participants. The group responded by narrating incidents and anecdotes from personal lives that pointed to similar images of social bias.

Principle 2: Initiation of Dialogue

The teacher/director as facilitator turned the question within the minds of the participants by asking them to define the word 'woman' through a series of presentation of metaphors and images. The groups presented scenes from everyday life where women are subjected to conformity of social and religious traditions. The teacher/director went to each of the groups keeping alive discussion on the question that was initiated in the first principle. The information within the group was structured cohesively to achieve linear progression of ideas whereby the group started at first with generalized notions and developed later into suggestions of alternatives to these notions.

Conflicting ideas from the dramatic presentations of the groups such as *fairer sex, weaker sex, shakti, Madonna, mother, nurturer, nourisher,* etc. emerged initially in the consciousness of the participants, leading to an acceptance of the ultimate meaning of woman as *human being*.

The process of dialogue within the groups helped to break down stereotypes erected by human institutions and to comprehend the totality of the image of the being of the woman.

Principle 3: Revelation to Reflection through Research

The teacher/director exposed the participants to experiences of women in history by narrating true-to-life incidents. For example, the struggle of Rukma Bai, a revolutionary freedom- fighter of Maharashtra, who had to first fight for her individual space to study medicine and to participate in the freedom movement inspired by Mahatma Gandhi, within an oppressive family into which she entered as a child bride; the reality of Pandit Ramabai of Pune, who faced social ostracisation because of her social-reform measures for women's education, the humiliating experiences of how women in India during the period of caste-struggle were not allowed by the higher castes to wear their upper-body garments; the spirit and verve of Smt. Muthulaksmi of Tamil Nadu, who against the norms of society gained admission into law school and also into the Legislative assembly to speak against the prejudices in society.

These narrations led to reflection on the part of the participants about the significant contribution of Indian women to the freedom struggle movement and an even more significant blanking out of these contributions in history books and documents.

The teacher/director thus moved from the experiences of the participants to the experiences of women in the past to establish through research the process of reflection about how the progressive silencing of women for centuries could be challenged and rectified.

Principle 4: Transformation of Knowledge into Action

The group was ready to transmit their knowledge of their past and their present to the outside world so as to bring about a change in perceptions in the outside world and within themselves. The culmination of the dialogue between the teacher/director and the participants; between the participants themselves; between the participants and the audience was realized when the play documenting women's struggles in private and public spaces was translated into action.

The transformation of the participants led to the transmitting of the essential understanding of their own past and present experiences to the larger community outside where transformation of knowledge is implemented in the form of action in real situations.

Through the four principles of drama praxis stated above, it is evident that when readers are acknowledged as capable of transcreating texts with multiple meanings and new insights, the process of reading becomes that much richer as an activity. Reading to reflect, respond and perform using multiple perspectives and fresh insights equips the language learner with the skill to make meanings of the text through constant reinvention and recreation from individual experiences. In this respect we may agree with Miller that 'the text is in fact an extremely impoverished promissory note with a view to performance. We don't know what it means until we tether it into a world, our world, and it doesn't become lucid or interesting or drama until it's in a world' (1988:2).

Thus, reading from the point of view of a higher order of language enhancement must materialize through lived/shared experiences for the reader to convert the words on the page to multi level interpretations. This transaction that happens between the reader, the process of reading and the text that is read has to be paid greater attention to if we are desirous of moving our learners to a higher level of proficiency in the use of language.

Works Cited

Fish Stanley, *Is there a Text in Class? The Authority of Interpretive Communities*, Cambridge, Mass : Harvard University Press, 1980.

Freire Paulo, *Pedagogy of the Oppressed*, tr. Myra Bergman Ramos, London; Penguin, 1996.

Iser Wolfgang, 'The Reading Process : A Phenomenological Approach', in *Modern Criticism and Theory A Reader*, 2nd edn, ed., David Lodge with Nigel Wood. U.K. Pearson Education Limited, 2000.

Jauss Robert Hans, 'The Theory of Reception : A Retrospective of its Unrecognised Prehistory', tr. John Whitlam in *Literary Theory Today*, ed., Peter Collier and Helga Geyer-Ryan, U.K. : Polity Press, 1990.

Miller Jonathan, 'From Page to Stage: Text, Interpretation, Performance', Strawberry Fare, Autumn, 1988.

Pennington M., *Perspectives on Second Language Classroom Teacher Education*, ed., J. Flowerdew, M. Brock, S. Hsia Knowloon : City Polythenic of Hong Kong, 1992.

Taylor Philip, *The Drama Classroom; Action, Reflection, Transformation*, London: Routledge Falmer, 2000.

25

Using Media as a Bait to Get Tertiary-Level Students Reading

Illango Ramasamy

The state of Tamil Nadu alone can boast of thousands of engineering graduates walking out of colleges every year but a majority of them are turned down by the prospective employers on the ground that they lack communication skills. 'While India produces the second largest number of engineers in the world, more than half of them are "unemployable". While 3,60,000 students passed out of engineering colleges last year, recent studies revealed that nearly 2,00,000 of them were unemployable' said Mr A. Satish Kumar, MD, Henkel India Limited, in his inaugural address of a state-level technical symposium organized by Sri Krishna College of Engineering and Technology, Coimbatore way back in 2006. And the situation is no different now.

That even after twelve years of English in schools, students need support in the basics of English at college level. The main culprits behind this kind of a situation are those in charge of planning and implementing education in our country. What sounds even worse is that till a few years ago, English was taught only in the first two semesters of their graduation, but now, it is extended to the third year students as well. The facile answer of the administration to the problem of paucity of English is to pile on a paper in English in addition to the regular first two semester papers.

When students are not able to communicate even after all these years of training, what good will the teaching of English for one or two more semesters do? Can larger doses of the same medicine administered all these years in all English classes that repeatedly found not so effective, really do much good? When I asked myself what is the exact problem and why students struggle to string a single meaningful sentence after years of formal classroom teaching, the answer that came to my mind was that they have nothing to communicate. I mean, it is 'what to say' perhaps even more than 'how to say' that cripples communication. I feel putting to use even their parsimonious English language can stretch their interlanguage. The point is borne out by the fact that even if they are asked to communicate in their mother tongue they find it difficult to speak or write coherently on a given topic. And even students who had scored 80% and 90% in English paper can at most talk or better still repeat what they have learnt or memorized as part of the learning, but when it comes to natural everyday communication, they dry up in less than a minute.

The reason for this kind of sorry state is that these students lack exposure and have not applied their minds and ingested even the little they have learnt. All that they do is just to memorize their essays and reproduce them in the exams. Though they have prepared themselves for so many English exams and successfully completed them, they aren't in a position to express themselves because for them, the process of learning English was never an enjoyable activity, but a drudgery carried out with disgust. So all the input they received in the English classes throughout their school and college days did not amount to intake at all. So our first responsibility is to make our students enjoy what they learn and learn what they enjoy. Grappling with syntax to communicate what they feel so much of an urge to share will be the answer.

We teach them or spoon feed the content of the lesson and they parrot it much as Freirre's 'banking system of education' describes. We may have the intention of teaching them the LSRW skills but we woefully neglect thinking skills. Without the 'T' added, unless there is an application of the mind, the LSRW would largely remain insufferable accumulation of junk. Unless the raw data is ingested mulled over syntacticized and is converted into reflected data, the input form cannot hope to become intake and subsequently be available as output.

One practical way out is to inculcate in them a love for and almost an addictive habit of reading. This is becoming a fast fading skill in danger of extinction. If you turn your accusing finger at televison, internet and the mobile telephony as the reasons for the dwindling interest in reading, can we, taking example from the mythical war, churn the sea and swallow the poison or even make through cleaver process of metamorphosis and alchemical transformation the poison itself into wholesome the *amruth*! Can watching good programmes on television channels, be it comics, movies, music and sports, be the source of replenishing the much lamented lack of knowledge of the world and thinking skills? That is turning television into a teaching tool!

And my humble and what might appear simplistic solution is to use television as a bait, make them read and listen for pleasure and slowly hook them into the habit of reading and listening. This was my hunch and my hypothesis: When students read and listen to English on topics they like and enjoy their exposure would improve, and it will be easier to turn what they learn into output.

Then comes the next step—how to make reading a habit? Now, all children are invariably inquisitive, they love to listen stories. So elders tell them fairy tales, events from the scriptures and tradition as well as bed time stories, and these children go on listening to various types of tales for the first few years of their life. As they grow older their longing for stories also increases and their parents run out of stock of stories to suit their growing intelligence and interest; nor can they find the time or inclination to spin imaginative tales to their now critical children! So the caretakers start to read out stories from books to the captive listeners. While listening to their parents' reading, children unconsciously learn to group words into meaningful clusters and also get the rhythm and intonation. This covert learning helps them to internalize vocabulary, syntax as well as features of pronunciation—segmental as well as suprasegmental. Hence in a matter of two to three years these children learn to read and understand short sentences and no longer depend on their parents to read out stories to them. Parents also are freed of telling or reading stories to their children by this time so they start to give them comic books. This is the first step in the formation of their reading habit and this leads to reading more children's literature found in magazines and books. As they grow older their interest also changes constantly from tales of fantasy to adventure to romance and thrillers. As they grow older their tastes change and they get wary of one genre after the other and read different types of articles, stories, poems, essays, novels, etc. that keep them engrossed till ultimately it becomes their most passionate hobby.

A child who grows like this will be exposed to different cultures around the world. This kind of children learn about the world, different traditions, politics, sociology, history, sports, crime, ethics, religions, etc. They will search for more and begin to seek a greater range and variety of topics and authors. Thus naturally their knowledge base and their attitude towards life would be on a much higher altitude compared to the children who do not have the habit of reading.

There is an abiding interest in stories for all of us, children or adults. Conversational storytelling and professional storytelling both are an absorbing part of growing. If only we could plan a stage of scaffolding that can provide a transition seceding control from adult caregivers to the learners themselves much would begin to happen as far as English language learning is concerned. This can pave the way for improved reading habit in children. This is how they become independent readers.

So how can a student of an engineering college who never had an opportunity or the exposure to reading a story or a novel for pleasure, read an article in the Science & Technology column of a newspaper or a magazine or a journal to strengthen his or her theoretical knowledge? So the students who have the reading habit at least in their mother tongue will certainly have an edge over the others who do not have the habit of reading. It will also be easy for those who have cultivated reading habit in their mother tongue to learn to read in the second language (in our context English). On the other hand if a student even though from an English medium school does not have the reading habit it would be certainly difficult to cultivate the habit at the age of seventeen and above and most of our students (above 90%) do not have the reading habit. So what is the alternative? How else can these kids expand their knowledge?

It is here we are advantaged since we are living in the digital era. We could make the very distractions serve the purposes at hand; we can make our children learn by singing, watching and reading what they fancy in the internet and the cyberspace. To a large extent our students do not like to read. They love to listen, even though the material is in English. They can take advantage of television since there are hundreds of channels with English programmes. For example, all the news channels broadcast debates, group discussions, interviews and expert opinions on various topics and channels like National Geographic, History Channel and Discovery give us programmes on Science and Technology and Historical Events; we have Animal Planet for wild life. But our students do not watch these programmes all that they watch on television is music and sports and that too in regional languages. There are many reasons for this lack of interest in our students.

The first and foremost reason is that they are scared and do not believe that they can understand or follow such programmes in English. They do not have the accessibility (lack of cable connection, lack of time, lack of freedom to watch English channels when the family members want to watch regional channels, lack of experience that leads to problems in comprehension, etc.), and thus, no idea about the programmes. Though a few of them have tried to watch such programmes, they say, they couldn't understand the programme so they swap to a more rewarding channel in terms of comprehension. But they also say that they have tried it only for a few minutes and not the whole programme. Channel surfing is another distraction that troubles a viewer. Lets imagine that on a rare occasion an engineering student sits to watch a good programme on Nat Geo, after nine minutes the programme has a commercial break during when the boy surfs other channels to see whether there is any other interesting programme just to kill time but when he returns to the programme that he has been watching, it would be on its final minutes. So obviously the boy hasn't got anything substantial.

So one fine day, I wondered if only I could remove all these barriers, won't I be able to get my students to watch useful English programmes beamed on television channels and eventually came up with a module to promote reading skills among the tertiary-level disadvantaged students using TV programmes? So I have started to identify and record some selected gripping and exciting telecast sans the annoying commercials in between and play them in our language lab. The average length of a programme is kept well within 50 minutes. To begin with, I have asked my students just to sit back and enjoy the programme and aim just at some global comprehension. Everybody in the class, except one or two said that they understood most of the programme and enjoyed watching it. I could notice visible joy in their faces as their confidence and comprehension improved. After a few such lab sessions, I asked them to take notes (with a semi filled in template supplied) while listening and at the end of the session I, put them into groups and asked them to share what they had understood, and then asked one from each group to speak for under two minutes about the programme.

After ten such classroom sessions, many students said they had started watching English programmes on television and many of them had started to borrow CDs from me. So through this I understood that students can acquire English watching programmes that excite them. And if the teacher can encourage and extend support to walk the way, these learners will soon cultivate the habit of independently watching good programmes in English which would certainly enhance their knowledge as well as their language skills. This habit will certainly enhance their listening skill and if properly guided and utilized, the same habit can be used to improve their speaking skills also. Thus, highly motivated, the learners can improve their vocabulary, spelling and even their pronunciation through this habit.

So I come to believe that among the two receptive skills one can be improved using this technique (listening) and I wanted to use the same to improve the other receptive skill (reading) also. For this purpose I transcribed three programmes (The complete speech text into written text). Each of the transcription runs into not less than 10 pages in an A4 sheet. I have also prepared short tasks based on these texts (Cloze tests, True or False, Match the following and Choose the best option). First I played the programme and then asked the students to do the comprehension questions. I have also provided the written text to them. Almost all of my students have read the whole script and did answer the comprehension questions quite satisfactorily, if not always accurately. So from this exercise I proved to myself that making students who haven't read even a single page in English, on their own in all their life, can be made to read around ten pages within an hour. I believe repetition of this activity will certainly increase their confidence and interest and eventually result in the reading and listening habit which will improve the receptive skills of our students.

If the proof of the pudding is in the eating, as they say the success of the approach in discussion is the following testimony. One of my students (Mahalakshmi, II Year Electronics and Communications Engineering) came to me with a novel I gave her to read during her vacation. (*The Client* by John Grisham). This is her first attempt at reading a novel and she had completed the book in just four days. She also told me that she had not used her dictionary while reading the novel. Hardly a year ago, I had to explain each and every word and phrase in a short story and she plodded on for one whole week through those ten never ending pages. But now after the intervention programme she could read a whole volume all on her own and that too in an astonishingly short-time.

It must also be said that I had earlier given her Sashi Tharoor's *India: From Midnight to the Millennium*, a non-fiction with a view to help her acquire the reading habit. It took her two months to complete it and not without a lot of assistance from me. The first thing that I gave her to read was a short story by Jeffery Archer – *Never Stop on the Motorway*. She took a week to read that but even then she could not understand it. She was thoroughly confused and had misunderstood the entire plot. But now after the media mediated training, she has taken another novel from me *The Rainmaker* by John Grisham. I promised her to give the movie once she finishes reading the novel. She also writes a summary of whatever she reads in a notebook and I use her errors to teach her grammar. I think this is the best achievement of my teaching career so far.

Once they start enjoying reading and listening in second language (achieving this itself would be a great feat) it would become easy for us, the English teachers, to get them to speak and interact in class and soon enough in real time in natural situations. Those who have read and watched something substantial and interesting would certainly like to show off to others that they have acquired something new, important and interesting. Since the input language was in English, it would be easy for them to speak and write in English when they want to communicate what they have enjoyed to their friends. Here as teachers, we should encourage them to do this and when they struggle, we should assist and also correct their errors without hurting them. We can use their errors to teach them the grammar. We can also teach them to use dictionary in this process which could become their lifelong teacher.

I also try some other activities to make my students listen and read. They are as follows:

1. I play English songs with lyrics (Karoake) and ask the students to sing along. (This helps them overcome shyness of speaking in English and helps them improve their pronunciation.)
2. Narrate a story and stop it half way through and ask the students to read and understand the rest of the story by themselves. The curiosity to know what happens in the climax makes them read the story at a pace they had never ever read before.
3. Use the audio texts and worksheets from *www.elllo.org* to improve all the four skills. Since necessary vocabulary, structure and pronunciation is provided to the students through the listening and reading of the given short conversations, students are able to answer the oral and written answers from their experience to the open ended questions based on the sample situation.

Appendix

'MEGA STRUCTURES – THE FASTEST, TALLEST, BIGGEST – MILLAU BRIDGE' TELECAST ON NATIONAL GEOGRAPHIC CHANNEL A SAMPLE OF THE ACTIVITIES

I. Who is Who? – Match the names of the persons given in column A with the designations given in column B.

A	B
1. Michael Virgeux	- Steel Project Manager
2. Lord Norman Foster	- Wind Tunnel Engineer
3. Jaques Godfrain	- The Project Manager
4. Jean Pierre Martin	- The Chief Engineer
5. Jean Marie Cremer	- The Architect
6. Marc Buonomo	- One of the Maintanence Engineers
7. Oliver Flamond	- Motion Control Monitor
8. Hosse	- The Mayor of Millau
9. Tierry	- Head Bridge Builder of the ministry of Transport, France

II. Who said what? – Following are the words of some of the personalities mentioned above. Try to find out who said what and write their names next to each statement.

1. When I've shown first the drawing of this bridge they really thought I was crazy ____________________________.
2. It was terrible for our reputation when you hear every day on the television or radio 'avoid Millau there is a traffic back up, a five hour wait in Millau'. ______________________.
3. We thought a solution to the construction which was the launch of the bridge from the two sides. One part from the Lassa Plateau one on the Rouge Plateau and to push them from the two sides and to make them come and meet here above the river Taarn. __________________________________.
4. If we've done the conventional launch we'd have knocked the piers over like the pins in a bowling alley. The basic principle can be demonstrated with a heavy

box and a wobbly table. ____________________.

5. The average wind speed was relatively low but because of such strong turbulence they created very fast big winds. ________________.
6. It was the maximum stress like poisoning your mouth. You don't forget that. I won't forget it. For four hours I was really scared. ________________.
7. Now remember because in construction sites there are often accidents. As that we have no serious accidents, nothing more than a minor injury.__________ ________________.
8. As you leave these plateaus you do fly; you fly across this bridge literally you're above the clouds. ________________.

III. Fill in the blanks using appropriate details:

A) Chronology of Events

1. ________________ - Ground breaking ceremony.
2. December 2001 - ________________.
3. ________________ - Pier construction was over.
4. February 2003 - ________________.
5. ________________ - Opening of Tukomenaros suspension bridge.
6. 22nd August 2003 - ________________.
7. ________________ - Launch from the northern side.
8. December 14th, 2004 - ________________.

B) What is what?

1. 28000^{0} c = ________the temperature of earth's _____.
2. 1 pylon weighing 700 tonnes = ________________.
3. Road deck weighing over 40,000 tonnes = ________________.
4. 10,000 tonnes – the combined weight of cable stays = ________________.
5. 25,000 tonnes – the breaking strength of the strongest stay = can hold back ________________.

C) Accidents

Bridge	City/Country	No.of Deaths	Year
Brooklyn	____________	_____	Not given.
____________	Melbourne	35	1970
Complends	____________	13	________.

D) Following are the problems faced by the construction team during the project period. Arrange them in their chronological order.

1. Laying road deck
2. Rippling effect
3. Land slides
4. Failure of the launching systems
5. Wind speed

E) Fill in the blanks:

1. The world's tallest bridge Millau's highest tower stretches about_________.
2. Millau Bridge is like building a series of Eiffel Towers then slinging up _______ lane highway between them. (a) 2, (b) 4, (c) 6, (d) 8)
3. The three big challenges faced by the construction team are:
   (i) Building the __________ bridge base in the world.
   (ii) Putting a _____________ tonne free way on top.
   (iii) Erecting _________ steel pylons weighing _______ tonnes.
4. The bridge was estimated to last for ___________ years.
5. How many pillars are to be erected and which is the tallest among them? (i) _________ (ii) __________.
6. Jamila in car _____ takes just ___ minutes to cross Millau through the bridge while Jamaima in car _____ take ____________________.
7. Lord Norman Foster is known for the buildings he built. He built ____________ in Hong Kong and ________________ in Barcelona.
8. Michael Virlogeux's design originally had (a) 5 piers, (b) 7 piers, (c) 9 piers, (d) 2 piers.
9. The bridge has to support the weight of ____________________tonnes in gail force winds.
10. The bridge required ___________ tonnes of concrete.
11. The _____________ must be just right; it needs _______________ strength to support the massive loads ______ it can't _________________ as it has to be in

position and poured hundreds of metres in air and it needs to be _________ to suit Norman Foster's vision.

12. Pier two was __________ above the grand __________ from the north and ______________ from the south.

13. The most difficult phase of the construction: (Choose the best option.)
    (a) Building the piers.
    (b) Putting the road deck on top of the piers.
    (c) Erecting the seven steel pylons.

14. The 2.4km road deck weighs ___________ .
    (a) 36,000 kilos (b) 36,000 tonnes (c) 36 tonnes (d) 36 hundred kilos.

15. The three major constructions of the famous Architect Eiffel are:
    (i) The once tallest bridge in the world; Garaby Viaduct in ____________.
    (ii) The framing of ___________________.
    (iii) _________________________.

16. The road deck was made of __________ separate sections weighing up to _______ tonnes and some of them _________ long.

17. Marc Buonomo automated the road deck manufacturing process with a _____ welding machine and a _____________________.

18. 28,000°C is the _____ times the temperature of the earth's____________.

19. *State whether the given statement is true or false:*
    There were two assembly plants at the construction site to assemble the 2200 sections of the road deck.

20. The largest temporary steel tower erected between concrete piers is _____ mt. tall.

21. Marck Buonomo & Jean Marie Cremer came up with a new technique to build this road deck. That is to use:
    (a) pushing systems (b) elevating systems (c) launching systems
    (d) pumping systems

22. What is the speed with which the road deck moved?
    (a) 600/4 minutes (b) 400 millie/6 minutes
    (c) 600 millie/4 minutes (d) 400 meters/6 minutes

23. The maximum wind speed at the top of the bridge could be:
    (a) 150 km/h (b) 130 miles/hr (c) 150 miles/hr (d) 130 km/hr

24. What conclusion did Oliver and his team arrive at after their wind tunnel testing? Ans: The winds they have _________ were strong enough to ______ the

unsecured deck ____________ its supports and send it ______________ hundreds of feet to the valley floor.

25. In total, how many launch systems have failed?
    (a) one (b) two (c) three (d) four
26. The two decks took months to meet each other.
27. Which of the following road deck is shorter, the deck pushed from the north or south?
28. The distance between each pier is:
    (a) 243mt (b) 342mt (c) 432mt (d) 423mt.
29. The first major problem in bringing the decks together is that the starting points were ______________________. Secondly, the bridge has a subtle __________ to it.
30. In the phase three of the launch there were _________ launching systems used at the same time.
31. Each pylon is ______ high and weighs 700 tonnes, the equivalent of 85____ _________.
32. Buonomo used the technique used before 4000 years in________ to lift the pylons.
33. What is the weight of the roadway with all the 7 pylons on top of it?
34. How many cable stays are there in the Millau Bridge?
35. What is the weight of the roadway after the cable stays were fixed?
36. The span bends just ______cms under the weight of over ___ tonnes.
37. The bridge was designed to cope with ___ cm bend in the span.
38. _________ vehicles in a day cross the bridge and they charge over _____ each car.
39. The total investment for the project was ____________________.
40. Tierry and franc's job is to test the ______________ system and ________ __________________ on each of the seven circle floors.

IV. What is what? Match the following.

1. 342 metres	(a) no. of individual steel strands that made the strongest steel stay.
2. 130km/hr	(b) the length of the bridge.
3. 36,000 tonnes	(c) weight of the steel bars.
4. 700 tonnes	(d) required amount of concrete.

5. 120 years	
6. 30,000$ (U.S.)	(f) the length of a single piece of road deck.
7. 2.5km	(g) wind speed
8. 200,000 tonnes	(h) combined weight of the 2200 steel sections of the road way.
9. 16,000 tonnes	(i) weight of the road deck.
10. 245 metres	(j) height of the bridge.
11. 90 tonnes	(k) weight of a single pylon.
12. 22 metres	(l) the height of a temporary pier.
13. 2000 (approximately)	(m) estimated life span of the bridge.
14. 342 metres	(n) penalty for a day.
15. 170 metres	(o) height of 2nd pier.
16. 600 millimeters	(p) the length of a single section of the 2200 steel sections.
17. 4 minutes	(q) accuracy of the alignment of the two road decks from north and south.
18. Over 18 months	(r) time taken to move the road deck to 600 millimeter.
19. Teflon	(s) distance pushed by the launching system at a single time.
20. 99.9999%	(t) wind analysis period.
21. 90 metres	(u) road trips taken to transport the parts of the road deck.
22. 25,000 tonnes	(v) the non-stick material used in the launching systems.
	(w) visitors in the first nine months.
23. 7	(x) height of each pylon.
24. 91	(y) breaking strength of the strongest cable in the stay.
25. 700,000	(z) no. of piers and pylons.

Bibliography

Peter Francis, 'Glossary of ELT Concepts and Terms'.

Focus on communication skills, students told, *The Hindu*, March 19, 2006.

26

Reading the BOOK: Reading the WORLD

Sridhar Bala

'Has the book been security-checked?', the strict tone of the inspector from the CISF (Central Industry Security Force) with a stern look to match roused me from my reverie while transiting through Chennai airport recently. Non-plussed, I looked at the innocuous book in my hands. The inspector took the book from my hands and ran it through the X-ray machine scan. This was new to me. On previous occasions, I had carried it with me and the security staff had only flipped the pages while doing the frisking. On previous occasions, the security staff had even commented on some of the more interesting titles like 'Houdini' and 'Genghis Khan'. But this time the title was quite harmless 'Great Carnatic Masters' and I wondered why it deserved a security scan.

My thoughts went back to another incident in a book I had read recently. This was 'The Unusual Reader' by Alan Bennett. It's a delightful read. A hilarious and fictional account of an unusual reader – the Queen of England and what happens when she begins to take an interest in books and in reading. Once on a ceremonial trip to open the session of Parliament, the Queen, a trifle self-conscious tucked the book under the seat cushions of the horse-drawn carriage. On her return, while gingerly feeling for the book under the cushions, the Queen is perturbed to find the book is no longer there. On her discreet inquiry, the equerry sends for the page who informs her that on a security check the sniffer dogs had unearthed the book. The security staff had removed it. The page replied 'They thought it might be a device that could explode, Ma'am'. The Queen expostulated, 'Explode? But it was only Anita Brookner!'. Later on, the Queen consoled herself with the thought that the book could indeed be a device that could excite and even perhaps ignite the imagination.

It is this excitement of the imagination that defines reading. We often wonder how avid readers are engrossed for hours reading . The book may be devoid of pictures, yet how does it hold the attention of the reader for hours on end? In addition to content, it's also the ability to imagine, to form mental pictures. When we read, we form pictures in our mind simultaneously. It is this visual aspect that supports and sustains reading. Children have a natural gift for imagination. If your book can excite the imagination of children, then you have a bestseller in your hands. In fact, no two reading experiences are ever the same. This experiment could be conducted in a classroom. Give the same chapter in a book to three children sitting in a row. After they have finished reading, ask each one to recapitulate what he or she has read. The content may be the same, but one will get three different experiences. This is because each child is blessed with a unique personality and the way each one internalizes what one is reading and then expresses it is unique.

Reading is now a total sensory experience. It's not just the mind but the whole body that reacts to reading. In 'Theories of Reading – Books, Bodies and Bibliomania' KarinLittau quoting Roger Chartier speaks about reading bringing the body into play. Littau goes on to say that reading affects the flesh and blood of the reader. Littau quotes from 'Blackwood's Magazine, 'the figure of the modern reader who tears his way through books, that appear to put through the whole gamut of passions'. 'He rolls his eyes, and clenches his fists, and snarls in the concentrated energy of indignation'. Lest this appear too masculine, Littau goes on to quote from Sharpe's London Magazine, 'to read in bed, is to injure your eyes, your brain, your nervous system, your intellect'. No wonder therefore, that young ladies withdrew quietly to the privacy of their bedrooms, so that they may lose themselves to the world of the forbidden pleasures of novel reading while safely removed from public, paternal or patriarchal scrutiny. A further illustration of young ladies losing themselves to, or totally engrossed in, the pleasures of reading are the figures of people reading made by tribal craft persons. A very popular figure is that of a young woman reading in a horizontal position with one leg slightly raised in the air. An example of total involvement with the act of reading and a reinforcement of the body as a sense perception reacting to what is being read.

In an excellent review of Alberto Manguel's seminal work, 'A History of Reading' , A.C. Grayling observes, 'To read is to fly; it is to soar to a point of advantage which gives a view over wide terrains of history, human variety, ideas, shared experience, and the fruits of many inquiries. A life thus equipped might not be happier ... but it is vastly richer'. When one opens 'A History of Reading' one is struck by a curiosity. Manguel opens the Last Page as the first. He describes the various readers through history. Aristotle, Virgil, Saint Dominic absorbed in the book he holds unclasped on his knees, deaf to the world, the Child Jesus explaining his reading to the elders in the Temple, Saint Jerome reading a tabloid-sized manuscript, while in the corner, a lion lies listening. Going down the ages, Manguel describes a Charles Dickens, drawing on his acting talents, holding up a copy of one of his own novels, about to read to an adoring public. The blind Jorge Luis Borges screwing up his eyes the better to hear the words of an unseen reader. In a dappled forest, sitting on a mossy trunk, a boy holds in both hands a small book from which he is reading in soft quiet, a master of time and of space. Manguel declares, 'All these are readers, and their gestures, their craft, the pleasure, responsibility and power they derive from reading, are common with mine. I am not alone'.

Stirring words these but with one small exception. Borges' readers were unseen to him but we now certainly have an identity to one of them. This was Manguel himself whom Borges met while the former was working in a bookshop 'The Pygmalion' in Buenos Aires. This was the beginning of a life-long friendship initially preceded by Manguel reading out to Borges over a four year period. Manguel has given a fascinating account of these years with Borges in a book titled simply 'With Borges'.

There is now a universal consensus that we need to strengthen the reading habit among young and old alike but specially among children and adolescents. This is especially true in countries where we may not have an adequate public libraries infrastructure. We speak of our children more glued to the television sets and computer screens than books. Margaret Meek-Spencer formerly Reader-Emeritus in the University of London pleaded for a symbiotic relationship between the world of media and that of books, sometime ago. In a country, where books are conspicuous by their absence in the audio and visual media and struggling to retain their presence in the print media, we cannot but heartily endorse her statement. We surely can give more 'entertaining' programmes on books and authors over television that might kindle children on to reading. This has been tried in other countries with a fair measure of success. For some years, the BBC in England sponsored 'The Big Read' programme which galvanized a whole nation into reading. The jury is still out on the future of reading whether it will continue to be from a print format or whether it will turn digital. Without getting into a debate about reading on the numerous E-readers currently in the market, can we use the novelty of these gadgets to hook children on to reading?

In an important book, 'Classic Connections – Turning Teens On To Great Literature', Holly Koelling speaks about classics and other books in a recorded format. She says teens may love to listen to the recorded classic while following the printed book and this enhances and enriches the whole reading experience. Similarly, music can draw the most reluctant teenagers into the classroom. The combination of the music of a world culture along with its classic culture will surely turn the teens onto the classics.

What is clear is that we need to find more innovative ways to strengthen the reading habit and get our people into reading. I would go further and plead for another national movement in the country – a movement for reading. The reading habit requires nurturing and it needs to be inculcated in children while they are young. We have enough examples of the positive effects of reading. I would like to quote only one example. While on an official visit to the city of Bogota in Colombia, four years ago, we were taken to a public library in a slightly rundown section of the city. We were curious as the architecture and design of the library looked anything but nut. We were right. The building had been the city's rubbish dump but had now been converted into a pleasant looking library. Inside was a beehive of activity with children and adolescents busy reading, getting books issued and returning. Small children were being taken to see films based on the books they had read. Speaking to the Director in Spanish, through an interpreter, we learned that the library had only been in existence for the last four years but was proving immensely popular. Previously, the neighbourhood was prone to a lot of petty crime and theft. While no definite study had been done, the director claimed that since the library came into being, there was a marked decrease in the crime rate in the area!

We would like to end this on a positive note. When the horrific events of 9/11 unfolded themselves in New York, it was learned that the authorities had a few precious minutes to clear occupants from the second tower before another plane struck. A few people were taken out through the underground passage and found shelter in a nearby Borders bookstore. While knowing that their traumatic experience would leave them in no condition to read, we can nevertheless believe that the sight of so many books in the calm atmosphere of a bookshop would have been a soothing influence on them and helped them to face the future with renewed vigour and confidence.

27

Schema Activation and Reading Comprehension

Shagufta Imtiaz

The ability to read is acknowledged to be the most stable and durable of the second language modalities (Bernhardt 1991)[1]. Reading involves the readers, text and the interaction between the two. Reading in L1 shares many important elements with reading in L2 yet the processes differ. A number of complex issues arise here, related to whether these are two parallel cognitive processes working simultaneously or whether these are common processing strategies accommodating both first and second language. Despite similarities, second language reading is quite unlike reading in MT. A number of complex variables contribute to the difference.This paper discusses the role of cultural, linguistic and educational schema in reading comprehension and demonstrates how activating them proves to be strong predictor of success in reading.

Schema as Widdowson 1983[2] defines it are 'cognitive constructs which allow for the organization of information in long term memory'. It relates the incoming data to what has already been embedded in the knowledge structure. This is how the reader is able to predict the written or oral discourses. In the words of Cook (1989) 'the mind, stimulated by key words or phrases in the text or by the context, activates a knowledge schema'[3]. And schemata are highly organized generic knowledge structures with slots for each component. Two broad types of schemata are content schemata and textual schemata. The profession classifies these variously as *content* schema (background knowledge), *formal* schema (textual) and *linguistics* (language) schema. Content schema

1. Bernhardt E.B., 1991, *Reading Development in a Second Language,* in Singhal, 1988 : 1.
2. Widdowson H.G., *Learning Purpose and Language Use,* in Singhal, *op.cit.* 1, 1983.
3. Cook, 1989: 69.

implies general or specific information on a given topic, while textual schema refers to information about standard rhetorical patterns into which texts are organized. They also include 'default values' for each slot. Thus if no information is available for the slot, the reader fills it with the value she knows to be typical in that slot. Schemata are organized hierarchically from the most important information to the least important ones (Anderson 1978)[4].

A considerable amount of work has been done on the influence of content schema on reading comprehension. Studies show that readers demonstrate better comprehension of text for which they have background knowledge (Spiro 1980, Taylor 1979, Langer and Nicolich 1971, Langer 1984, Kintsch and Greene 1978, Have 1982)[5]. Good and poor readers exhibit different approach to reading. It has been suggested that poor readers use top down processing when the material is familiar but resort to bottom up when the material is unfamiliar. Studies on the role of schemata in readers' comprehension suggest that different types of text structures affect comprehension and recall. It appears that concerns about linguistic difficulty of a text is partially misplaced. It is rather the lack of adequate and appropriate schema related to text or inability to use them that are of more serious concern.

Carrell (1984c) lists[6] a few factors that contribute to miscomprehension:

1. No existing schema (text assumes background knowledge that the reader may not possess).
2. Naïve schema (insufficiently developed).
3. Poor text (not enough cues for appropriate schema).
4. Multiple schemata (more than one interpretation of the text is possible).
5. Schema intrusion (reader chooses an inappropriate schema).

It becomes obvious that the greater the difference between L1 and L2 the greater the need for cognitive restructuring. (Segalowitz 1986)[7]. The L2 readers deprived of socio-cultural skills lack the content schema which enable them to perceive texts in a culturally specific way.Hence the need to activate the learners' schema is of paramount importance.

Schema Activation

Often most texts are not completely explicit and therefore the reader must rely on pre-existing schema to provide a bridge between the old and new. Evidence suggests that

4. Anderson R.C., 1978, *Schema Directed Processes in Language Comprehension* in S. Kathleen Kitao, 1995: 11.
5. Kitao, *op.cit.* 14.
6. Carrell P.L., 'Schema Theory and ESL Reading', Kitao, *op.cit.*, 1984c, p. 28.
7. Segalowitz N., 'Skilled Reading in the Second Language', cited in Singhal, *op.cit.,* 1986, p. 5.

not using schema appropriately or not recognizing similarities between the incoming schema and the existing one causes breakdown in reading comprehension. There are a number of prereading strategies to create a mind set prior to reading.[8] These include advance organizers (Ausubel 1960), structured overviews or graphic organizers (Alvermann 1981), previews (Graves et al., 1983), concept maps (Novak and Gowin 1984) and thematic organizers (Alvarez and Risko 1989).[9]

Bransford (1985) makes a distinction between schema activation and schema construction. It is possible to activate an existing schema but this does not imply that the learner can develop new knowledge and skills. Several teacher-directed and self-initiated activities such as problem solving lessons and activities can promote schema construction by providing a framework to help readers comprehend the input.

Culturally Familiar and Unfamiliar

Research has supported the causal relationship between comprehension and the reader's familiarity with the target culture. Rivers and Temperley, (1978) have emphasized the importance of providing background information, explaining high frequency but, culturally loaded terms and using illustrations to provide additional meaning to texts.[10] The goal of EFL/ESL reading teachers is to minimize reading difficulties and to maximize comprehension by providing culturally relevant information. Goodman (1979) puts the issue in focus when he says that 'even highly effective readers are severely limited in comprehension of texts by what they already know before they read. The author may influence the comprehensibility of a text particularly for specific target audience. But no author can completely compensate in writing for the range of differences among all potential readers of a given text'.[11] Grave et al., who developed previews for short stories that activated culture specific prior knowledge demostrate significant change in understanding a text. Gatbonton and Tucker (1971) in a seminal study suggested that inappropriate values, attitudes and judgments led to Filipino students misunderstanding of American literature.[12] However, when relevant cultural information was provided to them, their reading improved.

In yet another study conducted by Johnson (1981) it was found that reading comprehension was affected more by the cultural context of the passage than language

8. Ausubel D., 1960, 'Viewpoint from Related Disciplines: Human Growth and Development', in Alvarez M. and 1989 : 1
9. Alvarez and Risko, *Ibid.*
10. Rivers W.M. and Temperely M.S., *A Practical Guide to the Teaching of English as Second or Foreign* Language', Carrell and Eisterhold, *Ibid.*, 1978, p. 83.
11. Goodman K.S., 'The know-more and the know-nothing movements in reading: A Personal response', in Carrell and Eisterhold, *Ibid.*, 1978, p. 85.
12. Gatbonton C. and Tucker, 1971.

complexity in the case of Iranian and American subjects.[13] They understand and retained culturally similar passages in a better way. Studies have also shown that lack of cultural difference in the recall of events may be explained by conceptual relationships. In the case of narrative style, the chronological form could be considered universal. Therefore, readers of different cultural background would have a similar scheme for recalling the chronological sequence of events (Seliger 1971)[14].

In ESL/EFL classroom, one needs to be sensitive to reading problems that result from implicit cultural knowledge presupposed by the text. Study in EFL/ESL shows that the role of cultural knowledge has been a factor in reading comprehension. Rivers (1968) maintains that the strong bond between culture and language must be maintained for the students to have a complete understanding of the meaning of language.[15]

More recently in such a situation it becomes important to provide the necessary background information in order to fill up the gap in the readers' knowledge. Hayes and Tierney (1982)[16] found that presenting background information related to the topic helped readers learn from text regardless of how that background information was presented or how specific or general it was.

Analogy: A specialized instance of enriching background is the use of analogy. This is an expositional method for comparing information which is similar in essential respects to permit transportation usually from familiar to unfamiliar. Apart from providing students with analogies in the text, researches might focus on training learners to create their own analogies.

Activating Background Knowledge

If learners have the necessary background information, the question is, how this can be activated. Strategies that encourage students to relate new information to their background knowledge based on the assumption that learning is a constructive process rather than a reproductive process. Suggestions for activating the background can be teacher directed, learners or text-directed. Teacher directed strategies are: advance organizers, objectives, and pretests and pre-questions.

(i) **Advance organizers:** Ausubel (1968) had prepared the advance organizer 'to bridge the gap between what the reader already knows and what the reader

13. Johnson, 1981.
14. Seliger H.W., 1971, 'The discourse organizer concept in a framework for continued discourse in Johnson', 1986.
15. Rivers W.M., 1968, *Teaching Foreign Language Skills* in Carrell and Eisterhold, 1988: 83.
16. Hayes and Tierney, 1982.

needs to know before he/she can meaningfully learn the task at hand'.[17] It is suggested that advance organizers must be written at a higher level of abstraction than the material to be learned, address the conditions of their use and account for the unfamiliar concepts.(Ausubel 1978)[18].

(ii) Objectives: Providing students with objectives sets a purpose for reading. This enhances learning by making it more systematic.

(iii) Pretests and pre-questions: It has been claimed that pretests and pre-questions have a beneficial effect upon learning, for they 'increase a student's sensitivity to learning by alerting him/her to the nature of the task and its relevance as well as providing a means to evaluate, categorize or generalize' (Pressey 1926; Wilson and Putnam 1982; Levin and Pressley 1981).

The above three teacher directed instructional strategies are employed and directed on behalf of students, rather than by students, for background knowledge activation. However, as pointed out earlier, there are strategies directed at learners as well as at the text. Student-centered pre-reading activities are based on the notion that such activity has the potential to activate problem-solving behaviour as well as the ability and desire to examine ideas and generate alternatives. Making students read titles, prefatory statements, pictures, etc. some text-directed instructional activities make students better comprehenders, although with qualifications.

In this section two texts, one culturally familiar and other not, are presented along with a framework for activating the readers' schema.

Text A (Culturally familiar text)

Mrs. Packletide's Tiger by Saki (H.H. Munro)

Summary of the Text:

The following story by H.H. Munro 'Saki' is a humorous account of the attempt made by Mrs. Packletide, a resident in India, to kill an infirm tiger in order to outwit her rival Louna Bimberton.

I. Cognitive:

Activity 1: Using titles

The teacher uses titles/headings to facilitate understanding of the text.

(i) What does the title 'Mrs.Packletide's Tiger' suggest to you? Can you guess what the story is about?

---

17. Ausubel D.P., *Educational Psychology, A Cognitive View,* Robert Tierney & James Cunningham, Barr, R. et al., cited in R. Barr ed. 1984, *Handbook of Reading Research*, Longman, 1968, p. 614.
18. Ausubel D.P., 'In Defense of Advance Organizers', *Ibid.*, 1978, p. 614.

(ii) Killing a tiger today is a cognizable offence however, in earlier times killing for sport was common. What are your views on this?

Activity 2: Anticipating/predicting content.

(i) Can you guess how the story would end?

(ii) Do we normally associate women with shooting animals?

(iii) This story is about a woman shooting a tiger; suggest a possible sequence of events?

(iv) How would people have reacted to this killing?

Activity 3: Unfamiliar words.

You have to work out the meaning of the unfamiliar words. There are four stages to this, namely,

(i) Decide from your knowledge of English structure and word formation the part of speech of the unfamiliar word. Look at –

   (a) The unfamiliar word in relation to words before and after it. If it follows the definite article and precedes a noun it must be an adjective;

   (b) The grammatical ending (*-ed*, *-ing*, *-s*, etc.) makes the word a verb. The *–ing* ending indicates a present participle or gerund;

   (c) The affixes indicate meaning and tells you what part of speech the word is.

(ii) Unknown words –

   (a) The teacher invites learners to list some adjectives related to Mrs. Pakletide's tiger.

   (b) He/she points out some unusual collocation here and asks for its significance, e.g. Animal of respectable antecedents,Venerable herd robber.

(iii) (a) The teacher can provide a list of affixes to show how some words could be divided like antecedents, depreciation, speculation, dissipating, instructively, denomination, disagreeably, etc.

   (b) Contextual guessing

      (i) Infirmities of age

(The root word is *infirm*. It preceeds the noun *age*, so it could be an adjective).

Activity 4: Previewing text

The teacher asks the student to open the book.

(i) The reader previews to see how the text is organized and related to what they have already guessed.

(ii) The reader looks for mismatches between the text and the construction of the story.

(iii) The cultural familiarity of the learner can be evoked by asking certain questions

(a) You know that the text is set in pre-independent India. What clues reveal this?

(b) What are some of the words which are culturally familiar to you?

(*Memsahib, Hindustani, rupees*)

Can you think of other English words which are of Indian origin? Are they always borrowed in a similar way or are there some changes in the process of borrowing? Give examples –

(*Verandah, lathicharge, bandobast*)

(iv) The relationship between Mrs. Packletide and her assistant, Louisa Mebbin suggests a master– slave relationship. Can you think of other such relationships?

Activity 5: Analyzing collocation and grammatical structures

(i) Adj + N combination

respectable	*antecedents*
restful	*sleep*
venerable	*herd robber*
persistent.	*bleat*
morbid	*dread*
energetic	*intervention*
elaborate	*carelessness*

(ii) V + N

favoured	*rendezvous*
repressed	*emotions*
seeming	*irrelevance*

II. Memory:

Activity 1: Building on previous knowledge

Here is a list of prefixes with their meanings. Can you think of five related words in each.

a-an-(not)	*in*-(not)	*post*-(after)
ambi-(both)	*ir*-(not)	*poly*-(many)

Activity 2: Word grouping

List words with the same prefix to determine meaning.

antecedent	*denomination*
antedate	*denominator*
antechamber	*denominate*
anteroom	*desensitize*

III. Metacognitive Activities:

Flavell (1976) states that metacognition 'refers to one's knowledge concerning one's own cognitive processes and products or anything related to them'.[19]

(i) Pre-Reading Plan (PreP): Langer's (1981)[20] PreP is a 3-step assessment procedure. It determines the amount of information a reader has about a topic, the language used to express knowledge of the subject and to make judgments about the background knowledge and vocabulary needed for comprehension.

(a) Teacher selects a word, phrase pertaining to a major concept.

(i) What comes to your mind when you see, hear this word?

(ii) Why do you say that?

(ii) Structured Overview: Teacher guides students in developing a graphic hierarchy of a target concept that depicts:

(a) Superordinate concept

(b) Coordinate concept

(c) Subordinate concept

(iii) PQ3R (Robinson 1977): Preview, Question, Read, Recite, Review (PQ3R): PQ3R as suggested by Robinson (1977) makes the teacher motivate learners to activate their prior knowledge by applying the preview step in PQ3R to content area so that:

(a) the title is examined

(b) introductory statement is read thoroughly

(c) summary statement is read carefully

IV. Textual: Interpreting text/Relating text/Exploring text/Recognizing

Text B (Culturally unfamiliar text)

The Man with the Scar by Somerset Maugham

Summary of the Text:

This first person account of a person exiled from Nicaragua and later sentenced for execution has been written by one of the world's famous short story writers, Somerset Maugham. As his last wish before being hanged the protagonist wanted to meet his wife. When she came he flung his arms around her and stabbed her to death because he loved her and couldn't let her face the world alone. The general on the spot thought that was a noble gesture and ordered him to be freed. The ending is an anticlimax where he reveals that the scar on his face was due to a bottle which had burst.

---

19. Flavell J.H., 1976, 'Metacognitive aspects of problem solving, in Sanacore', 1984: 706.
20. Langer J.A., 1981, 'From theory to practice: A pre-reading plan', in Sanacore, 1983.

I. Title Familiarization:

Activity 1:

(a) Comment on the title of the text.
(b) How do you think the story would progress?
(c) What association does the word 'scar' bring?
(d) How is a *scar* different from a mark?
(e) How do people get scars? (*fights, wounds, wartime*, etc.)
(f) Does the title remind you of any thing in real or reel life?
(g) What wartime story, article or movie on a simlar there can you recall?

II. Making Mind Maps:

Activity 2:

(a) Invite the students to talk about scars and relate stories connected with them.
(b) Mind maps can be made by the teacher as the students speak.

III. Association with Key Words:

Activity 4: (The teacher writes a number of key words and the students are invited to recount associations which the words evoke.)

Activity 5: Students may be asked to give a one line definition of the selected key words which may be followed by a brief factual description of some of them.

IV. Strategies for Bridging the Gap between Learner's Prior Knowledge and the Text:

(a) Advance Organizers:

Activity 1: Simple account of the story with simplified vocabulary replacing certain apparently difficult concepts is presented to the students.

(b) Introducing new and conflicting situations:

V. Vocabulary: Difficult Words in Context:

Activity 1: Make a list of the difficult words (e.g. *scar, crescent, formidable, battered, affably, traverse, goal*, etc.).

Activity 2: Look at the word *affably* in the sentence: *But my companion nodded affably*.

(a) What part of speech does it belong to?

(Clues: (i) Look at the word before it.
(ii) Does *affably* modify this word?
(iii) words ending in *-ly* like *quickly, slowly,* etc. are often adverbs.
(b) Suggest other adverbs in the place of *affably* (e.g. *mildly, gently* etc.).
(c) Check your dictionary to see what part of speech would the word be when the suffix is dropped).

Activity 3: Look at the word *battered* in a sentence:

I never saw him in anything but a very shabby grey suit, a khaki shirt and battered sombrero.

(a) What part of speech is it?
(Clues: (i) It is followed by a word which means *broad, brimmed hat.*
(ii) The construction pattern is almost like *good hat, old man,* etc.).
(b) What additional information does it give about the noun '*somibrero*'?
(Clues: (i) The adjective-noun combination clue in the preceding words suggests that these descriptive words do not attribute anything positive to their respective nouns *suit* and *shirt*. *Shabby* suggests worn out and *khaki* suggests a colour worn in uniforms.
(ii) The conjunction *but* also reconfirms this because the narrator says that he *never saw him in anything but...*
(c) If it is not attributing something positive, then suggest some other adjective which give a negative attribute (e.g. *worn, damaged, dejected,* etc.).
(d) Can you make different degrees of comparison here?

Activity 4: Look at the word *traverse* in the first paragraph.

(a) What part of speech does it belong to?
(i) It is immediately followed by an adjective and noun e.g. *long distances.*
(ii) *The clauses associated with it are 'threaded his way', 'with a sort of rolling walk', 'long distances on foot'.*
(iii) Is some kind of an activity related to movement associated with it?
(b) If it is a verb then is it transitive or intransitive?
(c) Can you make past and present continuous forms of it?
(d) Can you replace it with some other verbs?

VI. Arrival at Meaning through Contextual Guessing:

Activity 1: Let's take the word *scar* and try to arrive at its meaning through contextual guessing.

(Clues (i) It is described by the phrase '*broad and red*' which is an adjective.

(ii) The verb associated with it is *noticed*. The man was noticed because of the scar.

(iii) Also, the phrase *on account of* further suggests that the *man* was noticed because of the scar.

(iv) Another clue is the word *ran* which talks about the *scar* and signifies its location between the temple and the chin.

(v) It suggests some features to do with the man's face. It could be a mark on the man's face.

(vi) The word *mark* is a noun and so is the word *scar*).

(a) Check up this word in the dictionary. Does it rightly confirm your guess?

VII. Word Formation:

Activity 1: The words below are from the text:

reasonable	*formidable*	*unexpected*
affably	*undistinguished*	*murderer*
possession	*execution*	*condemned*
Guatemalean	*suddenly*	*objection*
indifferent	*loveliness*	*impossible*
revolutionary	*government*	*leisurely*

(a) Isolate the prefixes and suffixes from these words.

(b) Isolate the roots.

(c) What is the syntactic category of the form without these prefixes and suffixes (i.e. is it a V, N, Adj, Adv)?

(d) What is the form after the suffixes have been attached?

(e) Does all the suffixation lead to change in the syntactic category?

(f) What kinds of changes result from the use of prefixes?

(g) Does prefixation lead to change in the category?

Activity 2: What other words can you make by adding the following suffixes:

-er	*-ful*
-ness	*-al*
-able	*-ed*
-tion/sion	*s*
-ly	*-ment*

Activity 3: Given below is a list of some prefixes:

ex-	*mis-*
pre-	*un-*
re-	*in-*
de-	*dis-*
	anti-

(a) Use the above prefixes in word formation.

(b) Indicate the meaning suggested by these prefixes.

Activity 4: Complete the following table (some of the blocks may remain empty):

Adjective	Noun	Verb	Adverb
kind	kindness		kindly
		execute	
	expression		aimlessly
different			
			suddenly
		possess	
		revolt	

Activity 5: Substitute the words in italics with a synonym:

(a) Strolling *leisurely*

(b) Terrific *scar*

(c) Reasonable *man*

(d) Great *crescent*

VIII. Sentence Structure and Substitution Exercises:

1. The examples given below are taken from the text. Using the prompts, produce other sentences with the same pattern.

   (a) *It was on account of the scar that I first noticed him, for it ran, broad and red, in a great crescent from his temple to his chain.*

   mark/forehead
   wound/head
   injury/temple

   (b) *He had small and undistinguished features, and his expression was artless*

   indiscernible/innocent
   uncharacteristic/guileless
   indiscriminate/unsophisticated

(c) *He threaded his way among the tables with a sort of rolling walk as through he were accustomed to traverse long distances on foot.*

familiar/travelling
habituated/cruising
used to/touring

IX. Discourse Recognition:

1. What type of co-referential relationship does the story begin with? Why?
   (a) Anaphoric
   (b) Cataphoric
   (c) Exophoric
2. Identify the conjunctive relationships marked by the linguistic markers (*but, for, although, then, when*) in the passage given below:

   'He was a powerful man of more than common height. I never saw him in anything *but* a very shabby grey suit, a khaki shirt and a battered sombrero. He was far from clean. He used to come into the Palace Hotel at Guatemala City every day at cocktail time and strolling leisurely round the bar offer lottery tickets *for* sale. If this was the way he made his living, it must have been a poor one, *for* I never saw anyone buy, *but* now and then I saw him offered a drink. He never refused it. He threaded his way among the table with a sort of rolling walk *as though* he were accustomed to traverse long distances on foot, paused at each table, with a little smile, mentioned the numbers he had for sale and *then when* no notice was taken of him, with the same smile passed on.'
3. What kind of relationship is indicated by the punctuation mark (-) used in the passage below:

   'The rebel advanced a step or two to meet her. She flung herself into his arm and with a hoarse cry of passion he pressed his lips to hers. And at the same moment, he drew a knife from his ragged shirt-I haven't a notion how he managed to retain possession of it – and stabbed her in the neck.'
4. In the passage given above whom does the *rebel* refer to?
5. 'What will you have, general?A brandy.' (lines 26-27)
   (a) Indicate the link suggested in the above sentence:
      (i) Ellipsis
      (ii) Referential
      (iii) Conjunction
   (b) How would you write the above sentence without using a formal link?
6. What/Whom do the underlined words in these sentences refer to?

(a) 'I was standing at the bar one evening, my foot on the rail, with an acquaintance...' (lines 20-21).

(b) 'The officer said that the general commanding the... awaited his arrival.' (49-51)

(c) 'It happened so quickly that...' (line 90)

(d) 'I loved her' (line 101).

(e) 'I never liked it, said I.'

X. Translation Exercise:

I. Context and Register

Activity 1: Pick out the unusual expressions or colloquial expressions (e.g. *I think he was for the most part a trifle the worst for liquor: Not so bad; everyday at cocktail times; he threaded his way among the tables with a sort of rolling walk; with hoarse cry of passion*, etc.) Work in pairs and try to give two suitable translations for these.

Activity 2: Compare your translation with others in the pair and choose the better suited translation for the purpose.

Activity 3: Pick out the words, phrases which are essentially culture-specific in this text (e.g. *cocktail time, a few pesos now and then, he spend the night in gaol, they were led into the patio of the gaol, dyed his shirt*, etc.).

Activity 4: Provide your own definition/explanation for the above expressions in L1 and then translate these into L_2.

Activity 5: In the passage below, the writer has used a number of unfamiliar words and has offered a brief explanation. Discuss the explanation and translate them as accurately as possible. You may use a dictionary.

(a) 'It was on account of the scar, that I first noticed him, for it ran, broad and red, in a great crescent from his temple to his chin.'

(b) 'It must have been due to a formidable wound and I wondered whether this has been caused by a sabre or by a fragment of shell.'

II. Word Order

Activity 1: Pick out some sentences and ask the students to suggest an alternative word order in L2 (e.g. 'They captured him, along with his staff, such as it was, and sentenced him to be shot at dawn'; 'I shook my head as for the twentieth time since my arrival'; 'He held out for my inspection his lottery tickets').

Suggest two translations, one closely matching the given word order and the other free. The students, in pairs, compare these and choose what they think is the best.

III. Reference and Meaning

Activity 1: Look at the word *it* in the passages below. Decide in each case what would be the most appropriate way of translating them.

(a) *It* was on account of the scar that I first noticed him, for it ran, broad and red, in a great crescent from his temple to his chin.

(b) *It* must have been due to a formidable wound and wondered whether...

(c) *It* was unexpected on that round, fat and good humoured face.

(d) *It* doesn't add to his beauty, does *it*?

(e) *It* happened so quickly that...

(f) And at the same moment he drew a knife from his ragged shirt-I haven't a notion how he managed to retain possession of *it*- and stabbed her in the neck.

IV. Back Translation

Give a small passage for translation from L_1 to L_2.Close the book and retranslate L_2 into L_1. Compare the translations with the original version in the book. Check to see the differences.

Post-reading Phase

Understanding

(a) Who is being talked about in the first paragraph?

(b) Who was the man with the scar?

(c) Why did the author think the scar on the man's face must have been caused by a sword or an exploding shell?

(d) 'They captured him (the General) along with his staff.'
Who captured the General? How did he come to be captured? What was the sentence passed on him?

(e) 'If this was the way he (the man with the scar) made a living it must have been a poor one.' What was the way? Why did the author think it was a poor way?

(f) Was the general upset by the sentence passed on him?

(g) What was the name of the general commanding the government troops?

(h) Pick out the words and phrases which describe the man with the scar.

Interpreting

(a) Why did the soldiers gasp in surprise when they looked at the general's wife?

(b) Why did the general kill his wife?

(c) Why did the officer in command, supervising the execution, spare the life of the general?
(d) Do you think the officer was influenced by some code of honourable conduct?
(e) 'He's a ruffian, of course, and a bandit, but not a bad fellow.' How would you justify this statement?
(f) What does the phrase *formidable world* suggest to you?
(g) What do you mean by *undistinguished features* and *expression was artless*?

Relating

(a) Did you like the man with the scar?
(b) Do you think you would want this character for a friend?
(c) Do you justify the killing of his wife?

Exploring

(a) The writer has described two people in the story. What techniques can be used to describe a person (sex, age, group, special feature, physical characteristics/ behavioural characteristic, etc.). Describe a person in 4-5 sentences.
(b) The writer has used the technique of narration here. What are some of its features? (sequence of events, how and why it happened). Can you think of other stories using this technique. What other techniques can the writer employ in writing? (first person narration, omniscient narration, etc.).

Recognizing

(a) What do you think is the purpose of the writer in this text?
(b) What do you think is the attitude of the writer with regard to revolution?

References

Alvarez M and Risko V., 'Schema Activation, Construction and Application', *ERIC Digest ED* 312611, 1989-11-00, pp. 1-5.

Barnett M.A., 'Reading through context: How read and perceived strategy use affects L2 comprehension', *The Modern Language Journal*. 72, 1988, pp. 150-162.

Carrell P.L., Pharis B.G. and Liberto J.C., 'Meta-cognitive strategies training ESL reading', *TESOL Quarterly*, 23, 1989, pp. 647-678.

Carrell P.L., 'The Effects of rhetorical organization on ESL readers', *TESOL Quarterly*. 18, pp. 441-469.

Cook G., *Discourse in Language Teaching: A Scheme for Teacher Education*. Oxford: OUP, 1989.

Gatbonton E.C. and Tucker G.R., 'Cultural orientation and the study of foreign literature', *TESOL Quarterly*, 5, 2, 1971, pp. 13-143.

Haswell R.H., et al., 'Context and rhetorical reading Strategies: Haas and Flower (1988) Revisited', *Written Communication*. Vol. 16, No. 1, January 1999, pp. 2-27.

Hayes D.A. and R.J. Tierney, 'Developing readers knowledge through analogy', *Reading Research Quarterly*, 17, 1992, pp. 256-280.

Imtiaz Shagufta, *Schema in Literature: Towards a Model of Comprehension Pedagogy*, New Delhi: Manak Publications, 2000.

Johnson P., 'Effects on reading comprehension of language complexity, cultural background of a text', *TESOL Quarterly*. 15, 2, 1981, pp. 169-181.

________, 'Effects on reading comprehension of building background knowledge', *TESOL Quarterly*, 156, 4, 1982, pp. 503-516.

________, 'Acquisition of schema for comprehension and communication: A study of the reading-writing relationship in ESL', *RELC Journal*, 17, 1, 1986, pp. 1-13.

Kitao S. Kathleen, *Theory and Application in English Language Teaching*, Tokyo: Eichosha Co. Ld., 1995.

Sanacore J., 'Improving reading through prior knowledge and writing', *Journal of Reading*, 26, 1983, pp. 714-721.

Sanacore J., 'Metacognition and the improvement of reading: Some important links', *Journal of Reading*, 27, 1984, pp. 706-712.

Singhal M., 'A comparison of L1 and L2 reading: Cultural Differences and Schema', *The Internet TESL Journal*, Vol. 4, No. 10, October 1-8, 1998.

Tierney R.J. and Cunningham J.W., Research on teaching reading comprehension, in Rebecca Barr et al., ed., *Handbook of Reading Research*, New York and London: Longman, 1991.

Contributors

Alan Maley, ELT Author & Trainer, UK. amaley@globalnet.co.uk

Amol Padwad, Head, Dept. of English, J.M. Patel College, Bandara Maharashtra. amolpadwad@gmail.com

Anam Govardhan, Professor, Western Connecticut University, USA. agovardhan@snet.net

Annie Kuriachan, Lecturer, S.G. Dept. of English, Women's Christian College, Chennai. anniku36@yahoo.com

K.S. Antony Samy, Lecturer, Dept. of English, Loyola College, Chennai. tonyrrr@loyolacollege.edu

T.S. Arul Kumar, Corporate Trainer, Coimbatore. amudhakumararul@yahoo.co.in

Aysha Vishvamohan, Asst. Professor of English, IITM, Chennai. draysha@iitm.ac.in

M.N.K. Bose, (Late) Professor of Applied Linguistics, Hodeidah University, Republic of Yemen. mnk_bose@hotmail.com

S. Devaki Reddy, Assistant Professor, IIT Madras. dre@iitm.ac.in

S.P. Dhanavel, Professor and Head, Dept. of English, Anna University, Chennai. dhanavelsp@yahoo.co.in

K. Elango, Professor of English, Anna University, MIT, Chennai. elangoela@rediffmail.com

Francis Peter, Reader, PG and Research Dept. of English, Loyola College, Chennai. peterace@loyolacollege.edu

Ilango Ramasamy, Senior Lecturer in English, Chettinad College of Engineering & Technology, Puliyur. illango-eng@gmail.com

J. John Love Joy, Lecturer, Dept. of English, St. Joseph's College, Trichy. johnljoy@gmail.com

Joseph Dorairaj A., Professor of English, Ghandhigrahm Rural University, Madurai. josephdorajiraj@gmail.com

Kirsten A. Anderson, Research Scholar AID India, USA. sistakaa@gmail.com

Lavanya Mavillapalli, Material Producer, Danseur Susikshaa, Chennai. susikashaa@gmail.com

Makhan L. Tickoo, ELT Expert and Author, Hyderabad. makhan.tickoo@gmail.com

Manjula Duraiswamy, ELT Consultant and Editor, Chennai. manjula92001@yahoo.co.in

N.S. Prabhu, Doyen of ELT, Mysore. prabhuns@airtelmail.in

V. Saraswathy, (Retd.), Professor Dept. of English, Madras University. saras_linguistics@yahoo.co.in

Sridhar Bala is an educational consultant.

Shreesh Chaudhary, Professor, Dept. of HSS, IIT Madras, Chennai. scc@iitm.ac.in

Stanley Mohan, Dept. of English American College, Madurai. stanley_mohan@yahoo.com

Shagufta Imtiaz, Women's College, Aligarh Muslim University, Aligarh.

Thilagavathi G. Joseph, Lecturer in English, Stella Maris College, Chennai. thilagajoseph@gmail.com

Usha R., Corporate Trainer, Chennai. ushangrila@yahoo.com